Charles Gavan Duffy

The League of North And South

An Episode in Irish history, 1850-1854

Charles Gavan Duffy

The League of North And South
An Episode in Irish history, 1850-1854

ISBN/EAN: 9783744713757

Printed in Europe, USA, Canada, Australia, Japan

Cover: Foto ©ninafisch / pixelio.de

More available books at **www.hansebooks.com**

THE LEAGUE OF
NORTH AND SOUTH.

An Episode in Irish History,
1850—1854.

BY
SIR C. GAVAN DUFFY, K.C.M.G.

"And let the Orange lily be
Thy badge, my patriot brother;
The everlasting Green for me,
And we for one another."—DAVIS.

LONDON: CHAPMAN AND HALL,
LIMITED.
1886.

DEDICATION BY WAY OF PREFACE.

My dear Mr. Justin McCarthy,

I propose to dedicate this book to you from a motive which probably never begot a dedication since dedications were invented—because I have a grave complaint to make against you. It contains the history of a period which you have seriously misunderstood and hence greatly misrepresented; and I desire to call your attention to the circumstance by way of friendly remonstrance rather than by refutation or controversy. I find in your speeches, and in the speeches of some of your colleagues, allusion to the Tenant Right party of 1852 as the "party of Sadleir and Keogh." It was no more the party of Sadleir and Keogh than you and your friends are the party of James Carey and Patrick Tynan.

Neither Sadleir nor Keogh were ever members of the Tenant League. They were sent to Parliament by Irish constituencies against the remonstrance of the League, and when they arrived there and made haste to betray the country, they only did what we always foretold they would do. For a time indeed they figured in the same division lists with the honest Irish members; but you are not unfamiliar with an identical experience in your own time, I think. Would you consider it quite fair to name the present Irish party not after its accredited leaders, but after the scabby sheep of the flock? But this is just what you have done in the case I have cited.

I know too well the difficulty of maintaining an Irish party in the House of Commons not to be patient with mistakes. But public men can scarcely commit a more wanton or gratuitous blunder in policy than to be unjust to their predecessors. You have fallen upon pleasant times. Electors are protected by the ballot, they have no occasion to fear ruin as the penalty of voting honestly; and young priests who fought in the *mêlée* during the movement of 1850-5, and fought unsuccessfully, are now archdeacons, canons, bishops, and archbishops, and lend

DEDICATION BY WAY OF PREFACE.

you decisive assistance. You travel by rail, *mon ami*, fifty miles an hour just now; but, pray, who surveyed the untrodden country, laid down the lines over quaking morasses at times, or through mountains of granite which might have dismayed a Stephenson, and so made this progress possible? If a member betrays his party at present he is denounced and discarded; in our time he returned to his constituents leaning on the arm of a bishop. The inevitable expenses of a political contest are plentifully furnished to you by the Irish race, we had to draw them in a large degree from our personal resources. We spent and were spent in that contest. An injustice commonly provokes a counter and compensating injustice; and when I took up my pen I was tempted to declare that the present Irish party in more prosperous days have simply administered the principles, and executed the designs, devised by their predecessors in the midst of famine and disaster; that a single concession has not been won for the Irish people, or sought on their behalf, which may not be traced back to the labours of the men sent to Parliament in 1852.

It cannot be denied that you taught the people

to rise in sterner wrath against their oppressors than the men of 1850 excited, and that you moved more effectually the Ireland in exile to co-operate with the mother country. But on the other hand, you failed to win the ear of the North—you failed to unite the four provinces on a common platform as your predecessors did. What signal results it might produce at this hour had you been able to emulate that memorable work?

If you do me the honour of reading this little book you will judge how much might be said on this thesis. But I can well believe that the men of to-day have often re-discovered for themselves principles and policy which were not new indeed, but had become forgotten. One of their shortcomings, I think, is to know imperfectly the unwritten history of the last thirty years—a history which concerns them so nearly. Mr. Parnell, as far as I have observed, never mentions the leaders of the Tenant League except with the respect and gratitude to which they are entitled, but he is strangely unfamiliar with the incidents of the period in which they lived. He recently spoke of Mr. Butt, for example, as the founder of Independent Opposition. Mr. Butt was not merely not its founder, but he was its steadfast enemy from the time it was first put into action in the House of Commons down to his dying day. He repudiated it as scornfully as he repudiated Parliamentary obstruction at a later period. Independent Opposition was formulated by the Young Irelanders in contrast to the place-begging policy defended in Conciliation Hall; and was propounded anew in 1847 as a more hopeful resource than Mr. Mitchel's proposal of refusing to pay poor rate. I have written the history of that transaction, and as I believe I may assume that you have read it, I will only ask you to note this fact; that the theory maintained by the majority of the Irish Confederates (embodied in the Report on Organization) insists on the principle upon which every success, great or small, gained for Ireland from that time to this has been won. A few years later George Henry Moore made a gallant attempt to induce the Irish party who opposed the Ecclesiastical Titles Bill to accept the same cardinal doctrine, but they had other ends in view, and it was adopted as a governing principle for the first time by the Tenant League members of 1852.

It used to be the habit of Irish Nationalists—of

that school, at any rate, with which I was connected and where you yourself matriculated,—to guard the reputation of their predecessors as a priceless possession of the Irish race. I do not think this spirit prevails universally at present. But such a spirit is not only just and generous, but on lower grounds it is prudent. You, in your turn, will have successors some day. I remember a story I heard at my mother's knee and have never forgotten, which I commend to you as a sample of the wisdom of our ancestors. In a famine year—so the legend ran—a comfortable farmer was persuaded by his wife to send out his aged father to beg. The old man was equipped with a staff, a bag, and half a blanket, and turned on the highway. After he was gone his frugal daughter-in-law inquired what had become of the second half of the blanket? After a long search it was discovered under the bed of her little boy. "Why, Mick astor, what did you want with a blanket?" his father demanded. "Father," says the boy, "I thought I'd keep it by me till I grew up to be a big man, and then it'll do for you when I send you out to beg." You are very far in the present hour of triumph from fearing that the blanket will ever fall to your lot. But it has fallen to the lot of men with whom the best living Irishman might be proud to be named. When we remember that Roger O'Moore was denied all control in the Confederation of Kilkenny, which his daring and inventive genius created—that Wolfe Tone fell into disrepute, for moderation, with the United Irish Societies which he founded—that Grattan was in the end denounced by the Volunteers whom he had led to one of the most memorable victories in history—that Smith O'Brien, Dillon, Meagher, Mitchel, and their friends were expelled from the Repeal Association, of which they were the most sincere and unselfish members, and that O'Connell lost his marvellous popularity in a few months after his last alliance with the Whigs—it may teach us all to be modest.

Let me cite a letter from your own pen, in which the same Independent Opposition which Mr. Parnell attributes to Mr. Butt, you in your turn attribute to Mr. Parnell:—

"I may say that the Irish members of Parliament stand aloof from the social influences of London, which used at one time to have such a softening and enervating effect on their political character. This isolation, for so I may call it, was distinctly the work of Mr. Parnell. It was not the way of O'Connell; it was not the way of Mr. Butt. O'Connell's relations of friendship with some of the Whigs of his day were often injurious to his influence over political movements; and similar relationships with English public men made Mr. Butt far too anxious to please or at least not to displease the House of Commons. .... It is a part of that policy of Independence which Mr. Parnell has come to carry out, and which is now tried in action for the first time."

You will learn from the narrative in this volume that "the policy of independence" was not tried in action for the first time by Mr. Parnell. And standing aloof from social influences is just as little a novelty. The Tenant League party had their own whip, and permitted no other to communicate with them; and not a man of them ever entered the *salon* of any political potentate of either sex. The necessity for this abstinence was preached in the *Nation*, and I will cite a few lines from a letter of Patrick McMahon, one of the honest members of the period, in answer to the exhortation:—

"Very, very glad that you have already enunciated the doctrine that we are to leave to our 'betters the duties of dancing and dining out.' Unless we act on a system that leaves us on terms of perfect equality with our richer fellow senators we will do no good. We must imitate the French *émigrés* who earned their bread by every humble lawful calling, and so maintained *their self-respect*."[1]

I make allowance, of course, for the fact that none

---

[1] August 14, 1852. McMahon to Duffy.

of your party, none of its leaders at any rate, were politically born at the period in question; that the history of that era has been hitherto unwritten, and that men rarely read old newspapers. I entirely disbelieve that you were wilfully unjust, but you had something to learn, which in your position it is almost criminal not to know; and with great respect and regard I have endeavoured to bring it under your notice. If I may cite so humble an example as my own, I have refrained from criticism on transactions of the Irish party which I could not approve, because I thought their enemies in front ought never to be supplemented by auxiliaries from behind; a similar tenderness is due, I think, to the men who bore the heat and toil of a contest which it has been your good fortune in a more favourable day to carry to successful issues.

Believe me,
My dear Mr. McCarthy,
Very faithfully yours,
C. GAVAN DUFFY.

Cimiez, Alpes Maritimes,
June, 1886.

CONTENTS.

CHAPTER I.
IRELAND IN 1850 . . . . PAGE 1

CHAPTER II.
PREPARATIONS FOR A NATIONAL CONFERENCE 38

CHAPTER III.
THE CONFERENCE 48

CHAPTER IV.
RECEPTION OF THE LEAGUE BY THE COUNTRY 64

CHAPTER V.
THE COUNCIL AND ITS FIRST TROUBLES 105

CHAPTER V.—(CONTINUED).
THE LEAGUE COUNCIL AND ITS TROUBLES 163

CONTENTS.

CHAPTER VI.
The General Election 181

CHAPTER VII.
The League in Parliament 215

CHAPTER VIII.
Another Rally of the League 274

CHAPTER IX.
Dr. Cullen and the Whig Bishops 301

CHAPTER X.
The Mission to Rome and its Results 330

APPENDICES.
I. Tour with Thomas Carlyle in 1849 385
II. John Mitchel, the League, and Gavan Duffy . . . 387

THE

LEAGUE OF NORTH AND SOUTH.

An Episode in Irish History,
1850—1854.

CHAPTER I.

IRELAND IN 1850.

WHETHER Irish Catholics and Protestants can transact public business together in good temper and good faith, as Catholics and Protestants in Switzerland, Belgium, and Hungary habitually do, is a problem which greatly perplexes sober Englishmen at present. The negative has been asserted so frequently, and with such emphasis, especially by eminent British critics who knew nothing of the matter, that many worthy persons have come to regard it as a truth which it is idle or temerarious to dispute. A generation ago the same question was equally a problem, and there were not wanting then, any more than now, men who answered authoritatively that such an alliance was impossible. But the experiment was made at that time; it lasted through four trying years; it was subjected to many critical tests; and it furnishes, I think, better materials for forming a safe opinion than any quantity of predictions and speculations.

I propose to write the history of that experiment. Many of the actors in it are still living to correct me if I fall into error, or to confirm my statements if they be accurate, as they certainly shall be to the best of my knowledge and judgment. There is nothing of which men commonly know so little as the unwritten history of the period when they were boys; and the facts will be new, not only to Englishmen, but to the generation entering on active life on both sides of the Channel.

When the nineteenth century had reached its midway no crux in the tangle of Irish troubles seemed more hopeless than to combine the North and South for any public end whatever. It had not been always so. Sixty years earlier, when Grattan was exhorting the Parliament in Dublin to concede Catholic Emancipation, he found his warmest supporters in Belfast; and when Wolfe Tone conspired for kindred and larger objects, he had more Presbyterian Ministers than notable Catholics, lay or clerical, among his adherents. But after the Union the sentiment out of which this fraternity sprang gradually died out in the North. During O'Connell's long struggle for Emancipation, few Presbyterian laymen, and not one Presbyterian minister, entered the Catholic Association. In 1842, when he accepted an invitation to a public dinner at Belfast, the Orange Lodges threatened his life; they wrecked the building in which he was about to be entertained, and he had to be escorted by police on board a Scotch steamer to escape their violence. Four years later some change had taken place, for Smith O'Brien and a deputation of Young Irelanders had a courteous reception in the same town, and a patient hearing for their opinions. But the change was not deep or wide, for in 1848 the Orange leaders demanded arms from the Government that they might be led against the Confederates. In 1850 it was still accepted as a truism in Irish politics that, whatever else might happen, Ulster and Munster would not join hands for any purpose that could be devised by man.

This was the state of public feeling when a rumour got abroad, early in 1850, that a Conference on the Land Question was projected in Dublin, at which authentic and accredited representatives of North and South were expected to meet and confer together. To the best-disposed the promise seemed too good to be true; the ordinary impression was that two or three stray

Northerns of no account would probably figure as mock plenipotentiaries of Ulster.

The condition of Ireland at that moment justified a truce in hereditary quarrels, had there never been one before. For nearly four years a famine following the potato blight had been in constant operation, and more than a fourth of the Irish race had perished of starvation, or fled in a panic to escape that calamity. Too often they fled in vain; emigrant vessels, as overcrowded as the slave ships of Sierra Leone, and the stifling hospitals into which those who escaped the dangers of the voyage were transferred, killed as surely as starvation, and the dead bodies of upwards of twenty thousand Irish exiles were dropped into the Atlantic or sown in the desolate wastes of Canada. The flight to the United States had been less calamitous, and it still continued unabated. Energetic young men and women, the seed of the future, fled from the country as fast as they could gather the essential passage money, and their first earnings were still remitted to enable their kindred to escape from the workhouse and the exterminating landlord. It was noted as a fact full of painful significance that it was no longer the wail of the exile which was heard at the ports of departure, but the cheerful bustle of a pleasant enterprise.

The construction of railways with the co-operation of the State, the reclamation of waste lands, reproductive public works and industrial enterprises, had all been successively proposed to Parliament as remedies for this tremendous national calamity, and always rejected. A Poor-law was substituted by official wisdom, which gave alms, but no employment. In addition to the aged and infirm, the youth of both sexes were shut up in Poor-houses. A native government would have made such institutions, if necessary at all, centres of industry the cradle of new manufactures; at lowest, training schools of agricultural education; but as it was, there were among the inmates a hundred and fifty thousand young men and women able and willing to work, who were rotting in idleness and demoralization, from which there seemed no escape but the pauper emigrant ships or the pauper grave. In a few cases guardians insisted upon trying spinning, weaving, and other industries for the immediate use of the paupers, but they received no encouragement from the authorities, and nothing effectual was accomplished. It is proper to note that when a famine threatened the artisans of Lancashire twenty years later a directly opposite method was adopted; they were employed on reproductive works, which yielded a substantial return for their labour. At the outset of the Irish famine there was generous sympathy in England with the suffering people. But it was the business of the Government to face the difficulty, and they were left in the end to deal with it at their discretion. The task fell on Lord John Russell and a Whig Administration. No man has ever appeared at the head of a great party less fit to be entrusted with duties which appealed to the imagination and the heart. He was of a cold, feeble nature and a limited intelligence, skilled in nothing but the arts by which office is won and kept; and he sacrificed the lives of the Irish peasantry mercilessly to preserve the votes of English ship-owners and corn-factors.

The bulk of the small tenantry and labourers who still struggled to escape the Poor-house were steeped in poverty. It was truly said that they were "clad like beggars, housed like beggars, and fed like beggars." Agricultural wages were lower than in any civilized country. A man, where there was still employment, could earn about sixpence a day, a woman scarce half that amount. A few benevolent ladies and clergymen had got embroidery, lace work, and other domestic industries established here and there among girls, and the support of a family often depended on this new resource. In 1850 the famine had not ceased, but had come to be regarded as a familiar phenomenon; it was computed that a hundred persons still died of hunger, or of the diseases begotten of hunger, every week, and were shovelled into pauper graves. In Connaught, where the soil is poorest, the distress was necessarily most intense; in Connemara it was alleged that some of the people only preserved life by eating the putrid flesh of dogs. There were districts where the land, or the tenure, being exceptionally good, the tenantry were still able to live, but when they met at market town or church, there were such huge gaps visible in the familiar muster that even in these districts the population looked like the remnant escaped from a shipwreck.

At a time when public alms were the only alternative of immediate starvation, an Act was passed forfeiting the possession of any small holder who accepted such relief, and under this inhuman law the country had been systematically depopulated. The Exterminators, as the landlords who cleared their estates came to be called, after a pitiless war extending over half-a-dozen years, were still busy at their accursed work. A traveller in any southern or western county saw the ruins of human habitations from morning till night. In 1841 there had been in Ireland 310,375 farms, from one to five acres, from which more than two-thirds of the cultivators had now disappeared. And the system was still in such vigour that within the two years then terminating, 21,000 small holders had been expelled. When an estate came into the market the first question an intending purchaser asked was whether it had been cleared of its paupers, cottiers, and small tenants? These wholesale evictions were justified to England by the invention that the over-crowding of the people had produced all the calamities of the country. Mr. Sharman Crawford demonstrated that farms were smaller and population thicker in the prosperous county of Down than in the most distressed districts in Munster or Connaught. Seventy-six thousand landholders, amounting with their families to over a hundred thousand persons, had been evicted in a single year. But sums total escape the imagination which can only fasten on details. In the Union of Kilrush, not larger than an average English estate, the habitations of fifteen thousand persons had been plucked down. Other proprietors proceeded more slyly and systematically. On the estate of Mr. Shirley, an English Member of Parliament, whose ancestors got a district in Ulster under Elizabeth, where the native chiefs had been murdered, and whose rental had gradually been raised in the progress of time from £500 a year to £20,000, another system prevailed. The original owners of property under the Brehon laws were expelled at the rate of three hundred tenants a year. A troop of bailiffs, grown skilful by practice, set out of a morning supplied with food and whiskey, crowbars and pickaxes, and, striking down the support of the couples on which the roof rested, brought house after house to ruin. There was not a county in the island where this practice did not sooner or later find imitators.

In Ulster, prosperous by its tenant-right chiefly, 3 per cent. of the population were receiving relief; in Leinster 7 per cent., in Munster 20 per cent., in Connaught, with the worst land and worst landlords in the island, 22 per cent. There were four million acres of reclaimable waste, and the half a million of able-bodied men who were competent to turn them into corn-fields were walled up in compulsory idleness, and fed at the expense of a class rapidly sinking into similar ruin. Men who had been elected Poor-law guardians when the system commenced were now receiving outdoor relief, and men who had been ex-officio guardians were administering it as paid officers.[1]

Depopulation had not, as its agents contended, diminished poverty. The country from end to end was poorer as well as less populous. Every kind of national wealth had decreased. The ordinary stock of

[1] A recent Parliamentary return gave the number receiving relief in the four provinces :—

	Indoor.	Outdoor.
Ulster	42,249	19,335
Munster	98,019	397,429
Leinster	54,075	86,310
Connaught	43,481	255,131
Total	237,824	758,205

a farm, cows, pigs, poultry and the like had dwindled away. The money in circulation was ascertained to be less by a million and a half than before the famine. A series of bad harvests, the decreased price of wheat, and the enormous increase of poor rates left a balance of farm produce which was often not equal to the landlord's claim, reserving nothing for the tiller of the soil. The consolidation of farms had not always worked well for the landlord; poor rates had to be paid, and the system had only begun which has since gained so prodigious an expansion, of growing beef as a more profitable pursuit than growing corn. The town population sank along with the peasantry; the bread they ate was dear; the goods they offered for sale faded on their shelves, or mouldered in their drawers without customers. Their savings were eaten up by poor rates levied to support in the mis-called workhouses tenants ejected from the neighbouring estates.

With the physical decline of the country the moral decline kept pace. The great temperance movement, a social revolution without example in the history of the world, died out. The political training of O'Connell and the Young Irelanders which "brought back a soul into Eiré," was in a great degree forgotten. The education in the National Schools had been stealthily altered in this time of calamity, till it became expressly such a training as might rear useful servants and dependents, not citizens. The national pride and sympathy which feed the spirit of youth in other countries were denied all nutriment. Mere book-learning is good for much, but it does not make men. The Chinese, after ample training in philosophy, permit themselves to be knocked on the head like swine; and if the Irish race was to be preserved from permanent vassalage, it was an urgent need to revive the discipline of soul and spirit which had been lost.

Old wrongs were forgotten in the throes of such a calamity as the famine, but it was a sensible aggravation of the public distress that the impoverished tenant-farmers had to bear the burthen of a Church Establishment from which they accepted no service, and which was endowed and officered out of all proportion with its duties. To pay the clergy and build the churches of the gentry, while their own clergy and churches were sharing the decay of the time, was a hard trial. The churches built by their ancestors for Catholic worship had been transferred to the minority by law, and under another law, Catholic rate-payers had been compelled to erect whatever additional churches the minority considered necessary for their accommodation, while they had not themselves in the whole island as many edifices suitable for the ritual of the Catholic religion as often exist in one town on the Continent of

Europe. The extreme cases of hardship which continued even after Catholic Emancipation, will scarcely seem possible to the present generation. When I was a boy the only place of Catholic worship in the chief town of my native county was a barn, long used as a rustic theatre. And after I was a man, I have knelt in the rain to hear mass outside of a cow-shed in one of the show-places of Wicklow, because the proprietor not only refused to sell a site for a Catholic chapel, but forbade his tenants to permit the temporary use of any building on his estate for that purpose.

The root of all these wrongs and disasters was a land code unparalleled on the earth. Great estates, like principalities, which subsist at present only in England and Russia, were created in Ireland by the Norman conquerors, with a calamitous condition, which they strictly prohibited in England, that the new proprietor might habitually reside out of the country from which he derived his income. The best land was enjoyed by powerful nobles who lived in London and governed Ireland by open or secret influence. The resident proprietors for the most part were their clients and dependents, and between the visit of Henry II. and the era which we had now reached, the policy pursued towards Ireland on any cardinal question was a policy dictated by these Absentee proprietors.

But a more fatal enemy to national prosperity than

the Absentee was the black stranger who lived in Ireland half the year that he might levy his tribute effectually to be spent in London or Paris. He was commonly too straitened in circumstances and too self-indulgent to be considerate of his tenantry, and he had grown accustomed to regard their whole earnings, and any surplus savings created by their frugality and enterprise, as his natural property. When the potato blight began, landlords of this class hurried the cereal crop out of the country to secure their rents, in disregard of the just claims of their tenants to a subsistence out of the food they had raised. When the danger became universal they began to eject the small farmers—sometimes for rents barely due, often for arrears which were fraudulent in amount and character. The nominal rents in a number of cases were impossible to be paid, and were retained at an obsolete standard only to ensure the political subjection of the tenantry. In the war with Napoleon the prices of cattle and corn had risen prodigiously, with peace they fell thirty per cent.; but the rent, secured by lease, and if not by lease, by competition, did not fall. When Free Trade was established in 1846, the wheat of Dantzic, Belgian corn, and French flour competed successfully with the products of Irish farms in Mark Lane, and the cattle of Spain and Holland in Smithfield, but the rents remained unabated. The famine came and destroyed twenty millions worth of the people's property. They could no longer count on the potato for subsistence, and had to purchase Indian corn as the cheapest substitute; they were loaded with the moiety of an exorbitant poor rate, with a county cess which ought to have fallen exclusively on property, and with a rent charge in lieu of tithes, which was collected by the landlord. When they paid over the sum total of their earnings to the agent, they commonly got a receipt on account, which kept the claim for arrears alive for any happy windfall on which it could be levied; and in former famines, where relief in money was granted to the tenantry, a substantial part of it, by this device, found its way into the pockets of the landlords. The fall of agricultural prices was pressed on the Treasury by landowners as a reason for remitting a portion of a loan made them by the State, and their claim was allowed; but in the majority of cases they gave their own debtors the benefit of this consideration no more than the unjust steward of the Parable gave his. If a reduction was demanded, the ordinary answer was a notice to quit. Some provident agents were said to have a notice to quit printed on the back of their receipts on account. It is needless to say that there were exceptions, that some of the gentry strove to do their duty, and that, among those who did not, there were better and worse; but a class takes its character from the disposition and action of the majority, and the majority were cruel and unjust.

The history of the Irish working people has yet to be written. It is a history of astonishing courage, perseverance, and industry. Under native law they were joint owners with the chiefs of the soil of the country, of which they could not be dispossessed; but English statesmen, shortly after the Reformation, substituted feudal law which enabled the king to confiscate the land on any real or imaginary offence of the chief. They had been expelled from the best counties of Ulster by James I., and driven to the mountains, in order to make way for settlers from Scotland and England. Under Cromwell the mass of the nation were transported into Connaught, because the soil of Connaught was the worst in the island. But they maintained their courage and constancy. Under the penal laws the native gentry who did not fly to the Continent, sank gradually into the condition of peasants and labourers, and probably fortified the class into which they descended with new intelligence and intrepidity; their devotion to their faith, which was heroic in its constancy, purified and elevated them, and they emerged from long persecution, ignorant indeed, but morally sound and sane. When, in modern times, O'Connell led the movement for Emancipation, the most effectual stroke was struck, at immense risk to their own interests, by the small farmers of Louth, Monaghan, and Clare.

Their industry was a greater marvel than their courage, for they toiled without any security that they would enjoy the fruit of their labour. They turned the heathy hill and the rushy bog into arable land, and their recompense in the end was often an increased rent or an ejectment from the farms which they had re-created. Down to the middle of the nineteenth century (the period with which we have to do here) a great proprietor living in London could pluck down a village or depopulate a town-land with the same supreme indifference to the interests of the inhabitants as a Norman king who wanted a hunting ground six hundred years earlier. The petty proprietor was less of a tyrant, but often more of an extortioner. He took, in the language of an indignant priest, "the cow which gave milk to the poor man's family, the horse which tilled his land, the bed on which he slept, the pot that cooked his food, and sold them to meet demands which were inordinate and extortionate."

This system necessarily produced resistance and retaliation. There has never existed a community of God's creatures who would have endured it with submission. But the resistance was isolated and immethodic; Secret Societies were formed consisting solely of peasants· their retaliation was commonly the murder of other peasants who had served processes of ejectment, or executed harsh orders for the agent; it was rarely they presumed to strike at the landlord in person. When a people are reduced to a condition bordering on starvation, it is impossible to restrain disorder. "Hunger," says the national proverb, "will break through stone walls," and it will assuredly break through the laws of God and man. But the peasantry were fighting for existence, and, to borrow the language of a Protestant clergyman, "what strangers regarded as rapine and disorder, to the peasantry were only ambuscade and military strategy." A benevolent Englishman said it was undoubtedly a war of Thugs, but he was not quite clear whether the true Thug was the tenant or the landlord.

From the earliest existence of a Press in Ireland, newspapers had been maintained to slander the native race to England, and whenever agrarian disturbances broke out, the peasants were described as "rebels" in concert with some foreign power levying war against the Crown; and judges and soldiers were despatched to reduce them to submission. During fifty years there had not been three in which Coercion Acts were not in operation to strengthen the hands of the gentry against the people.

When the famine was four or five years in operation the contest between the owners and tillers of the soil had become so manifestly a struggle for life that the ingenuity of resistance was sharpened. Adventurous farmers of late had hit on the device of cutting their crop on Sunday, when it could not be seized, and carrying it out of reach of the landlord. It was a miserable spectacle to see an honest and generous people driven to such a stratagem; but let the moralist, before he is too vehement in his condemnation, consider whether a proprietary who refused to regulate rents by any reference to the standard of prices, who, after they got hold of the harvest which the peasant had reared, made no scruple of ejecting him from the farm he had fenced, and the house he had built, were quite spotless in the eyes of abstract justice. The device had only a limited success; lawyers professed to have discovered a statute which rendered any person aiding in the removal of property of this nature liable to a penalty of double its value, and as this was not deemed sufficient protection, a bill was before Parliament at the time our narrative opens, which prohibited the practice altogether.

This was the condition of an island rich in soil, in position, in climate, in a circling sea which united it with two continents, and in a manly and pious population, when the century which is now drawing to a close was at its mid-point. And let it be noted that while Ireland was sunk in this abject misery England was as prosperous as ever she had been since Liverpool rose from amid her marshes or Manchester from her coal-pits. And the prosperous island kept on foot in the unprosperous one an army nearly as large as she is able to bring into the field in a great European emergency—an army of thirty thousand veteran troops—to maintain the system which wrought these calamities.

It would be a perpetual reproach to the Irish race if they had not made persistent attempts to protect themselves. In the House of Commons projects which a native Parliament would have adopted with enthusiasm were proposed by Irish gentlemen and contemptuously rejected. The remonstrance of public meetings, of boards of guardians, and even of grand juries against ignorant mismanagement which was killing the people faster than plague or guillotine, were ignored. A courageous journalist, to whom the universal misery made life intolerable, exhorted the people to save themselves as other people in sore emergency had saved themselves, by force and arms; and the law seized him and carried him into penal exile. A country gentleman of long descent, whose family had been hereditary leaders of the nation since before the English invasion, and many associates of undisputed honour and ability staked their heads in the attempt to overthrow a system which was annihilating their race; but they failed to awaken the stricken people. "Young Ireland," in the gracious language of the *Times*, was now "picking oakum in the convict settlements"; and public feeling fell more prostrate because such an experiment had been made in vain.

It was at this lowest point of despondency that a local attempt to arrest the tide of ruin was made which had notable consequences. Callan, a populous town in the county of Kilkenny, is the centre of a purely agricultural country. The principal proprietor is the Earl of Desart, and the Earl of that day was an active exterminator. Between four and five hundred persons had been expelled from his estate since the commencement of the famine. In the autumn of 1849, the Catholic curates of Callan determined to found a society to give confidence to the disheartened people in their struggle for existence, by bringing a class less dependent on the landlord—the local shopkeepers and professional men—to their aid. On the 29th of October in that year the "Callan Tenant Protection Society" was established. Its objects were specified to be "Fair Rents, Tenant Right, and Employment"; and the member's card bore as motto the famous *dictum* of Thomas Drummond, "Property has its duties as well as its rights," and the principle recognised in Holy Writ as the basis of agricultural contracts—that "the husbandman who labours must be the *first* partaker of the fruits." The senior curate, the Rev. Thomas O'Shea, whom popular affection distinguished by the endearing name of "Father Tom," belonged to the class who find a straight road to the popular heart. Masculine in frame, frank and prompt in utterance, genial and cordial in expression, of dauntless intrepidity, and moved by a sympathy and sincerity which were mesmeric, the people would have followed him anywhere and at any risk. His comrade, Father Matthew Keefe, possessed gifts which were the complement of these qualities for a popular tribunate. Thoughtful, circumspect, forecasting, he estimated the difficulties to be encountered, and pondered on the next step in advance. The "Callan Protection Society," which was reported in the Kilkenny newspapers, soon attracted attention. Local oppression was exposed, the principles of a permanent remedy were debated, and a constant reliance in the invincible justice of their cause taught to the trampled multitude. The example was contagious. Tenant Protection Societies were formed in other districts of Kilkenny, and soon afterwards in Tipperary, Limerick, and Waterford. After a little time, they began to be heard of in Connaught—generally the last province to move, but where the need was greatest; and in Meath, Westmeath, and Wexford, where a still prosperous population were in a better condition to maintain a contest with the landlords. At length it was noted that the movement spread to the North, and, in the spring of 1850, there were Tenant Protection Societies at work at Strabane, Banbridge, Newtownlimavaddy, Newtonards, and other towns in Ulster. It was a gallant struggle, but necessarily desultory and immethodic, as it wanted not only a common centre and system, but the confidence which springs from wide-spread union and co-operation. They all demanded an alteration in the law of landlord and tenant, but there was no agreement as to the precise alterations which would be effectual, or on the best method of obtaining them.[1]

Neither the Parliament in Dublin nor the Parliament in London had ever granted any relief to the Irish tenantry. The Land Code, as an Ascendency Judge boasted, was framed solely in the interest of the proprietors, and was modified from time to time only to increase their power. Complaints and disorder had indeed led to inquiry. Select Committees every dozen

[1] The *Nation* newspaper, revived in 1849 after having been suppressed in 1848, claimed to have first suggested such an organisation. "In our sixth number (of the revived *Nation*), published on October 6th, 1849, the formation of Local Tenant Protection Societies was demanded. At that time there was not a single Tenant Society in Leinster, Ulster, Munster, or Connaught."—*Nation*, Sept. 7, 1856. But the man who accomplishes a work is its true author, rather than the man who projects it, and the Callan Curates were the authors of the Local Societies.

years heard evidence, and sometimes made useful suggestions, but they were never acted on. From the time of Swift, Berkeley, and Burke to the time of De Beaumont, Michael Sadler, and Poulet Scrope, there had been moving exposures of the condition of the people. Grattan, and after him O'Connell, told a tale to move the coldest hearts; but to obtain any remedy proved impossible. The great Absentees forbade legislation on a question raising so many dangerous collateral issues. Sharman Crawford, a large proprietor in Ulster, is memorable as the man who first dealt with the question in a practical spirit. He attempted so early as 1836 to secure ejected tenants compensation for improvements made with the landlord's consent, or which the condition of the farm manifestly required; but the Bill embodying this modest project never obtained a second reading. In 1843 Sir Robert Peel appointed a Royal Commission (known by the name of its chairman as the Devon Commission) to inquire into the occupation of land in Ireland. It reported two years later, and a Bill was framed by the Government granting compensation for future improvements in certain cases, but taking no notice of the millions' worth of improvements already in existence; it contented neither landlord nor tenant, and it was finally abandoned. In the summer of 1846 the Whigs came into office, and O'Connell supported them on the promise (which he alleged they had made) to propose eleven important reforms in Ireland, one of which was the establishment of tenant-right on an equitable footing. O'Connell was now dead, and neither the Tenant-Right Bill nor any other of the promised measures was forthcoming. An opportunity of making an effectual reform without wrong to any one had presented itself, and had been deliberately thrown away. In 1849, an Encumbered Estates Act was passed, giving creditors a prompt remedy against embarrassed landowners. In the six months which had already elapsed, thirteen millions worth of property had come under the operation of the new law, but none of the land was sold to tenants, and no conditions favourable to tenants were imposed on the purchasers. Such a policy had been urged in Parliament and in the Press, but the English Government at that time was under the direction of the feeble, selfish old man already specified—a man of the dimensions and demeanour of Quilp in the popular story—who had no higher purpose in public life than to make his place secure, and who understood that low art imperfectly. He refused to listen to a proposal that the new proprietors, in return for a Parliamentary title, should be required to grant the tenants a tenure under which they could live and thrive. Never was a fairer opportunity thrown away of effecting a great public good. Since that time land to the value of nearly fifty millions sterling has changed owners, with the result of giving the peasantry more absolute and more pitiless masters.

In 1848, and in a succeeding session, the government had proposed a Tenant-right Bill, without pressing it seriously on Parliament; and now in 1850, when the measure was renewed, it was discovered that one of its consequences would be to destroy the tenant-right of the North. It provided that certain specified improvements, if made with the consent of the landlord, should entitle the tenant to a limited compensation in case of ejectment; and lawyers were of opinion that all rights not included in this formula were *ipso facto* forfeited.

The Ulster tenants who had been organized into a Tenants' Association since 1848, took alarm at this danger and despatched a deputation to London to oppose the Bill. The Whig concessions, they affirmed, would be their ruin. From the period of the Plantation of Ulster by James I., the English and Scotch planters had allowed their tenants a special tenure, which came to be known as the Ulster tenant-right. It consisted of continued occupancy at a fair rent, and the right of selling possession to a *bona fide* purchaser at its market value. But in recent times, many Northern landlords had come to impose unfair rents, a practice which curtailed or extinguished the hereditary tenure of the province. A Northern poet at this time expressed the historic origin of the tenants' claim in vigorous ballad rhetoric:

> "We have been kinsmen of your blood, and clansmen to your name;
> No bond we asked but nobles' words when to this land we came;
> And now our rights, but favours none, we're seeking at your hands;
> We gave our Yeomen services—we'll keep our Yeomen lands.
>
> Was it for fate like this, my lords, our people crossed the sea,
> From Niall's and O'Donnell's swords your race's guard to be?
> Did for such serfdom many a year our yoemen fathers strive
> From wolf, from woodkerne, and from want to save your souls alive?
>
> Bethink ye well before ye try to grind us down to earth,
> The hands that kept a hostile land can keep a yeoman's hearth.
> We look around our hills and vales—are recollections there
> Of failure or defeat to bid our fathers' sons despair?"

This right did not exist in the Southern provinces, but there was the root and foundation of a still clearer right. For the Southern tenants were the descendants of the clans who had owned the land in common with the chiefs under native law, and who had been tricked out of their property without their knowledge or consent by the substitution of the feudal for the patriarchal system. They understood their claim imperfectly indeed, but they knew that their fathers and their fathers' fathers had tilled the same soil, had fenced it and erected whatever farm buildings it possessed at their own cost, and that the landlord's sole share in the enterprize had been to draw the rent.

The discontent of the North furnished an opportunity for national concert on the land question, but Ireland seemed never less prepared to turn an opportunity to account. The members of Parliament on whom the duty properly lay were the despair of honest Irishmen. They were lower in character and personal influence than Irish members had been at any time since the Union. A general election took place in 1847, shortly after O'Connell's death, and many of the constituencies, as a tribute of respect to his memory, had allowed his sons to nominate candidates, and persons got elected under their patronage who had made the name of Repeal member a target for contempt and curses. They had been all duly pledged to fidelity to Mr. John O'Connell, but by this time they regarded his wishes less than the wishes of the doorkeeper of the House of Commons. They were in general, indeed, men whom you might as profitably send to Westminster pledged to resist temptation as cast flax into the furnace with an exhortation not to burn. It was an exaggeration of course, but an exaggeration with a strong savour of truth, to say, as some one did, that the Irishmen fittest to enlighten and persuade senates had been sent into penal servitude, while men selected to enlighten and persuade Parliament would have been more at home in the hulks. A well-known writer, in a satire on the era, describes the House of Commons at this time as a place

> "Where Irish members make a holy show,
> And ruffian R—— blackguards Billy K——."

The capacity of the people to help themselves was at the lowest. The peasantry were broken by famine, pestilence, and extermination, and their hopes turned towards the emigrant ship rather than to agitation or resistance. A substantial minority of the middle class were Unionists, and those who were Nationalists took slight interest in any measure which did not aim to restore self-government to the country. Their principles had been subjected to a hard trial, but " faith," says the apothegm, "cannot be drowned in water or burned in fire." A considerable body of students and artisans still conspired for an insurrection to explode within a given number of months. Anything short of an immediate revival of the struggle with England, these honest Hotspurs rejected with contempt. There was unselfishness, sincerity, and genuine passion among them, but it was a passion so mixed with folly and gasconade, so little accustomed to take the ways and means of its enterprises into account that it drove reasonable men to despair. A year earlier, during the Queen's visit to Dublin, a plot had been framed to seize her person and carry her into the Dublin mountains as a hostage; and less than two hundred persons mustered at the appointed *rendezvous* for this prodigious service. A little later, a day was fixed for a rising in Munster, and it ended in an unsuccessful attack on a single police barrack. But these examples did not cool the ardour of these young men, and they treated the attempt to procure any change by peaceful agitation, or through Parliament, as hopeless and criminal.[1] But in politics you have to choose not what you would prefer but what you can accomplish. Though the Irish people had exhibited a constancy of purpose which has few parallels in history, it was certain that they were now sunk in a torpor from which it was hopeless to lead them to heroic enterprises. And there is profound truth in the saying of Burke that "All patriotism which is impracticable is spurious"—or at any rate it is unfruitful.

The more mature and far-seeing of the National Party did not believe that the edifice of Irish liberty could be built on the quagmire on which we found ourselves, like Aladdin's palace, in a single night. On the contrary, they saw that they must exercise infinite patience and work for a future which was

---

[1] There were some notable exceptions; among the earliest contributions to the League was a sum sent to me from Mullinahone by Charles Kickham, afterwards one of the Fenian Directory.

painfully distant. National revolutions have everywhere been the ultimate result of a long train of antecedent causes; and if Irishmen could regain their forfeited rights in the end it was plain that they must be content to do what was possible at this moment. It was by preliminary successes, piled like granite upon granite, that the lost path might be re-constructed. What could be attempted at the time with some probability of success was to shelter the peasants from being cut off in detail by extermination. The tenure of land had become the main Irish question. Sensible men attempt one thing at a time, and not more than one; for the national proverb warns us that "those who hunt two hares catch neither." All that could be done directly for Nationality was to re-commence teaching its principles and duties to the young. The mind of a country, like the skin of the chameleon, is of the colour of what it feeds on; and the future of Ireland was in its schools and colleges, and the teaching of the national Press.[1]

After the state trials of 1849, an unhappy destiny

---

[1] "The green acres have not rotted with the blight, the 'fishful rivers' have not fled in a panic into exile. Nowhere east of the Atlantic is the raw material of national prosperity plentier than in this island at this hour. Like the magic castle in the fairy tale, it stands with its door ever open, and stored with all imaginable wealth, if we but knew how to enter and take possession."—*Nation*, 1850.

left me almost alone to vindicate the practical capacity and generous aims of the Young Ireland party; and this was the course I recommended and insisted upon. If the priests and the Nationalists could be reconciled, if the North and South could be induced to act together even for a time, it would be possible to stop the destruction of the people. This was a result I could by no means hope to accomplish, as the representative of a lost cause on whom the cowardly and selfish looked with alarm or derision; but I had personal relations with men who were better situated to attempt it.

At the commencement of 1850, Frederick Lucas, who for nearly a dozen years had edited the *Tablet* in London, as the chief organ of Catholic opinion in the Empire, transferred it to Dublin, with my active sympathy and co-operation. Lucas, who had been born a Quaker and educated as a barrister, became a Catholic in his twenty-seventh year, and shortly afterwards relinquished his profession to become a journalist. Of the laymen who have written on Catholic politics and theological questions in recent times there are only two, Veuillot and Brownson, who in my judgment can be compared to him for power, originality of genius, and profound integrity of purpose. He was at this time forty years of age, of a reserved demeanour, which did not solicit, but seemed to shun attention. But it was difficult not to be struck by his shapely head, well-poised manly figure, and lucid blue eyes. When he talked confidentially his thoughts were sometimes like electric shocks, for his subdued demeanour covered a powerful will, prodigious energy, and a courage which, when it was tried in the end by the fiercest test, no difficulties could repress. He had come to Ireland to defend the interests of the Catholic Church and to serve the interests of the poor, with whom he had a tender sympathy. He acknowledged the right of the Irish people to manage their own affairs, and was an advocate of local government from the parish to the Parliament. But these were the decisions of his judgment; the passions of his heart were given to the Church and the poor. To be educated a Quaker, one of his admirers said, and turn Catholic was memorable; but he did a more notable thing than that—he was educated an Englishman and he had turned Irishman. More than any contemporary publicist, he enjoyed the confidence of the bishops and clergy of the Catholic Church, and any course he recommended was sure of favourable consideration at their hands.

In the Summer of 1846, the Northern farmers had founded a Tenant-Right Association, which was still in existence in 1850. The honorary secretary of the organization and the leader of the movement for the defence of their local rights was Dr. M'Knight. Like Lucas he was a journalist, and somewhat of a theologian, for his newspaper, the *Banner of Ulster*, was the official organ of the General Assembly of the Presbyterian Church. By birth he was descended from the Ulster settlers with a strain of native blood, of which he was proud; in opinion he was a Nationalist of the Scotch pattern, eager to foster the native music, manners, and literature of the country, but disposed to leave its politics to the Imperial Parliament. With him too I had long maintained intimate relations, and he was not indisposed to a closer union for any purpose on which we were agreed. He was the leader of the deputation sent to London to remonstrate against the Government Land Bill at this time, and was exasperated at the apathy of Lord John Russell.

For the purpose in view he was a factor of still more importance than Lucas, for it was hoped that he could move the hitherto immovable North. Dr. Gray, editor of the only daily paper in the popular interest, when he was consulted, entered warmly into the project of organizing the tenants' cause. The Tenants' Protection Societies must necessarily be the foundation of any such attempt, and Father Tom O'Shea, with whom they originated, knew how infinitely reformers struggling for a difficult object multiply their strength by union, and he threw himself into the movement with all the enthusiasm of his nature. When these men were brought together the basis of a powerful confederacy was laid. After consultation and correspondence, we agreed upon a programme. To give the proposal a broader basis, the assent of several persons who had not been consulted in the first instance was obtained, and then an invitation to a Conference on the Land Question was issued, signed by men who would have influence in all the provinces. It was designed to hold it in June or July; but when it became necessary to postpone it till August, in order to enable Presbyterian ministers, who were pre-engaged by the General Assembly of their Church, to attend, the country began to understand that there was to be a genuine union between North and South. The majority in the Northern province belonged to the Church of Scotland. They had clung to the faith of the early planters, not only from natural preference, but because it had long been repressed and insulted by the State. In modern times however they had been courted by the landlords and invited to make common cause against the growing power of the Catholics. The Northern proprietors had run serious risk of losing their estates in 1798 by revolution, and as a safeguard against a recurrence of this danger, they systematically fostered religious bigotry among their Protestant tenantry. They founded the Orange Lodges from the same motive which induced the planters in the Southern States of America to encourage the Mean Whites, that they might have a retinue who would need no other pay than impunity for party excesses. The farm labourers, many of whom were Presbyterians, were delighted to be admitted to the same lodge with the squire, and joyfully pledged themselves in return to abjure "Pope and Popery, brass money, and wooden shoes"—four hobgoblins equally dangerous to their peace at that time. The Presbyterian clergy, who had been the soul of political action in the North up to the Union, were placated by another device. The savage insolence with which they had been treated by the Established Church was greatly mitigated, and for two generations they had received a subsidy from the Treasury which was not without effect in reconciling them to the State.

NOTE ON CHAPTER I.

ORIGIN OF THE TENANT CONFERENCE.

This was the original summons to the Conference :—

"We, the undersigned, being strongly impressed with the conviction that in order to secure speedy and good legislation on the tenant question, it is essential to frame a measure which, in its principles and details, may unite the suffrages of the nation, and present a definite object of agitation until it be granted, respectfully request you will attend at a Conference to be held in Dublin (about the second week in June) to devise some specific measure of legislation to be sought for, and some plan of united action for its accomplishment :—

"JOHN REYNOLDS, M.P., Lord Mayor, Dublin.
"J. M. CANTWELL.
"C. GAVAN DUFFY.
"WILLIAM FORDE.
"JOHN GRAY.
"S. M. GREER.
"FREDERICK LUCAS.
"JAMES M'KNIGHT, LL.D.
"JOHN O'CONNELL, M.P.

"*May 11th.*"

Mr. Reynolds headed the list *ex officio* as Lord Mayor of Dublin, and Mr. Forde as Town Clerk ; Dr. Gray, and Mr. Cantwell, a solicitor, were proprietors of the *Freeman's Journal ;* Mr. Greer was a Northern gentleman who had written effectively on the Tenant question, and had been one of the deputation to London ; Dr. M'Knight was the founder of the Ulster Tenant-Right Association. The two members of Parliament, Mr. Reynolds and Mr. John O'Connell, never took any part in the Conference or in the subsequent proceedings of the Tenant League; Mr. Greer (afterwards M.P. for Londonderry) could not concur in the principles adopted by the Conference when it met, and retired immediately. The other signers, with the exception of Mr. Forde, prepared agenda for the Conference, and framed the rules of the Tenant League, and afterwards conducted the movement in union with the ablest men elected on the Council of the League from the provinces. As respects the origin of this confederacy (which has sometimes been a subject of inquiry) I will quote a single sentence from an article in the *Nation* (August 1855), while all the leaders of the League were still living and busy in its ranks, which may throw some light on the point :—" Before I was three months out of prison (in 1849) I had personally visited Mr. Lucas in London, Dr. M'Knight in Derry, Mr. Maguire in Cork, Dr. Cane and Father O'Shea in Kilkenny, Mr. Shine Lalor and Mr. Shea Lalor in Kerry, Mr. Godkin in England, Mr. Thomas Dillon (brother of John Dillon, then a political exile) in Mayo, and other friends elsewhere, to debate the feasibility of a Tenant Right movement." Some account of this journey, which I made in company with Thomas Carlyle, will be found in a note in the Appendix.

CHAPTER II.

PREPARATIONS FOR A NATIONAL CONFERENCE.

THE interval was not wasted. The men who projected the Conference employed it in preparing the necessary agenda, and the Press was busy debating the principles on which the Land Question ought to be settled, and the method by which these principles could best be established. Plans and projects were nearly as plentiful as in Paris between the summons and the assembly of the Tiers Etat in '89. I naturally took occasion to specify the policy of the *Nation* in the premisses, all the more because the claim of the tenants for complete justice had been first formulated by the *Nation* eight years earlier. There ought to be a plan, I contended, so just and adequate that it could be accepted by North and South, and might become the Tenants' Charter. It must provide, once for all, perpetuity of tenure.

"Over three-fourths of Europe (I said) the tenant is as immovable as the landlord, where landlords are not unknown.

From the British Channel to the Sea of Azof the tiller of the soil sits firm. Even under the British flag in Guernsey and the Channel Islands no one can divorce him from the land. This fixed tenure turned the rocks of Switzerland and the harsh sands of Belgium into cornfields. It would turn the spectral graveyard of Skibbereen into the cheerful and prosperous home of men. It is the custom of the civilised world on both sides of the equator. Here, then, the Irish tenant is entitled to take his stand. 'Give us the custom of the civilised world; your boasted freedom surely cannot deny us this.'"

The second essential point in a tenants' charter was a just rent. To fix a just rent it was necessary that the land should be valued. The proposal had been scoffed at as something new and monstrous, but this was a mistake; it was neither new nor monstrous.

"Every estate, and every farm upon it, is valued by order of the proprietor to ascertain the rent it can pay. The demand of the tenant is only that this process shall be *fairly* performed; that such valuation, instead of being private or partial, shall be a public one, made upon established principles and by competent persons. The County Cess and the Poor-rate, levied by the direct authority of the State, cannot be assessed arbitrarily, like rent, so much on this man and so much on that. The law provides that there shall be a careful *valuation* of the land beforehand, and that the rate assessed shall correspond with the value. The tenant only asks to put upon the private landlord (insatiable in the pursuit of his own interest) that restraint which the State puts upon itself." [1]

To obtain the recognition of these rights it was necessary to have a popular organisation and a Parliamentary Party representing it. An organisation which

[1] *Nation*, May 11th.

could appoint and cashier members of Parliament would become more formidable in the House of Commons than if its principles were specifically approved of in the decalogue.

The time was come when a settlement must be made if the Irish race were not to be extirpated, and I warned landlords that if they would not accept a fair rent they might evoke a spirit which would strike against rent altogether till a settlement was accomplished.

"In the front, like a dwarf, stands the just and moderate demand of the people soliciting a just and moderate arrangement, and willing to be content with it if, haply, it can be obtained. Behind is the giant who will settle the battle at a blow, if in any perilous extremity it becomes necessary to call in his aid. For it is to be noted that the whole system which grinds the people to death is supported by a subsidy 'paid in two equal half-yearly payments, at May and November,' by the people themselves; wanting which subsidy the system could not keep itself together for a year. And it is to be further noted that there is a great constitutional remedy known to her Majesty's Commons in Parliament assembled, and also to her Majesty's Commons *not* in Parliament assembled, reserved for great exigencies of State, called 'stopping the supplies.' The specific difference between this agitation and all that have preceded it is the existence of this resource. It is not one to be used—not to be so much as named lightly—but which, nevertheless, will act as a potent mediator between a Tenant League and the 'lords of the soil.'" [1]

[1] *Nation,* May 11th, 1850.

Correspondents and contributors were also busy on the subject, and two or three writers made themselves heard above the hurly-burly. Michael Macoboy, a barrister of wide reading, but in whom knowledge had not extinguished enthusiasm, specified the principles which lay at the bottom of the great land codes of Europe, and applied them to the case in hand.[1] The other was a cultivated young priest, who had been educated in France, and was able to look at Irish questions from the outside. The object which the Conference had in view, he said, was the *only* purpose to which agitation could profitably address itself at that period. To be successful one object must be taken in hand at a time, and it must be an object not sectional or sectarian, but genuinely national. It must, moreover, have a fixed plan and policy. The great Repeal movement, after a boastful and unprofitable existence, died an ignoble death, because it had neither. The plan he would suggest was this. Let there be established in each parish a Tenant Society including, if possible, every tenant farmer in the parish, whose members would take a pledge in these terms—" We promise God, our country, and each other never to bid for any farm of land from which any industrious farmer in this district

---

[1] Mr. Macoboy's letters appeared with the signature of "Agricola" in the *Nation* and in the *Weekly Chronicle* of London. He died a County Court Judge in Victoria, Australia.

has been 'ejected.'" Should any person violate this pledge, his name must be struck off the registry, as unworthy to associate with honest men. To sustain the tenantry there should be established at the same time in the chief town of the district a Tenant Protection Society, consisting of shop-keepers, professional men, and artisans, which would collect a fund for the sustenance of tenants unjustly evicted. If any member bid for land from which a tenant-farmer had been ejected, he must forfeit his membership, and, at the same time, " the call and patronage of his townsfolk and the district." [1]

Here was a practical proposal; but it is the misfortune of Ireland that she is seldom ready to adopt any project till the opportunity of using it effectually has vanished. Some months earlier Father Tom O'Shea suggested a nearly identical pledge to the Callan Protection Society, and printed it on the back of members' cards, but the lawyer to whom he submitted the formula declared it to be illegal. Mr. Lucas, on the other hand, was of opinion that he could bring it within the law for the protection of trade combinations; in short, that a farmers' strike was as legitimate as an artizans' strike, and both he and I, in our respective

[1] The young priest who made this proposal in the *Nation* signed it "J. W. Croke, C.C., Charleville." He is now Archbishop of Cashel.

PREPARATIONS FOR A NATIONAL CONFERENCE. 43

newspapers, recommended it for the consideration of the country.[1] But there was a marplot prompt to raise an alarm. The great name of O'Connell was at this time represented by his son John. Four years earlier, on his father's death, he had been conducted to the tribune of Conciliation Hall as hereditary leader of the Irish people, as solemnly as Richard Cromwell, two centuries earlier, was proclaimed Lord Protector in Westminster Hall. But a leader is one who can and will lead, and neither of these pretenders could lead anywhere. During the troubles of Forty-eight Mr. John O'Connell fled to France, and when they were over returned in the uniform of a captain of Militia to reopen Conciliation Hall in the interest of the Whigs, from whom he was expecting an office, which he finally obtained. But a few bishops and priests still sent him a little money for his father's sake, and when this supply was supplemented by the sale of the Hall, which was the property of the Irish people, it enabled him to keep up a delusive show of agitation. His meetings were not attended by a dozen persons; he had nothing to propose

---

[1] "The compositor who sets these lines, the proof-reader who revises them, and the mechanic who prints them, belong to a society which by its own act fixes their rate of wages, and they will not accept employment at a lower one. The law protects them in these proceedings as a necessary defence against extortionate employers. Why not the farmers?"—*Nation.*

which any rational creature would listen to; no person of name or weight ever appeared on his platform, but he was still worth something as a mischief-maker. This tribune of the people raised a clamour that the pledge in question would deliver over the tenant societies to the toils of the law. The peasantry were dying at the rate of a hundred a-week from starvation, and it might well seem that they could afford to run a little risk for their own protection: but the prudent shook their heads portentously, and the timid and ignorant took alarm, for Conciliation Hall was still a word of significance in a few rural districts. There was another difficulty to be taken into account at the date of this suggestion. An indispensable condition of success for any cardinal proposal was that our new allies, the Northerns, should accept it, and this proposal was one which it might be feared they would not accept. Nevertheless, I answered on my own behalf that the scheme was a reasonable one, and might be carried out successfully, if the people had the necessary pluck and perseverance. This system is what is now known as "Boycotting," and there was a quite recent case in point, which I cited.

"The Cape of Good Hope furnishes a pregnant example of the magnetism of indomitable will. The English Government commanded the Colonists to open their country to convicts. They refused. The Government entreated them to receive even one shipload, and no more. They refused. The Government persisted, and ordered the convict ships to sail for St. Simon's Bay. The Capemen did not fly to arms. They were too few, rather fewer, for example, than the men of Tipperary or Limerick. But they stood still. They declined to buy or sell, or barter or traffic with the English authorities. They refused to furnish them with bread or meat, or service of any kind. They refused, and they were faithful to their refusal. They stood together, and sustained each other. The result was inevitable. In six months the British Empire struck to the little handful of Colonists on the verge of the world, who knew their rights, and, what was better, knew how to maintain them. The Tithe Agitation has left another memorable lesson behind it. All the power of England was pledged and committed to the collection of tithe. A speech from the Throne commanded its immediate payment. The army in Ireland was doubled to enforce it—the police were turned into tithe collectors. But not one shilling of tithe could be drawn from the people. Royal speeches, and Royal army, and Royal Constabulary were all in vain. It was a war, with all the expense and danger and weary toil of war to the army; but without plunder or victory. The people *stood still*, and paid nothing. Their cattle and crops were seized and set up for auction. The whole country-side attended, but among the multitude there was not one buyer. Tithes were dead and buried, if one fatal mistake had not brought them back to life."

But to get such an experiment tried with the assent of the Conference proved impossible. The preparatory committee could not agree upon it. The Northerns thought it would alarm and, perhaps, alienate Ulster; and Dr. Gray and his friends were persuaded that it could not be attempted without exciting agrarian outrages against pledge-breakers.

In the mean time the landlords were not idle. They also had remedies to propose. Lord Lucan submitted a bill to his peers providing increased powers of eviction, and facilitating distress for rent, which he conceived would meet the real difficulties of the case. Lord Westmeath introduced another bill inflicting severe penalties on tenants who cut their crops after sundown to the peril of the landlord's claims on the entire cereal harvest. Some more politic proprietors, advised apparently by Mr. Isaac Butt, who was the leading spokesman of their opinions, declared that the true specific for the public distress was a revival of the Corn Laws. This simple reform would enable the tenants to pay both current rent and arrears, and restore general harmony and prosperity to the agricultural classes. Meetings to advocate protection were called in various parts of the country, but the popular Press spoiled this device; and the tenants, who generally attended in great numbers, declared that the protection they wanted was protection against aggressive landlords and exorbitant rents. In the clumsy fashion in which popular dissent is commonly expressed, they refused a hearing to Protectionist orators, and even Mr. Butt— who was still popular as counsel for Smith O'Brien, Meagher, and other political prisoners—was shouted down. The Free Traders in England took alarm; Mr. Cobden denounced this new panacea for Irish distress as a "mixture of shallow cunning and base hypocrisy;" and after a little it was heard of no more.

The men who had the management of the preliminary business by constant consultations, extensive correspondence, and the practice of printing and distributing the agenda among leading men, laid the basis of unanimity. In the three or four months between the issue of the invitation and the assembly of the Conference they were as assiduous as the ministers of a great State, and it was during that time that the seed of all future success was sown.

There was work indeed to make the brain ache and the heart quail, when they brooded over the social chaos that needed to be restored to order, and measured the formidable difficulties in front, or listened to the groans of the perishing multitude behind.

CHAPTER III.

THE CONFERENCE.

AT length, on Tuesday, the 6th of August, at nine in the morning, the Conference of Tenant Farmers and their friends met at the Royal Exchange. There were nearly three hundred delegates in attendance, mostly representative men, carrying the proxies of a district. There were Presbyterian Ministers, afterwards to be Moderators of Synods, and professors in colleges, farmers who had manned the local societies, and some of whom were to ripen into members of Parliament, priests, destined to be Archdeacons and Bishops, and nearly a dozen professional men, who afterwards entered the House of Commons or were legislators in some of the great colonies. I have seen deliberative assemblies in free countries from the Thames to the Arno, and from the German to the Pacific Ocean, but I am persuaded that the picked men of the Tenants' Conference would match any of them in practical ability and debating power. It was an authentic Parliament of Ireland as far as the assent of the people can make one, and in the fundamental fact of representing the whole nation. Reserved stern Covenanters from the North, ministers and their elders for the most part, with a group of brighter recruits of a new generation, who came afterwards to be known as Young Ulster, sat beside priests who had lived through the horrors of a famine which left their churches empty and their grave-yards overflowing; flanked by farmers who survived that evil time like the veterans of a hard campaign; while citizens, professional men, the popular journalists from the four provinces, and the founders and officers of the Tenant Protection Societies completed the assembly.

As the names were called over each delegate rose in his place, that the members might come to recognise each other; and whenever the name of a man who had done good service in the past, or whose character and position were guarantees of good service in the future, was announced, it was welcomed with ringing cheers. Dr. M'Knight, who had founded the Ulster Tenant-Right Association; Father Tom O'Shea, who had founded the first Tenant Protection Society; Pat Lalor, of Tinakill, who had organised the anti-tithe agitation of 1833; Rev. John Rogers, the orator of the General Assembly of the Presbyterian Church; young

Girdwood, who had induced his Northern society, crowded with Lurgan Orangemen, to recognise the justice of the movement for Nationality; William Connor, who had been imprisoned for the cause, and was known as the "Tenant's Friend;"[1] Michael Banim, the survivor of the famous authors of the *Tales of the O'Hara Family*, as dear to Ireland as the *Tales of my Landlord* are to Scotland; Henry Fitzgibbon, a milder type of the Church of England patriots led by Charles Lucas three generations earlier; Dr. Spratt, second in command to Father Mathew in the Temperance movement; Rev. David Bell, who had proclaimed a truce of the Lord in the Orange town of Ballibay; John Martin, who had laboured to keep the Dublin Corporation pure and public-spirited; noted priests or presbyters, whose names had a significance from events then fresh in the public mind, but now forgotten, and men destined to be eminent in the future in the legislature and justiciary of free States, and others of whom it was enough

---

[1] William Connor, of Inch, a gentleman farmer, who was a Protestant entitled to carry the arms of General Arthur Condorcet O'Connor of 1798, with a bar sinister, was prosecuted in 1841 for alleged sedition, found in a speech delivered to the farmers of the Queen's County. He advised the adoption of valued rents and permanent holdings. O'Connell expelled him from the Repeal Association in 1843 for recommending a strike against rent till the claims of the tenants were fairly adjusted. He had sincere sympathy with the people, but it was not supplemented by adequate capacity and judgment, and he accomplished nothing.

to say that they represented Derry, Limerick, Ballibay, and Clonmel—names as significant and symbolical to Irish ears as Rome, Geneva, or Rochelle.

Among the men of the future were Robert Stirling Anderson, afterwards Minister of Justice in the Colony of Victoria; Edward Butler, afterwards Attorney-General in New South Wales; and Wilson Gray, a distinguished member of Parliament in Victoria and a Judge in New Zealand. Before the Conference Michael Macoboy, afterwards a County Court Judge in Victoria, helped to shape the programme, and Samuel Bindon, afterwards Minister of Justice in the same Colony, became Secretary of the Tenant League. Young Ulster included a few dashing Ministers like David Bell, a few generous cultivated professional men like William Girdwood, and a few enthusiasts who inherited the historic blood of '82 or '98. The tone and temper of these men justified us in believing that there was a new Ulster familiar with the history of the Volunteers and the United Irishmen, who still sang the songs of Drennan and "remembered William Orr." Thomas Neilson Underwood, Secretary of the Strabane Tenant Protection Society, was in appearance a sickly sentimental boy, but with a manifest reserve of passion and will. He was known to be a lineal descendant of Samuel Neilson, one of the founders of the *United Irishmen* and Editor of the *Northern Star* in '98, and he was himself in the fulness of time destined to found the organisation known as the Brotherhood of St. Patrick, the forerunner of the Fenian Societies.

Sharman Crawford, who would naturally have presided, was detained in Parliament, and his place was filled by Dr. M'Knight. The secretaries were Father Tom O'Shea, Rev. William Dobbin, P.M., and William Girdwood. Two classes of great social importance were alone unrepresented. The gentry, with the exception of Mr. Crawford and one or two small proprietors of recent growth, held quite aloof, and with them the clergy of the Established Church. Many of the clergy had taken a warm interest in measures for the protection of the poor in the early years of the famine, but remedial legislation was necessarily political, and in politics their traditional place was with the Government and the gentry. Among the Irish parsons, numbering nearly three thousand, those who supported Catholic Emancipation, Parliamentary Reform, or Free Trade, might be counted on the fingers, and among the friends of Tenant Right there were none to count.

The risk run by an assembly consisting of such various elements was not that it would go too far, but that it would flounder into some feeble compromise. The work of the Preliminary Committee in framing specific proposals minimised this danger, and it disappeared altogether when it was seen that the bulk of the Conference manifestly longed for strong food.

It sat for three days, having a morning and evening meeting each day, with an interval for refreshment which served also for private consultation among the leaders. The gravity and urgency of the business to be dealt with was great, but no greater than the gravity and dignity of the Assembly. Day by day capable and energetic Presbyterian ministers worked side by side with Catholic priests of the same calibre in perfect harmony and good faith. When difference of opinion, which is inevitable among honest and intelligent men, arose, it was never a difference between North and South. The debates were free and full, but invariably courteous. There was no attempt to stifle dissent, a weak device very common in Irish counsels; and the result was a definite plan framed on principles which have since been recognised as just, and which, after long resistance and delay, have all got established by law.

Rents, it was declared, must be fixed by valuation of the land; and the power of raising them at will or recovering a higher rent than the one so established taken away from landlords.

The tenant must have a fixed tenure, and not be liable to disturbance so long as he paid the rent settled by the proposed valuation. If he chose to quit, or if he could not pay his rent, he must have the right to sell his interest, with all its incidents, for the highest market value; neither the landlord nor any other person being entitled to enter on possession, except on condition of buying it at a just price. The tenant's property, and his improvements, past and future, must be sacred; his to hold or to sell as freely as the landlord could sell his estate. One principle which has since been recognised by law, but evaded in practice, is worthy of being set out in the *ipsissima verba* of the Conference—

"Nothing shall be included in the valuation, or be paid under the valuation, to the landlord on account of improvements made by the tenant in possession, or those under whom he claims, unless these have been paid for by the landlord in reduced rent, or in some other way."[1]

---

[1] This is the principle known in the present day as "Healy's Clause." The local societies sometimes gave their delegates to the Conference precise instructions; the Strabane society in their instructions declared that "in estimating a fair rent the tenant's investments should not be made a subject of rent; and that in any periodical revision any subsequent improvements should not be taken into account, these being the tenant's property." On the subject of labourers, their instructions would form the basis of a just settlement at present. Labourers, they declared, in proportion to the size of a farm, ought to be provided each with a rent-free house, and a rent-free field, and have his wages paid in money, not on the truck system; and be released from the practice of "conacre," which imposed an endless burthen on him; and in case of lengthened possession, or when improvements were made, have the right of sale.

The political and non-sectarian character of the debates is illustrated by one that took place on the valuation of rents. Mr.

There were a million of agricultural labourers whose bread was put in peril by the consolidation of farms. Specific measures of relief for this class were still imperfectly understood, but the Conference ordered—

"That it be an instruction to the League (which it proposed to call into existence) to take into consideration at the earliest possible period the condition of the farm labourers, and to suggest some measure for their permanent protection and improvement, in connection with the arrangement of the question between landlord and tenant."

These principles have since blazed like beacon-fires in Ireland, sometimes obscured and apparently extinguished, but only to revive again. Sir Robert Peel thought it his duty when he passed the Catholic Emancipation Act to recognise that it was not to him, but to agitators in Ireland and to Whig statesmen in England, the success of the cause was due; and

Lucas wished the valuation to be made in each case by arbitrators appointed by landlord and tenant respectively, with an umpire chosen by the arbitrators. Mr. Gavan Duffy contended that a public general valuation of all the lands of Ireland ought to be made as the future basis of rent. Mr. Lucas's views were supported in debate by Dr. M'Knight, Rev. Mr. Dobbin, P.M.; Mr. Girdwood, Mr. Wilson Gray, Mr. Cantwell, Dr. Gray, Father Tom O'Shea, C.C.; Mr. Cody, Rev. Mr. Maloney, P.P., and Mr. Henry Fitzgibbon. Mr. Duffy's views by Rev. David Bell, P.M.; Rev. Dr. Kearney, P.P.; Rev. James Godkin, I.M.; Rev. John Rintoul, P. M.; Mr. Connor, of Inch; John F. Maguire, M'Carthy Downing, Shea Lalor, and Mr. Underwood. A compromise was finally agreed to, leaving the method of valuation open for future consideration.

when he repealed the Corn Laws he attributed to the labours of the anti-Corn Law League and the unadorned eloquence of Richard Cobden, the triumph of which he was the agent. I do not remember that either Mr. Gladstone, Mr. Parnell, or Mr. Davitt has thought it necessary to acknowledge where the principles of the Land Act of 1881 were first successfully formulated and made articles of popular belief.

There had been too much speechifying and haranguing in Ireland, and the Conference marked the opening of a new era by furnishing the newspapers with a mere skeleton of the debate, but with a full and exact statement of the principles adopted. It closed its labours by establishing the Tenant League at a public meeting at which Catholic priests and Presbyterian ministers succeeded each other in the tribune in support of each resolution. A Council was appointed fairly representing the entire country, and it was agreed to raise a fund of ten thousand pounds, for the purposes of the movement, by assessing the counties in proportion to their capacity. They asked for money that many things might be attempted, which, without money, would be impossible—deputations, tracts, and contested elections being the most familiar. The meetings of the Council were ordered to be held successively in different parts of the country, each to be followed by a county meeting, which should be invited to adopt the principles of the League.

The feeling of the country at these proceedings was divided between satisfaction at the cordial union of the provinces and alarm at the startling programme. But satisfaction greatly predominated. The journals friendly to Tenant Right were jubilant. The *Fermanagh Mail*, a strictly Protestant journal, circulating in one of the most Orange districts in the North, broke into poetic prose, which represented characteristically the delirium of the hour—

"It was a grand, an ennobling sight to see the children of the Covenant from the far North, the Elizabethan settlers from the Ards of Ulster, the Cromwellians of the centre, the Normans of the Pale, the Milesians of Connaught, the Danes of Kerry, the sons of Ith from Corca's southern valleys, the followers of Strongbow from Waterford and Wexford, and the Williamites from Fermanagh and Meath—all, all uniting in harmonious concert to struggle for the dear old land."

And a young poet of the *Nation* sung the event in authentic verse, of which one couplet passed from mouth to mouth—

"The news was blazed from every hill, and rung from every steeple;
And all the land, with gladness filled, We're one united people."

The right word spoken at the right moment is often magical in its effects, and there was a ring of sincerity and reality about these decisions which arrested immediate attention. But did they lie within the region of possibility—of practical politics, as the phrase now runs ? This was the difficulty to be first encountered. An aristocracy trained from boyhood to command and to obey, and knit together by a common interest as by ribs of steel, and who could count on all the power of the State to sustain them in the last resource, seemed nearly impregnable. It was waste of time to assail them except on principles so just that they would command the assent of reasonable men everywhere, and so adequate that they would content the people. The new party must not only know what they wanted, but be ready to justify it before the world. They performed this duty with notable success. Valuation, they insisted, was not a fantastic novelty, but the natural remedy for a distinct wrong. Less than a century earlier rents did not average ten shillings an acre over the whole island; in many counties they did not exceed four shillings, but they had shot up to thirty or forty shillings. This enormous change had to justify itself, and valuation was the natural and legitimate test. The Court of Chancery ordered a valuation before fixing rents, so did the Dublin University in dealing with its tenants, and even the London Companies. The State did the same thing before fixing the amount of its rent called Poor-rate ;

the landlord invariably obtained a valuation for his own guidance, and it was only sought to insure that this essential process should be publicly and fairly performed. Neither was it a novelty to make the valuation compulsory. A railway company could insist on a valuation to protect themselves from extortion by landowners, and the same protection was manifestly more necessary in the case of tenants than of a public company. Three-fourths of the property of Dublin had been compulsorily valued under the powers conferred on the Wide Street Commissioners. Landed property was a public trust; when the trust was abused the State was entitled, and bound, to restrain the abuse. It was on this principle alone that the Encumbered Estates Act (passed to make insolvent landlords yield up their property to their creditors) could be justified. The Irish landlords got their estates through their predecessors in title on specific conditions which had been universally evaded. Their legitimate position was that of stewards between the State and the people, and Parliament was entitled to inquire and ascertain whether they had been just stewards. This inquiry was, for simplicity, called Valuation.

As to perpetuity, it was the common custom throughout Europe, and the condition without which agricultural prosperity was impossible. It was one of the incidents of Tenant-Right in the North, and in the remainder of Ireland the tenants' right to possession was older than the landlords'. They had inherited the land from their ancestors, and they had bought it over again by their labour, for confessedly all the improvements were made by them. It had been suggested that a certain number of years' enjoyment exhausted the tenant's right to improvements; but if he put his savings in a bank he got the annual product, and afterwards the entire capital was returned to him. Why should he be content with the annual product alone in the case of investment in a farm? The landlord who declared that the law must not presume to regulate the tenure of land was in a strange dilemma, for there was scarcely an Irish estate which had not been taken from the original owner by Act of Parliament; and the present proprietors were the very creatures of law. It was known, indeed, that scarce one in twenty had a title with which he could go into the market, though it was always good enough to exterminate his tenantry with. The farmer in Ireland, as everywhere else in Europe, except Great Britain, must have perpetuity.

The popular journals and their correspondents carried the defence of the fundamental principles farther than it would have been discreet for the Council to go. The reforms proposed, they insisted, were the most moderate with which an injured people had ever been satisfied. When the existence of an aristocracy living on exorbitant rents became incompatible with the existence of the people on the Continent, landlords and rents were either abolished by revolution or strictly regulated by law. This change has happened throughout all Europe irrespective of race, government, or religion. In Austria the farmer enjoyed a perpetuity of tenure and a fixed rent. In France the farmers were generally proprietors, and paid no rent. In Prussia the country was in the hands of peasant proprietors, who either paid no rent or only a *quasi* rent as instalments of the purchase money of their farms. In Switzerland and the Alpine Valleys there were neither landlords nor large proprietors. In Norway every fifth man was a proprietor, and the agricultural labourers had secure farms for life at a fixed moderate rent, paid in labour. In Belgium the mass of the farmers were owners in fee, and had created a garden on a sandbank. In Holland the same system prevailed. In Tuscany, Piedmont, and most of the States of Italy, the farmer paid the landlord a certain proportion of the produce, usually one half, after deducting what was necessary to keep up the stock. And in the Channel Islands, within an hour's sail of England, which are a paradise of prosperity, farmers had perpetuity of tenure. On the Continent, wherever the Code Napoleon was in force, the landlord, when there were landlords, must let his land supplied with every improvement necessary for its profitable enjoyment; if he fail to do so the tenant has an action against him. If the crop was destroyed by such a visitation as the late famine, instead of the food which should support the occupier being carried away, the farmer has a legal right to a proportional deduction of his rent.

The enormous leap opinion had made on this question may be gauged by a significant fact. A few years before, O'Connell suggested a tribunal consisting of a competent judge and jury to fix a fair rent. The tribunal was to ascertain the expenditure of the tenant on useful and valuable improvements on the premises; and after a reasonable deduction for the profits derived by the tenant from his own expenditure one-third of the surplus should be attributed to him, and only *two-thirds of the improved value* charged by way of rent for the new tenure. The principles of agrarian reform were so ill understood that even O'Connell admitted the vicious practice of charging the tenant rent on his own improvements, and counting the enjoyment of them as a gradual compensation.

The landlord Press at first declined to debate these abominable propositions — they shrieked in hideous chorus that the principles of the League were sedition and communism. The outcry was as loud as it is against Mr. Gladstone's bills to-day. Even the *Times*, ignoring the courtesy and mutual forbearance exhibited in the debates, represented them to be as rude in form as they were unreasonable and impracticable in purpose.

"Never were fatal mistakes so eagerly insisted on—never was dissent more rudely treated—never was worldly wisdom more completely set at nought, than during the debates of the delegates sent to discuss the question of what is termed Tenant-right in Ireland. Amidst this vast farrago, the mind vainly seeks for some resting-place afforded by common sense and ordinary prudence."[1]

Mr. John O'Connell, whom the support of two or three bishops still kept in some degree alive as an agitator, solemnly announced his conviction that the main principle, rents regulated by valuation, was a ridiculous impossibility.

"Any man who pretends to have the least idea of agricultural affairs, who would say it was practicable to settle the rents of the country by a system of valuation, I would not argue with him, for it is evident he knows nothing of what he is speaking of."

To those who could interpret the signs of the times, this furious opposition was almost as solacing and hopeful as the enthusiasm and applause of the people.

[1] *Times*, August 31.

CHAPTER IV.

RECEPTION OF THE LEAGUE BY THE COUNTRY.

THE preparations for county meetings began in several districts, and the Council set to work on the instant to turn them to the best account. It took up the business in a practical spirit and by practical methods. As Parliament was still sitting, Mr. Shea Lalor was despatched to London on the part of the League to induce the Irish members to obtain, if possible, an act protecting tenants from eviction for exorbitant arrears during the recess, and he was furnished with a draft bill to give effect to this purpose. Mr. Lucas was appointed chairman of a sub-committee to answer the dangerous misrepresentations of the *Times*; and Mr. Gavan Duffy, chairman of a sub-committee on Organisation, was authorised to prepare a plan for conducting the local meetings and preliminary conferences, and to frame model resolutions for the county meetings and rules for the local societies. The report of this committee recommended that county meetings should be held in quick succession, that the temporary Council should be replaced by one consisting of a hundred and twenty members, elected by ballot; and that, in addition to its weekly meetings in Dublin, it should meet at least once in each province during the year. It was agreed to send deputations of Presbyterian ministers and laymen to the South and West, and of Catholic priests and laymen to the North. Ecclesiastics could speak with an authority of individual cases of injustice, and would represent in the most intelligible and significant way the new union which was our strength.

It is a penalty which a subject country never escapes that its complaints are treated as unreasonable, and its demands as extravagant. The principles of the League were met in England with contemptuous scorn. The philosophical *Spectator*, then edited by Mr. Rintoul, affirmed that the League, in seeking fixity of tenure and rents founded on valuation, was seeking impossible ends, and ends which, if attained, would prove not a blessing, but a curse. The *Times*, whose immense influence made it a power to be reckoned with, declared that the exposition of our case, sent by Mr. Lucas, though courteous "in phrase and rational in manner, was wholly without value, either as evidence or argument"; a death-blow would be given to every hope for Ireland if such principles prevailed. The *Law*

F

Review, as a specialist, was pained to see such ignorance of common law as the League displayed, and "the existence of such an organisation for the accomplishment of a ruinous impossibility." The *Standard* described the Presbyterian clergy as "freed from the proper restraints of morality and decency"; and its confederate, the *Morning Herald*, spoke of the "hungry, half-fed, and wholly untaught dogs of Maynooth, who longed not only for power and predominance, but for the pleasant enjoyments of a material and sensual life."

The *Daily News*, on the other hand, recognised the substantial union which had been effected.

"Hereditary feuds and recent squabbles are alike forgotten in the common feeling and universal impulse of the hour. Sects that have long been at variance, and parties that have long looked upon each other as enemies, mingle cheerfully in the same multitudinous assemblages, and learn to act cordially together in the same Tenant League."

Their appeal to Parliament was signally unsuccessful. Mr. Lalor held a consultation with Mr. Cobden, Mr. Bright, and a number of the Irish members, and laid before them the bill to prohibit eviction for arrears till the amount necessary to cultivate the farm and to furnish a reasonable subsistence to the farmer and his family had been deducted from the value of the harvest. The Irish members consented to introduce him to Lord John Russell, but declined to sanction the Bill, and took occasion to assure the Premier that their presence must not be construed into any approval of it. Under these circumstances the Premier did all that could be expected when he took a copy of the document and bowed them out without prolonged parley.[1] But it was a cause which could afford reverses. "It is as just a cause," some one said to Father Tom O'Shea, "as that which was preached by Peter the Hermit." "Yes," he replied, "as just a cause as that which was preached by Peter the Apostle; for it is the lives of the people we protect, which are the seed of the Church." One of the Northern deputies cited the Russian proverb, "With God's aid one may go safely over the sea; without Him not over the threshold."

But when they turned their faces from treacherous members of Parliament and scornful newspapers to the people whom they desired to serve, they met a success, which for promptitude and enthusiasm had no parallel in Irish history.

The first meeting was held at Enniscorthy on Saturday, September 21st,[2] among a population who

---

[1] The Irish members who accompanied Mr. Shea Lalor to Lord John Russell were Messrs. Frank Scully, Ousley Higgins, O'Gorman Mahon, Morgan John O'Connell, J. P. Somers, E. B. Roche, T. C. Anstey, Torrens M'Cullagh, and John Thomas Devereux. It is proper to say that the two latter in the end gave valuable assistance to the League.

[2] 1850.

inherited the blood of the invaders under Strongbow, but which had long been as Irish in spirit and temper as the clans of Connaught. The farmers of the county Wexford within twenty miles of the place of meeting attended on foot and on horseback, and there were said to be voters enough present to control the county election. A correspondent, for whose accuracy I am particularly bound to vouch, described the scene in the next *Nation*—

"It was a monster meeting. An immense area was covered with men on foot computed at twenty or thirty thousand. The horsemen formed a belt round this huge semicircle, and, as of old, bands sent up cheerful music to the sky. There is a subtle electricity in a mass of men of one mind—courage and hope passed from breast to breast, and it was plain every man felt that this cause must win. Be assured, the heart of the South is kindled anew."

The shire and borough members who had been invited to attend sent excuses, but there was no lack of more important recruits. Priests from nearly every district and citizens from the chief towns were present in force. The Northern deputation consisted of Dr. M'Knight, Rev. John Rogers, of Cumber, and Rev. David Bell, in whose person Ballibay had come to Vinegar Hill. Mr. Lucas, Mr. Lalor, and Mr. Duffy attended from the Council in Dublin.

Mr. Rogers explained and justified the principles of the movement. They met, he said, not to spoliate others, but to protect themselves—not to touch the fee-simple of the landlord, but to prevent him from appropriating the property of the tenant. He had been taught in the Word of God to "do good unto all men," but the Church of which he was a member had never been the sycophant of power, and he was in no mood to pay unmanly court to the landocracy. Valuation he regarded as indispensable, because the failure of the potato had rendered the payment of present rents impossible.

"I have never met any one (he said) who thoroughly understood the loss of the potato. It is a loss which every living thing about a house, down to the very mice, concur in deploring. For whether you consider the want of potatoes at the table, or to horses and black cattle, or whether you consider the privation of the pig, which Phelim O'Toole said was the gentleman that paid the rent, or the poultry, or the honest watch-dog, which bays a deep-mouthed welcome at his master's return—you must feel that the failure of the potato is an irreparable loss. On the ground, then, of the potato failure, I hold a fair valuation of land indispensable. In the North there had been an unfair valuation because the valuator was generally an Englishman unacquainted with the country; but whether English or Irish he was invariably in the interest of the landlord. When a tenancy terminated, no matter from what cause, the improvements effected by the tenant went as an addition to the fee-simple of the landlord. He would not refer to cases where the tenancy had been made to terminate before in equity it ought, or to districts where the landlords had driven their carriages and four through the leases of a whole tenantry, and then clutched their beneficial interests. He would not recall the harrowing scenes of eviction where the population of entire villages had been turned out onto the road-side to weep and die, and deprived of the Christian sepulture, except it could be called Christian to leave the evicted dead to the wild dogs' carnival, growling and gorging over carcase and limb. But he would notice an equally effective but less repulsive system, by which the aristocracy accomplish their purposes—the power of arbitrarily increasing rent. He expressed his satisfaction at the union of North and South in one glorious brotherhood for the regeneration of their common country. The Irish people had suffered too much and too long already to wish to perpetuate their own misery by needless agitation ; but, whereas, hitherto North and South had allowed themselves to be played off against one another to further the designs of political charlatans who fattened on faction and waded to place and power through the blood of their country, this game was now to cease. We will not allow ourselves (he said in conclusion) to be put into a wrong position. We love our Queen as well as our country; we respect constituted authority; we will keep within the Constitution; we will honour the law; but, by the blessing of the Most High, we will labour energetically and determinedly, till by legal and constitutional means we obtain the victory which the Irish Tenant League is destined, I trust, soon to win."

Mr. Bell followed in the same spirit. The omnipotent power of truth, justice, and humanity were the weapons on which the League relied—

"By these, and by these alone, they would conquer; and ere long men would see the black ensign of the pirates, who have long scourged this beautiful land, hauled down, and the Union flag, which bore upon its folds the Catholic green and the Protestant orange and the Presbyterian blue, unfurled to the breeze, to float over a prosperous, a free, and a happy people."

Like his colleagues, he insisted that the agitation which the League had begun was forced upon them by the aggressions of landlords. The property of the working farmer was being systematically confiscated. Extortion and eviction had rendered the right of the Ulster tenant, which was supposed to be an inexhaustible treasure, practically valueless. He instanced a significant case: a Presbyterian clergyman held a large farm under one of the members for a northern county which he had purchased from a previous tenant. Notwithstanding the potato failure, free trade, excessive poor rates, and the sinking of everything by which farmers were formerly enabled to pay high rents, he was kept up to the old figure. The consequence was, that he was losing largely every year, and last season was obliged to leave it without a penny of compensation for his purchase of the Tenant-right. But this system must end, for the earth is the Lord's, not the landlord's.

Dr. M'Knight declared that the men of Wexford were far in advance of anything he had previously conceived. Wexford was a model county in every sense of the word, and he trusted that the admirable habits of regularity and the high order of intelligence they had seen would have a beneficial influence, in the way of example, on the members of the Ulster deputation. If their movement was conducted with caution and a determination to be always in the right, Heaven would smile on their labours and success would crown them. But to succeed they must be united. Among many of the Orangemen in Ulster Tenant-right had extinguished party animosities; let the same spirit spread throughout the island till there was no longer Young Irelander or Old Irelander, Conservative or Repealer, Orangeman or Ribbonman, but only one great and united brotherhood.

The priests of Wexford reciprocated the cordial sentiments of the Northerns, and confirmed their statement that it was not an aggressive, but a defensive, contest in which they were engaged. The landlords, indeed, declared that they were the natural protectors of the people. But the people had no confidence in men who took advantage of the famine to fall upon them with more ferocity than they had ever experienced from a foreign foe—who, instead of consoling and assisting their unfortunate tenantry, extracted the last penny from them by rack-rents, and then demolished their humble dwellings, casting them forth to die on the road sides.

Resolutions were adopted accepting the principles of the League, and undertaking on behalf of Wexford to contribute 500*l.* towards the 10,000*l.* fund, and dividing the county into districts, in each of which a local society would be established, answerable for a fixed proportion of the amount. It is a fact worth noting that before the public meeting a County Conference was held, at which the resolutions were considered in committee, with the aid of the best local men. The correspondent of the *Nation* already quoted describes the scenes behind the curtain like one who had mixed in them—

"The social arrangements were made on a munificent scale. One enthusiastic priest carried off the two ministers as his guests; a young attorney seized upon a brawny editor; a hospitable doctor captured a meagre one, and a contest arose over the body of Dr. M'Knight, of which some Wexford poet might make a striking episode in the epic which in the fulness of time this invasion must beget. Mr. Shea Lalor (who acted as hon. secretary) was to be separated by no entreaty from his beloved tin box (containing the documents of the League), and he sat in perpetual committee at the hotel, giving and taking counsel like a general on the eve of battle."

A public dinner to the deputation closed the proceedings.[1]

[1] The Committee of the County Wexford Tenant Protection Society, a week before the Enniscorthy meeting, issued an address calling on every parish to send representatives to the county meeting and conference, and reminding them that if out of the present crop the rents, cesses, and rates to which they were liable were enforced, no adequate surplus would remain for the support

After two days spent at Enniscorthy the deputation proceeded to the county Kilkenny, where the first Tenant Protection Society had been planted. To receive them eight thousand farmers flocked into the city from the neighbouring districts, and the priests of Ossory were present in great force. The chair at the county meeting was occupied by Sergeant Shee, one of the leaders of the Common Law Bar in England, but an Irishman with local relations by property and family with Kilkenny. To bring the weight of his professional and personal character to bear on public opinion in England was a happy stroke of policy. The Sergeant defended the principles of the League—

"In England, if a landlord lost a tenant he found it hard to replace him, there were so many other paths open to energy and capital. But in Ireland, if the tenant did not accept the landlord's terms he might lie down in a ditch and die. Hence there was unnatural competition, and to regulate it valuation of rents was essential. The condition in which the land was let was a scandal; he had recently travelled through the most prosperous counties of the south, and he did not, except in the vicinities of the great cities, or the resort of fashionable recreation, see any building which would deserve the name of a farmhouse in England, Scotland, or in the north of Ireland. He did not see one single cottage which would bear comparison with the dwellings

---

of their families, the cultivation of their farms, and the purchase of seed for next year. Mr. John O'Connell warned all concerned that this was an illegal address, and would deliver those who attended the meeting into the hands of the Attorney-General; but by this time he had arrived at the point that no one took the slightest notice of his vaticinations.

of the labouring poor in any of the counties he was acquainted with in England. As regards fixity of tenure, it was ridiculous to describe it as a new principle. It was perfectly well known to civil law, and it was established in England by the system of copyhold, and was introduced into many countries of Europe by aid of the sovereign power. The death of Sir Robert Peel would give rise to new political combinations, and if the Tenant League was ready to throw in its influence with the party who proposed a good Land Act they would soon get one."

Dr. M'Knight reminded the people how they had been divided and deluded hitherto. The landed aristocracy connived at party dissensions—they set Irishman against Irishman, and succeeded in crushing and oppressing them all. Let them give up, and at once, all aimless and meaningless distinctions of party, and establish a community of brotherly feeling, a community open to Irishmen of the Presbyterian faith, such as he was, as well as to Irishmen of the Catholic community, and of every other persuasion. Let each, with singleness of heart, take the hand of his brother-Irishman, even as he now did. He suited the action to the word, by grasping the hand of Father O'Shea, an incident which raised the popular enthusiasm to a tempest.

Father O'Shea, in his turn, described from local experience why the principles of the League were necessary. "The people were compelled at present, as when Swift wrote against oppressive landlords, to coin 'their very vitals into rent—to starve themselves and their children to satisfy the excessive demands of their rapacious taskmasters.' Within a circuit of six miles around Callan, 280 houses have been levelled with the ground, though, with one notable exception, the local landlords could lay claim to a fair share of clemency and humanity."

Rev. Mr. Rogers told them good tidings from Ulster—

"Presbyterian Ulster (he said) is not Orange. Presbyterianism is incompatible with, and destructive of, Orangeism. Orangeism is Toryism, and the genius of Presbyterianism is utterly antagonistic to such a despotic creed. Orangeism is intolerance, and Presbyterianism has ever been foremost to rebuke intolerance, and to vindicate and defend civil and religious liberty. I know little of Orangeism, except this, that those who are baptised with its baptism bind themselves to uphold the present Constitution in Church and State. Presbyterians could not do this without denying their own principles. No one but an ignorant and apostate Presbyterian could be an Orangeman. The Orangemen of the North are landlords and agents, at one extreme—bailiffs and the tag-rag-and-bob-tail of society at the other."

Dr. Cane, Father Keeffe, and others well known to local men applauded and confirmed the union of North and South.

"We hold in our hands (said Father Keeffe) a weapon sheathed for three hundred years—a weapon never yet tried against England, keen, sure, and unerring—a weapon whose strength, because untried, can scarcely be estimated—a weapon before whose dazzling sheen the eye of the Viceroy blinked in the North—that weapon which shall achieve our victory is the union of all Irishmen. The landlords pursued the policy of 'divide and conquer,' and they succeeded; but that cry is hushed for ever. The people of Ireland have raised the holier cry of 'Unite and Conquer.'"

The second week the League crossed the Boyne, and made its formal entry into Ulster. A dozen counties were competing for the distinction of taking an early part in the movement, but it was determined to alternate provinces, and the chief question was where the most significant beginning could be made in the North. Mr. Bell was persuaded that we ought to begin in a stronghold of Orangeism, to make plain to friends and enemies that the League had none of the old parties opposed to it. Monaghan was known as the "Gap of the North," and Ballibay since before Catholic Emancipation was a headquarter of the Orangemen of three counties. Being a resident minister there he understood the state of opinion and he advised that we should plant the tricolour of the League where civil war was threatened a generation earlier.

"The 'bad eminence' which we have until lately occupied in consequence of our political feuds (he wrote to me) will render a united manifestation of our principles and purposes infinitely more telling here than it could possibly be in either Monaghan or

Carrickmacross (which were substantially Catholic towns). Besides, the landlord party might attempt to create disturbance in Monaghan—*here* they dare not show their faces."

When the meeting was announced the landlord Press warned us that we would have to meet the historic men of Ballibay, as Jack Lawless had of old;[1] and we did meet them, but with a difference. Masters of Orange Lodges moved resolutions, tylers of Orange Lodges helped to keep order, and one of the managing committee was son of the once famous Sam Gray. On the other hand, the "Farney freeholders," whose predecessors had opened the county in 1826 by electing an Emancipator, came in procession, extending, it was said, for nearly two miles; and a few veterans among their leaders who had elected a Dublin barrister against a combination of the Whig and Tory gentry, were on the platform with their old antagonists, where a flag of green, orange, and blue, typified the new union. Letters from Richard Cobden and Poulett Scrope were read, giving guarded sanction to proceedings in which they had still probably only imperfect confidence.

Mr. Bell recalled the threats of the landlord Press, and asked the Presbyterians of Ballibay to disavow them, which they did with ringing cheers for the

[1] In the era of O'Connell's agitation for Catholic Emancipation a civil war was nearly provoked by the mission of John Lawless to Ballibay. His opponent was Sam Gray.

League. John Francis Maguire, one of the deputation from the Council, asked them whether, as a Munster Catholic, he was welcome amongst them to help to regain for the people the rights in the soil which they had lost, and was answered with enthusiastic assent. Rev. Mr. Godkin, editor of the *Derry Standard*, invited the deputation to visit the Maiden City, and have the welcome of the North confirmed under the historic walls of Derry. He described the wrongs which had forced humane men to unite—

"I declare, before heaven (he said), my firm conviction that it would be more humane and merciful in the law, when the levelling brigade goes forward to destroy a village, to pull down houses over the heads of families, the frantic mother instinctively clinging to the roof-tree as for life—I declare, solemnly, that I think it would be more merciful to order out the police, to make them surround the village, and shoot dead on the spot every one of the men, women, and children, than doom them to the moral death and physical degradation of those pesthouses—the overcrowded and disorderly poorhouses."

Priest and minister followed each other on the platform, and were equally well received by the reconciled audience. In the evening there was a soiree to the deputation, Rev. Gunn Browne, P.M., presiding. Mr. Lucas, whose speech consisted of an exhortation to perpetual union, read letters which he had received from the Archbishop of Tuam and the Bishop of

Meath, encouraging and applauding what had already been accomplished by the League. They were welcomed by Orange cheers. Mr. Duffy answered some of the objections directed against their principles.

The deputation left Ballibay escorted by Catholics and Orangemen in fraternal union. It was such a sight as Thomas Davis had predicted—

> "Tories and Whigs grow pale with dismay,
> When from the North bursts the cry forth
> Orange and Green shall carry the day."[1]

---

[1] Our first embarrassment arose in connection with this meeting. Lucas and I (who agreed to take little part in the public meetings as long as we could get competent new men to speak, but who always attended to assist at the preliminary conference and watch over the proceedings) were met as we approached Ballibay by a local shopkeeper, or perhaps innkeeper, named J. J. Hughes, to say that the Catholics understood we had been advised by Mr. Bell to put up at the York Hotel, the famous Orange house, kept by the family of Sam Gray, from which a Catholic had been shot, and that they felt insulted by such an arrangement, and sent us an invitation to go elsewhere. We told him that our consent to the proposal was the sign and seal of the union we had accomplished, and that if we shrank from it the fact might prove disastrous. Some of the objections he stated, however, finally induced Lucas to accept the invitation, of which he was the bearer, while I kept our appointment with Mr. Bell at the York Hotel. It is easy in Ulster to move party passions. Next day I found the amiable Mr. Hughes had whispered about that I preferred the society of bitter Orangemen to my own relations in my native country; and on the other hand a distrust of Lucas was sown in the minds of the Northerns which, as we shall see, bore evil fruit. Before many weeks the Council found it necessary to publish a notice in relation to this

The next county meeting was summoned at Navan on the banks of the Boyne. Much was expected from Meath, the site of the greatest of the monster meetings held by O'Connell in 1843; and expectation was not disappointed. The solid farmers and graziers of the county and the whole body of the Catholic clergy were present. The meeting was held in the market square, which proved insufficient to supply standing-place for the immense attendance. Mr. Henry Fitzgibbon, Mr. Lucas, and Mr. Duffy, represented the Council of the League, and the occasion was signalised by the presence of Sharman Crawford. The county members declined to attend. Mr. Henry Grattan was willing to consider the land question, but "could not with propriety pledge himself to any particular body of men or any set of principles they might think fit to adopt." Mr. Corbally was more emphatic in his refusal; he believed the proceedings of the Tenant Conference "had materially injured a good and just cause, and therefore it was impossible for him to identify himself with them." But the men destined to represent great Irish constituencies in the near future were of a different

Ballibay Leaguer which it may be desirable to recall—"That the Council having read statements put forward by Mr. J. J. Hughes, of Ballibay, relative to certain proceedings at the League we have no hesitation in declaring that in all their essential parts those statements are utterly false."—(Signed) FREDERICK LUCAS, Hon. Sec.

opinion. Sergeant Shee sent his warm sympathy in a letter to the Secretaries, and vindicated the necessity of the movement. It was amply justified, he insisted, by facts stated by Sir Robert Peel in the House of Commons—

"More than half the houses in ten Irish counties, containing a population of 3,350,000 souls, and one-fourth of the houses in all the other counties, were," he said, "mud cabins, having but one room, inhabited by rack-rented tenants-at-will; and in the year 1849, 50,000 families were cleared out of such houses, to die in lanes or ditches, or part like strangers at the workhouse door."

Mr. M'Carthy Downing, afterwards member for the county of Cork, in a similar letter urged that a pledge to support the League programme should be everywhere obtained from members and candidates. Without exercising this duty in every county and borough in Ireland, regardless of political feeling or friendly ties, the agitation had better cease, for in that case he predicted it would end in discomfiture and disgrace. It was excellent advice, but the difficulty of complying with it was curiously illustrated by the fact that in a county Cork election four years later, where the candidate was a Whig lawyer, who frankly admitted his intention of supporting the Whig Government instead of the League, Mr. M'Carthy Downing succeeded in sending him to Parliament (as we shall see) to the "discomfiture and disgrace" of the cause to which he was pledged.

The speech of the occasion was Mr. Crawford's. He insisted on the principle of Valuation. The intervention of the State was necessary, because tenants could not protect themselves. Landed proprietors were protected by the usury laws from paying exorbitant interest on mortgages; and if the State protected the landlord from the claims of the usurer, why was it not to protect the tenant from the usurious claims of the landlord? The practice of defending the weak from the strong by law was a common one.

"The workers in manufactories had been compelled to work a greater number of hours than it was right they should work. A law was passed that women and children, and young persons should not work more than a certain number of hours; and when protection is given in that case, why should it not be given to the tenant, who is under greater power of compulsion —the alternative of life or death? We know (he said) that in other countries extreme remedies were used. We know what was done by an arbitrary monarch in Prussia. We know also that in India— our own territory—Lord Cornwallis, seeing the power exercised over the Indian tenant, altered that system and fixed the rents by valuation, and established perpetual tenure. That was done by one of our own officers; and if ever there was a case which justifies extreme measures it was the case of the Irish tenant; and it was right and just that measures should be taken to afford an adequate remedy for the evil."

Language like this from a great proprietor was equal to a battle won; it put to shame the objections of newspaper and platform critics.

Mr. Crawford justified Valuation, but he was unfavourable to the other cardinal principle of the League —Perpetuity. His limit was "a holding on the soil equivalent to the value which the tenant's labour and capital created"—a principle which neither covered the Tenant-right of the North, springing from original contract between the planters and their clients, nor the joint ownership which had existed in the South before the introduction of feudal law. Mr. Duffy, in defending Perpetuity, however, had to beware of alienating the indispensable Northern leader.

"Take up the map of Europe (he said) and you will find but a single State where it does not prevail in one shape or another. Our next neighbours in France have perpetuity. Their next neighbours in Belgium and in Italy have perpetuity. Cross the Adriatic and you find it in Austria and Prussia. Cross the Baltic, and you will find it in Norway and Sweden. Cross the White Sea, and you will still find perpetuity of a base kind in the vast dominions of the Czar. Take up the map of the whole world, and you will find that the practice of arbitrary ejectment—or, as we have learned to call it, 'extermination'—exists only in two small islands on the western rim of Europe, called England and Ireland. In the dominions of Great Britain herself —in every latitude beyond these seas—the practice of perpetuity exists. If a farmer from Meath emigrates to Canada, to Australia, to Newfoundland, the English

Government will give him the land for ever. Who ventures to assert that there is any just reason why he should not get the same tenure of the land which he and his father and their father before them have moistened with the sweat of their brows? Some of you, my friends, may have been in Jersey or Guernsey. They are flourishing and happy little islands in the British Channel, and under the British Crown, overflowing with comfort and plenty. What tenure of his lands do you think the farmer possesses? Nothing less than this daring novelty of the Tenant League, this invention of the Dublin Conference—Perpetuity."

Mr. Godkin renewed the welcome theme of the new union, and illustrated it by instances which had fallen under his notice—

"At the Monaghan meeting the band played 'Garryowen,' and the Orangemen listened to it with respect. There was another playing up the 'Protestant Boys,' and the men of Farney had nothing to say against it. The men of Farney marched into Ballibay in thousands, and, instead of being repelled by the Orangemen, were welcomed. Some of the most zealous people of Farney dined in the York Hotel, which was kept by the son of Sam Gray; and in the room where they dined was suspended the document that conveyed the freedom of the city of Dublin to Sam, for resisting the invasion of Jack Lawless. All the old animosities of the people were forgotten, buried in oblivion; and whoever attempted to disinter them ought to be considered as the most infamous of resurrectionists."

Mr. Fitzgibbon insisted that the League was fighting the battle of landlords as well as tenants. It had risen against a system which was pulling the whole community down to ruin; a system which lived on the plunder of industry, dried up the springs of employment, palsied the national strength, and tended to general anarchy. The leaders of the League were men who lived by industry, and understood the interests of industry; they knew well that its interests were never promoted by violence or crime. Mr. Lucas defended the League from some newspaper imputations, which, though they were a trouble at the moment, are now quite forgotten. The county was assessed towards the Ten Thousand Pounds Fund, divided into districts for local societies, and the electors pledged themselves to vote for no candidate who did not adopt the principles of the League.

The week following, the county Tipperary assembled at Cashel. The extent of the population and its repute for public spirit drew universal attention to this meeting. The "matchless men of Tipperary," as the poet named them, were in fact generous and public-spirited, though they had been befooled into electing as county members some of the most contemptible party hacks Ireland ever sent to Westminster, and the boroughs were long the refuge of Whig placemen. The honest freeholders attended in great numbers, and seemed to understand that this was a work in which they had a direct and special interest. The clergy were also largely represented, and among these were some new men in no way responsible for past elections, who proved the most steadfast friends of the League. Three of the district members attended, Mr. Frank Scully, M.P., taking the chair.[1] It was an evidence of progress, doubtless, that members of Parliament considered it necessary to commit themselves to the movement; but it was a doubtful advantage; for to put the new wine of the League into these cracked utensils would be wanton waste of public power. It was a case where, in the language of the national proverb, their places would have been better than their company. Dr. M'Knight opened on behalf of the League.[2] He told them that Ireland had been apathetic hitherto, and he read them a fearful catalogue of results—

"Within the last few days there has appeared the official report of the Board of Works, by Captain Larcom, for the year 1849, and it states the number of evictions that year to be—In Leinster, 8,253 holdings were made vacant; in Munster, 14,500; in Ulster, 5,357; in Connaught, 17,931; making a total of 46,041. In 1848 the total number amounted to 71,147, making, in 1848, and 1849, 117,178 holdings from which poor people were evicted. Those farmers were turned out to perish on the roadside or to die some lingering death in the workhouse, or to take care of themselves as best they could. The usual number of a family amounted to five individuals, and if they multiplied 117,178 by 5, they would have 585,890 poor Irish men, women, and

[1] The others were Sir Timothy O'Brien and Mr. Cecil Lawless.
[2] The deputation consisted of Dr. M'Knight, Mr. Bell, and Mr. Girdwood from the North, and Mr. Lucas and Mr. Lalor from the League.

children, who were turned out on the world in a state of starvation. Was there (he asked) a country on the face of God's earth in which that could occur but in Ireland?"

Father Cahill, a young priest who possessed many of the gifts of a popular tribune, described the sufferings, struggles, and rights of the people in language of passionate conviction. At the dinner which followed the meeting, Shea Lalor made a telling appeal to national feeling. He described a boy learning geography from his father over a school map then in use—

"In the margin there were drawings representing characteristic scenes in the different countries. England had its happy harvest home, Scotland its prosperous manufactures and well-cared-for fishermen, France its vintage, Prussia and Switzerland comfortable peasant proprietors; Holland, Belgium, Russia, Poland—all and each of them something emblematic of prosperity. But how was wretched Ireland figured forth? On a car, drawn by a jaded horse, driven by a ragged peasant, sat a half-starved woman and her naked children. 'Oh, father dear,' said the child, 'look at Ireland.' They might all look at Ireland, and ponder on the moral the picture conveyed."

At the County Conference Tipperary was divided into districts for local societies, and undertook to contribute £600 to the League Fund. A few days later[1] the League, fresh from Tipperary, was welcomed into

[1] Thursday, October 24th.

Orange Tyrone. The meeting was held at Omagh, within half an hour's drive of the Protestant church, where, two generations earlier, the Volunteers of '82 declared for Catholic Emancipation and the independence of Parliament.

At an early hour mounted men began to throng into Omagh. Every part of the county was represented from as far north as Donagheady and as far south as Dungannon, from Ardboe on the east and on the west from the borders of Donegal. At the front of the platform ornamental banners were placed with appropriate devices, and over all waved a giant tri-coloured flag of orange, blue, and green—colours which had not met in Tyrone in the memory of man, except in open conflict. An excellent band struck up in succession "St. Patrick's Day" and the "Protestant Boys." Thomas Montgomery, a Presbyterian Nationalist, of advanced years and solid position, who had belonged to the Young Ireland Party in '48, presided.[1]

Dr. M'Nally, the Catholic Bishop of Clogher, sent his good wishes, and expressed his conviction that there was urgent necessity for the immediate interference of the State for the protection of the lives of the tenants. The principles of the League would be fully explained

---

[1] The League deputation consisted of Mr. Lalor, Mr. George Fuller, who brought for a short time brilliant abilities and great information to the cause, and Mr. Duffy.

and powerfully advocated by the able men who took the lead; he only felt it necessary to urge that all intemperate language and all topics tending to exasperate ought to be studiously avoided.

Mr. Poulett Scrope, who had been invited to attend, sent congratulations on the union of creeds which the League had effected —

> "The unhappy divisions created by religious differences have alone (he said) permitted the Government to neglect so long the material interests of the Irish people. I rejoice, too, to see the cause of the tenant-farmers supported at their meetings in a peaceful, constitutional manner, and by able and temperate argument, which their opponents appear to me to meet only by unreasonable abuse and invective, in which the whole question at issue is begged."

Mr. Scrope formulated a principle which lay at the root of the entire movement. "Property," he said, "*can* have no rights inconsistent with the welfare of the people."

Rev. Mr. Chambers, P.M., rejoiced that union and peace prevailed. Sectarian rancour had vanished before the doctrines of the League; and the assembly of Tyrone, under the flag of Orange, Green, and Blue, would make the day an historic one in Ireland. The Rev. Mr. Gordon, P.P., warned the people that if they did not free themselves from the burthens of the present system the land would become a desert. When hereafter it was asked what had become of Ireland, it would be told that it was once inhabited by a brave, athletic, and courageous race, who served God and were faithful and honest citizens; but all they produced was devoured by two-legged monsters, who left them to perish of starvation. Mr. Underwood reminded them that the landlords claimed to have immutable titles. Immutable titles! Why, Cromwell made titles, Charles II. made titles, William III. made titles; surely Parliament was equally competent to make them to-day! Rev. Mr. Ferguson, P.M., justified the popular organisation. Tyrants met to consult together how they might oppress the people. Why should not the League meet to consult how they might give them liberty and prosperity? Bad landlords (for there were good landlords) had put their heads together to see how they could hunt from their estates the poor and desolate; but the Leaguers were putting their heads and hearts together, that they might preserve their homes to the fatherless, and secure to hoary-headed age the fruits of that labour which the old man had wrought in his youth. The Rev. Mr. Doherty, P.P., said the League admitted that the land was the landlords', but they utterly denied that the buildings, fences, and improvements were theirs. He had always been the friend of moderation, and he said now, " Let the landlords, even at the eleventh hour, grant valuation and perpetuity, and there would be peace once more." The arrangements for local societies and a contribution to the League Fund having been made, a banquet to the deputation closed the proceedings.

So many districts now competed for a place in the movement that a weekly meeting no longer sufficed. County Conferences were fixed for North and South on almost the same day, and the Council divided its available men to supply the essential deputation. On Monday, the 29th October, the farmers of Donegal and their friends met at Letterkenny. They desired to meet at the Courthouse, but the High Sheriff refused it, as the requisition did not contain the names of the class whom he regarded as entitled to that concession. The first fifty-five names, he remarked, consisted only of Presbyterian ministers and Catholic priests. It was true they were only priests and ministers, but a better judge of political forces would understand that this was a fact of more significance than if the requisition had been signed by the whole *posse comitatus*.

Again there was the pleasant evidence of union and harmony; parties which had long stood as jealously apart as castes in India mingled at every stage of the proceedings. A priest and a Presbyterian minister acted as joint secretaries. The Rev. Dr. Rintoul, P.M., who opened the business, rejoiced in their blended hearts and blended colours.

"What is there (he asked) in the strain of a musical air or in the colour of a piece of ribbon that should alienate the hearts of Irishmen from each other? Though he was as staunch a Protestant as any man in the community, he could admire the sweet music of 'Patrick's Day' as well as that of the 'Protestant Boys.' There floated above the platform a flag blended of orange and green; and he trusted orange and green would ever combine, and that no rude hand would rend them asunder."

He reminded the farmers that there was another class besides themselves who needed protection.

"Every farmer should be bound not only to provide neat cottages on their farms, but to provide also plots of ground for the labourers and their families whom he employed in the cultivation of his land."

Rev. John Kinnear, D.D., the Presbyterian minister of the town, applauded the career of the League. It had been founded by men of large intellect, and its bases were laid on the principles of justice. Its first success must be sought in Parliament; and the result lay with the electors; let them catechise candidates strictly; if they answered to their satisfaction on the catechism of Tenant-right let them bid them God-speed, but not otherwise.[1]

The Rev. Edward Glacken, P.P., also promised success, on condition that their union was maintained;

---

[1] Mr. Kinnear was afterwards one of the members of Parliament for the county Donegal, and has helped to secure the victory which he predicted.

and the Very Rev. William Brown described the urgent need of straining every sinew for success. On his way to Letterkenny that day he had seen 1,000 acres of waste land which could be profitably cultivated by men squandering away their lives in poorhouses.

"In 1846 he had invited the farmers to pay a small sum weekly to employ the poor; but what was their answer? That if they expended their money in improvements the landlords would come, in a year or two, and charge them an additional rent in consequence. He suggested the propriety of asking leases; but they replied that leases were of no value, as the land was not worth the present rent. This state of things in his own parish taught him the necessity of the two great points contended for by the League—Valuation and Fixity of Tenure."

Mr. Duffy explained and vindicated the creed of the League. The tenants' property in work done on their farms by their own hands or at their own cost was denied; but their claim did not stop there.

"That great Courthouse on the hill (he said), from which the High Sheriff has shut us out to-day, is a tenant's improvement. That bridge over the Struel, behind our back; those roads on which you marched to the meeting to-day, are tenants' improvements. Your money made them, and they are part of your stake in the country. They are part of the purchase money you have paid for perpetuity of tenure. Against perpetuity a new objection has been started by the *Times*, and echoed by every enemy of the League. 'If we give the tenant farmer perpetuity (they exclaim) we will next be bound to consider the condition of the labourer.' Why, sir, I rejoice in the necessity. There are still nearly a million of labourers in Ireland; and any arrangement that left them helpless beggars in the land no honest man would accept as a settlement of the land question."

He warned them that the cause for which they were fighting was in effect their existence as a people—

"As I passed through the titular capital of Donegal the other day, the withered town of Lifford, dead as Herculaneum or Pompeii, I thought it was a significant type of what the exterminators would make of all Ireland if we failed to arrest them. There was the enormous jail, the stately courthouse, a palace for the police, lodgings for my lords the judges, the messroom of their worships the grand jury; but not a human creature on the streets, not a pulse of industry—nothing but the grim, silent castles of authority and the miserable cabins of the poor. And this is our fate—to have nothing left of this ancient nation but a herd of miserable peasants and their hard taskmasters, if we cannot save ourselves."

The freeholders of Clare played a decisive part in the establishment of religious liberty in 1829, but in recent years they had been scourged by famine and by the more deadly plague of exterminating landlords, till public spirit was nearly extinguished. It had fallen so low that Colonel Vandeleur, the worst exterminator, got elected to Parliament for the county which he had helped to lay waste. It was not a promising task to move such a population to self-assertion, but the League undertook it. While Donegal met at Letterkenny, Clare was meeting at Ennis. The Council sent the Rev. Mr. Black, P.M., and Rev. William Rintoul, P.M., as delegates from the North; and Mr. Lucas, Mr. Lalor, and Mr. Connor from the headquarters of the League. The attendance was considerable, the peasantry marching into the town by parishes, led by their local clergy, as at the historic election of 1828; and the traders of Ennis swelled the popular muster.

Mr. Black described the principles on which he and his class had joined the movement. They did not desire to deny any of the landlords' legitimate rights. They held and taught that he was entitled to a fair rent, but they insisted that the same legal security should be spread over the property created by the tenant's toil and industry as over the mansion of the pampered lord who is clothed in purple, and fares sumptuously every day.

"I was asked (he said) by a landlord what business have the clergy with all this. I could give an answer, which, like an arrow, would pierce his conscience. What business had Elijah the Tishbite with Ahab when he took by violence Naboth's vineyard? Ahab was the king of Israel; he coveted the vineyard of Naboth; he took it by violence, and the prophet of the Lord was sent to tell the oppressor of his sin and coming punishment."

Rev. Mr. Rintoul followed in the same strain. Religion required him not only to love his neighbour but also to feed the hungry, to clothe the naked, to visit the widow and the fatherless in their affliction;

and it required him to do good to all men without distinction; and in coming to the South, in place of bartering his convictions, as the *Dublin Evening Mail* suggested, he was carrying out the religious principles that should influence all Christians.

Mr. Lucas spoke a language which came still closer to the bosoms and business of the people—

"We have now (he said) come to the extreme southwest of Ireland—to that country which may be freely called the Golgotha of Ireland, the place of skulls and skeletons—the classic land of famine and fever-sheds—the county in which starvation-deaths are regarded as natural deaths; in which the crowbar brigade assist at many a ghastly tragedy; in which the population of two or three moderately-sized towns are shut up within the walls of the Ennis Workhouse and its auxiliaries; and in which every possible persecution is committed against the tenant, on whom the law bestows no protection.... I think I have a right to say that there are twelve thousand adults in the workhouses of this country, who, if landlord cruelty and inhumanity had not driven them from their farms and made them the miserable recipients of alms, would be here to-day to swell this meeting."

Some of the local clergy, who had striven hard to keep public spirit from extinction, rejoiced in the hope of effectual help, and exhorted the people to second the efforts of the League.[1] The customary local arrange-

---

[1] Notably Father Vaughan, P.P., of Ruan and Dysart; Father Quaed, P.P., of Callaghan's Mills; and Father Sheehy. The contribution to the League was fixed at £300.

ments were made, and the deputation proceeded to the county of Waterford, which met on the 1st of November. It is unnecessary to follow the march of the League in detail. Ten thousand farmers of Waterford, which, like Monaghan and Clare, had struck an effectual blow in the contest for Catholic Emancipation, assembled on the hill of Ballybracken, overlooking the city, declared for valuation and perpetuity, and pledged the county to contribute £600 to the League Fund. Westmeath mustered immediately afterwards at Mullingar, and the entire county, from the Bridge of Athlone to the Bog of Allen, was represented by competent local men. The High Sheriff granted the Courthouse for the meeting, but it proved too small for the immense attendance, and the county Members were present, and, failing to satisfy the people, were warned that they must make room for better men. Dr. Kearney, a suave dignified parish priest, and Father Mullen, a vigorous young curate, explained the wants and feelings of the district in plain popular language, and Mr. Lucas and Mr. Fitzgibbon expounded the principles of the League. The work of local organisation was performed in the manner which had now become familiar to the people.

It was no longer possible to furnish deputations as quickly as they were demanded. Carlow, Longford, Kildare, Mayo, and Cork announced that they were ready to move as soon as the League could meet them. But the available missionaries did not exceed a dozen. The movement could not now be arrested, however, and the East Riding of Cork met at Mallow without a deputation. The chair was taken by Dr. Power, M.P., who, in the absence of the founders of the League, thought it safe to affirm that however good their principles might be, Parliament would never accept them. Dr. Power was one of the impostors smuggled into Parliament by Mr. John O'Connell after his father's death, who declined to take a pledge against place-begging as an insult. While he was disparaging the principles of the League from the chair of a League meeting this adroit gentleman was negotiating with the Whig Government to exchange his county seat for the government of a crown colony.

The Rev. Justin M'Carthy[1] defended the fundamental principles of Valuation and Perpetuity, and Father Corkran indicated the *motif* of the movement—

"I am asked by the landlords (he said) 'Why do you interfere?' Because my Master who is in Heaven told me to bind up the wounds of the bruised and bleeding man on the roadside, and pour oil into them. Great God! how many of them have I seen! And if it be mercy to save one man from the danger of death, what exalted mercy must it be to save thousands from the slow death of starvation!"

[1] Uncle of Mr. Justin M'Carthy, M.P.

The Bishop of Cloyne wrote to express his sympathy and concurrence;[1] but the country missed what was now the supreme charm of public demonstrations, the union of Orange and Green. It was the first at which no Northern had appeared.

The time had nearly come to hold the first general meeting of the League, at which the Council would report progress. They had marvellous progress to report. The greatest counties of Ireland had promptly declared for their programme, half the fund they demanded was already voted, and new districts, North and South, were preparing to be enrolled. They were about to knock at the gates of Derry, and the gates of Limerick, once the citadels of contending armies, and they were assured of a cordial welcome in both. Hope, which had died out of the hearts of the people, rekindled like a torch; money, which had been long refused for all political purposes, came in a golden tide. They had commenced in autumn, and when the winter was half over local societies were planted in nineteen counties.

[1] "Surely no man—I shall not say with a Christian, but even with a heart of flesh in his bosom—can contemplate unmoved such harrowing scenes, unless all the kindlier feelings and sensibilities of our common nature be extinguished within him. Under those circumstances, I deem it the bounden duty of every man, no matter what his rank or order, who values the existence of order among us, to aid and assist in every legal and constitutional effort to introduce and establish fair and equitable relations between our landlords and tenants."—Letter of the Right Rev. Dr. Murphy.

out of thirty-two: an agency which gave the Council more eyes than Argus and more hands than Briareus; and, above all, the bases for obtaining a Parliamentary party were being silently laid. More than thirty constituencies had pledged themselves to elect only Leaguers, prepared to work in and out of Parliament for the establishment of our principles. Other signs of success were not wanting. Abatements of rent were constantly reported in the newspapers. The Marquis of Ormond, the Marquis of Lansdowne, Lord Ashburton, and other proprietors, had adopted the practice of public valuation. In England one of the Protectionist leaders, the Marquis of Granby, told his tenantry that he would select two men acquainted with their feelings and their wants to consider what their rents ought in reason and justice to be. The work accomplished was estimated alike by men of widely different politics. A hard-working barrister declared that it had struck a blow which, in the words of Grattan, would " resound through history " in asserting the great principle that the rights of humanity were paramount to the rights of property. And a journalist living in a focus of factions recognised that it stood high above all party feeling. "No petty intolerance," he affirmed, "no rivalry for leadership, no partisan bigotry, intruded on its peaceful course"; and he pronounced that the independent yeomen of Fermanagh "would give the southern brogue as hearty a reception in Enniskillen as the old Scottish twang of the Covenant was greeted with beyond the Boyne." The survivors of the Young Ireland poets brought to the movement the inspiration of song. An English poet[1] foreshadowed the new Ireland which the League might create—

> "Studded with cheerful homesteads fair to see,
> With garden grace and household symmetry,
> How grand the wide-browed peasant's manly mien !
> How sweet the matron's smile serene !
>   Oh happy, happy land ! "

The common sentiment of the time was "Each for all, and all for each;" and it was with genuine and touching piety an eminent ecclesiastical Leaguer exclaimed, when the result was laid before him, "Glory be to God on High, and on Earth peace to men of goodwill."

[1] W. J. Linton, the artist, who wrote in the *Nation* under the *nom de plume* of "Spartacus."

NOTES ON CHAPTER IV.

DEPUTATIONS.

Comic incidents sometimes befell the deputationists. On one occasion I was the guest of a young poet; when dinner was over he locked his study door to secure an uninterrupted *tête-à-tête*, and then produced—literally—a tragedy and two epic poems, on which I was to favour him with my candid opinion. In another district a hospitable country priest insisted on providing shelter for an entire deputation. Next morning the supply of towels ran short, and a Dublin dandy rang for more. Lucas, returning from an early walk, came into the bedroom (which had more than one occupant) in time to hear the gentleman's wants. "More towels," he said with the profound gravity which is the basis of Saxon humour, "Oh, certainly; is there anything else you would like to mention? It was very negligent of our host (a country curate) not to assign a body servant to each of us to look after his special requirements."

It is a common experience of life that if every pleasure comprises unexpected pain, almost every labour has unexpected compensations. Many of the journeys to the country were as refreshing as open air, agreeable society, and exciting conversation could make them to dusty citizens. Some of the talks on the business in hand, on experience of life, on books and men, were memorable. I can recall the surprise of his associates when Lucas illustrated his opinion of Thackeray's ballads by reciting from memory the story of Jacob Omnium's " Lost Hoss," as narrated by Policeman X. And we were becoming more familiar with the attractions of the country and the habits of the people—a study which a lifetime does not exhaust. Here is a scrap from the private letter of one deputationist in a prosperous district—

" Heavens! but I have had such delicious days. This is a country for demigods to dwell in—men to make love in, or worship God. Such trees, such grass, such skies, such air, and the river, and the old holy mounts! And the friendly people. And here there is actually no appearance of poverty, and the crops look well and the people hopeful."

Another philosophised in a different vein—

"A great physiognomist of nature might write a book on the character of races, as exhibited in their agricultural fences; and tell us, perhaps, why the Galwayman erects miles of loose, ragged stone walls, so feeble and rickety that a vigorous brogue might kick them down of a morning, and often does; while the Wexfordian raises a fence that would shut out the waters of the Rhine around every patch of his little holding. 'Ah,' exclaimed an impetuous friend, 'what incomparable peasant proprietors these fellows would make, when they foster the landlord's acres so tenderly!'"[1]

---

[1] *Nation* Correspondence.

CHAPTER V.

THE COUNCIL AND ITS FIRST TROUBLES.

IN popular movements the control has a tendency to fall into the hands of an informal Cabinet. The men who take most pains naturally obtain most power. There is rarely any special appointment to such an office, it springs from the nature of things; a good deal probably from a silent concurrence in the national proverb that where all are captains the ship sinks, but most of all from the fact that there are not many men who will undertake constant and onerous labour when there is not a stiver of pay. The duties of one of the leaders in such a movement are not confined to the council room, still less to the platform: his essential and governing power is exercised in correspondence and consultations which correct misapprehensions and smooth away difficulties. The office requires constant attention to details, patience with folly in all its forms, and a decision of character which can act promptly in emergencies.

The most indispensable element in the new organisation was the Northern contingent. Dr. M'Knight was their undisputed leader. He had won the confidence of Ulster, and deserved it by a genuine devotion to the interest of the tenant-farmers. For their sake he transformed himself in middle-age from a dreamer loitering in the flowered fields of literature and philosophy, into a practical man, armed with Blue Books and Acts of Parliament. He had, indeed, always a leaning to metaphysics, which gave a speculative character to his thinking, but he corrected it by constant attention to details. He was earnest, acute, well-informed, and on the social side as free from bigotry or distrust as any man with his discipline and experience could be expected to be. He was the incarnation of cautious good sense, little disturbed by passion or prejudice, and he entered into the League fixedly determined that it should never fail from any fault of his. He could rarely attend the préparatory meetings, but I was in constant correspondence with him in relation to whatever was done or projected, and we had always the advantage of his advice, which was sound and generous, but cautious and discreet.

The confidence of the Catholic clergy was chiefly given to Frederick Lucas. He was a man of prodigious industry, and could always be counted on to be at his post. Though he was easily moved by the moral indignation which is never wanting in a profound and generous nature, it was held in check by patience and an imperturbable composure. In discourse he was close and vigorous, rarely lifted by imagination or passion above the lively, lucid, common sense fittest for the transaction of business in popular assemblies. Those who saw him indefatigable in committees and conferences knew imperfectly the constant and exhausting labours he undertook elsewhere. His position imposed a wide correspondence and constant interviews with persons from all parts of the country; he not only edited, but in great part wrote, a weekly paper, and he watched over the business of the League with minute attention. He had little sympathy with the Nationalists who scorned any project falling short of self-government; and still less with the Whigs who scorned any project which had not received the preliminary sanction of English statesmen. But he fulfilled the condition which Pascal considers the evidence of a nature fit to control and reconcile, which does not go to either extreme, but touches both, and fills the space between. He was not alone a writer and thinker; he possessed the fundamental condition of success in politics—the capacity for action; and he had, besides, the physical equipment all but indispensable to public success—a massive head, a deep chest, a full and flexible voice, and the general robustness which belongs to such an organisation.[1]

Mr. Henry Fitzgibbon was a draper, with a good deal of the public spirit with which Swift endowed an imaginary "drapier" a century earlier. One of his brothers was a successful barrister; another is still remembered in London as a man with a grievance. He had been an officer of militia in Upper Canada, and was persuaded that his promptitude saved that colony to the British Crown in the troubles of 1837—a belief which the British Crown apparently did not share. Henry Fitzgibbon had intelligence and generous sympathies, and represented adequately the Protestant shopkeepers of Dublin, both in their interests and their prejudices.

---

[1] Lucas had a simple manliness in transacting business which was a lesson to Irish pride. There were several writers of the *Nation, Freeman*, and other Irish journals on the League Council from time to time, and there was probably not one of them who would not have been insulted at the proposal of taking a subscription for his paper, and transacting business in a place where he attended for public ends. They saw with amazement, and not without scorn I fear, Lucas counting the shillings paid by some country priest for his subscription to the *Tablet*, and giving him a receipt with as little sense of incongruity as if it were the coupon of a national loan. His journal addressed itself to clerical readers mainly, and, as I learned from himself, yielded an income on an Apostolic scale. He accepted "holy poverty" cheerfully as one of the conditions of the task which he had undertaken.

He felt keenly the wrongs inflicted on tenant-farmers; but in other respects accepted the British connection with all its penalties rather than face the perils supposed to reside in a native Parliament.

John Shea Lalor had been a lawyer and a landed proprietor—both on a limited scale; but the disorders of the time broke up his relations, not only with his profession but with his estate, which fell into the hands of the new Land Court. He was a man of popular talents, had long experience of the country, and possessed in an extraordinary degree the power of recalling it with dramatic effect. He was an actor in the sense that Demosthenes considered acting an essential part of oratory, and could make the commonplaces of politics shine with unexpected light. He entered on his duties of honorary secretary with the zeal of a new Minister of State.

I have already named in connection with public meetings the most energetic of the ecclesiastical Leaguers; but some of the most laborious and influential never mounted a platform. I can still recall Father Ennis, from the diocese of Meath, a man of sweet and gentle disposition, which, when it is united to honesty of purpose, wins confidence more than great ability; Father Dowling, from the same diocese, who gave to the details and the accounts the care a selfish man bestows upon his own ledger and day book;

Father Aylward, from Ossory, ex-President of the College of Kilkenny, silent and retiring, but with the courage of a lion; Father Bernard Daly, a handsome young priest from Dublin, who had been a Young Irelander in '48—a man of fertile and cultivated intellect, and an apostolic love of the suffering people; the two Dobbins, Presbyterian clergymen, and brothers, I believe, but who only resembled each other in zeal for the common cause.

The condition of Ireland was not favourable to the growth of trained capacity. The primary and intermediate schools were bad, and there were no public functions to discipline men in the transaction of business. The insight which flashes a sudden light upon a point at issue belongs to the national genius, but the practice of collecting knowledge patiently, and pondering over it till guiding principles are attained, was rare, and the movement at its outset depended on the men I have indicated and one or two others.

The unbroken and unexampled success which had attended the League for three months furnishes an adequate measure of their silent labours. The process by which the convictions of the ideaful few become the common opinion of a community has seldom worked more decisively. But it is rarely the fortune of human affairs to long resemble a triumphal march The inevitable check may be expected; and political sagacity consists in a larger degree in the habit of anticipating and providing against it.

Their first serious embarrassment was the withdrawal from the Council of John and Wilson Gray, who had brought a fund of practical sagacity to its deliberations.[1] They desired to disconnect the local societies from the League, under the apprehension that the peasantry would be sure to run into illegal excesses for which the Council would be responsible. The leading members, lay and clerical, were of a different opinion; they considered the local societies the strength of the League, and that, exactly in proportion as they spread, illegality would diminish. For the League would have what no Government possessed—two or more officers in every parish, North or South, enjoying the confidence of the people and bound by their profession to watch over the public safety. The Grays replied that to insist on their opinions, which they were bound to do if they remained, must create dissension and to avoid this evil they would retire. We next heard from the North that our friends there were paying some of the penalties of patriotism. Certain professors of the Queen's College, Belfast, complained that the organ of the General Assembly was edited by a man committed to dangerous opinions, and they demanded

[1] The Messrs. Gray were the principal proprietors of the *Freeman's Journal.*

to have Dr. M'Knight ousted from that office. The landlord Press in Ulster kept up a lively cannonade on Mr. Rogers, Mr. Bell, and the other Presbyterian Leaguers, and a few of their brethren lost no opportunity of expressing their displeasure with the new movement. And Mr. John O'Connell announced once a week that Mr. Duffy had proved a dangerous leader in 1848, and would be sure to tempt the people into illegal courses. These were troubles which might have been anticipated; but a more alarming danger sprang up in a quarter where nothing was foreseen. It was Lord John Russell who gave the League its first serious check.

Towards the close of 1850 the Pope placed the control of ecclesiastical affairs among the Catholics of England on a new footing. The Bishops since the seventeenth century had been named Vicars-Apostolic, and, after a long eclipse, he revived the titles, organisation, and jurisdiction of the Hierarchy as they originally existed. The Court of Rome is not accustomed to act rashly, and it had taken unusual precautions in this business. A year earlier Lord John Russell, then Prime Minister, presented a scheme to Parliament with a view to revive diplomatic relations with the Holy See, and his father-in-law, the Earl of Minto, who was in Rome on this business at the time, was shown the proposed arrangement for the new Hierarchy, to which

THE COUNCIL AND ITS FIRST TROUBLES. 113

he made no objection. Under ordinary circumstances the transaction would have scarcely attracted attention in England, for the Catholics, in organising their Church, did no more than Methodists, Presbyterians, Independents, and other sects of Protestant Dissenters were in the habit of doing. But there had been numerous conversions to Catholicity among the propertied and cultivated class, and especially among the clergy of the Established Church, and the middle and lower orders were amazed and angry. The Whig Government at this time, as always happened under the feeble lead of Lord John Russell, had lost public confidence, and he suddenly bethought him that he might regain it by making himself the mouthpiece of resistance to this Papal aggression. Without consulting his colleagues, he wrote a letter to the Bishop of Durham on the transaction, which was an appeal to the most sectarian passions. The sudden zeal for the Church of a man who pendulated in his own religious attendance between a Dissenting Chapel and a gorgeous Puseyite Church, and who had clambered to office by demanding the appropriation to secular purposes of Church property in Ireland, was well understood to be a party device. But his precise motive was anxiously scrutinised. In England the desire to make his position in the Treasury more secure was considered motive enough; in Ireland there

I

was a suspicion that he aimed to break up a confederacy which he hated and feared. For the first time for generations the Irish people were united. They were laying the foundations of a Parliamentary Party which might hold the Whig Ministry and all succeeding Ministries at its mercy, and to counteract this danger they were persuaded he had had recourse to the traditional weapon, sharpened in succeeding generations by the skill of Bacon, Strafford, Boulter, and Saurin, and which often struck as silently and surely as death—religious bigotry. The Northerns had entered the League with the most generous intentions, and had pacified, if they had not converted, the Orangemen; but to raise religious questions was to carry a torch among gunpowder. The business did not properly concern Ireland, and we hoped for a time that it might be dealt with as an English question, in which, while we insisted upon the right of Christian communities to manage their own ecclesiastical affairs according to their own will and conscience, we were not called upon to take a more active part in the contest than the English Catholic community took in Irish affairs. Some marplots demanded a series of county meetings in Ireland to protest against the Durham letters, insisting that no reasonable Protestant could object to such a defensive movement. But the League wanted the assistance of unreasonable

Protestants, of Orangemen, and of bigots. Its strength and success sprang from this unprecedented combination; and if it were dissolved by any mischance, the exterminator would be unchecked, and another million of the Irish race would die in torture and ignominy. Meantime England took fire; passionate denunciations of Pope and Popery were heard on all sides, and every post brought exhortations to Irish Protestants to join their brethren against the common enemy. The problem whether the North and South could act together could scarcely have been subjected to a more sudden and crucial test.

Immediately after this difficulty arose, the county of Louth met at Dundalk, and both parties to the new union behaved admirably. The Chairman an aged clergyman,[1] announced that the county would be won for the League, and by the League, against all competitors—

"I know this county well (he said). I have served in all parts of it, from the bar of the Boyne to the borders of Monaghan. I have taken an active part in establishing and sustaining the registry. If I, joined by all the priests of the county, and all the Protestant rectors of the county, and all the landlords of the county, put forward candidates opposed to Tenant Right, we would inevitably be defeated.'

Letters from the county and borough members were read. Mr. Bellew, head of a Catholic family which

[1] Rev. Mr. Bannon, P.P.

had ugly traditional relations with the Castle, understood that the Government were about to take up the question, and considered a county meeting premature; Mr. Torrens M'Cullagh,[1] though unable to attend, heartily concurred in the object of the movement; but Mr. Chichester Fortescue was of a widely different opinion. He was for reasonable reforms; but the proposals of the League were manifestly not reasonable. He was quite willing to support a measure acknowledging the right of the tenant to be reimbursed for *bona fide*, unexhausted, improvements executed by him upon his farm, either by a continued occupancy at the same rent, or, in case he was dispossessed, by compensation in money. But what the League desired he unequivocally repudiated—

"A right of occupancy beyond the term of the contract made between owner and occupier (he said) is a right which I cannot acknowledge; and the principle of regulating rents by public authority, is a principle, in my opinion, so unsound, that no legislature would entertain it for a moment. Men might as well ask to be protected against the exactions of the retail dealer, or to have their wages fixed, by some legislative enactment."

His elder brother, Mr. Thomas Fortescue, afterwards created a peer—not in recognition of his wisdom and foresight, it may be hoped—was still more emphatic in his condemnation—

[1] The present Mr. M'Cullagh Torrens.

"I look upon the so-called tenant-right movement (he said) as mischievous in its immediate effects, and its avowed objects of fixety of tenure and compulsory valuation of land as more suited to those American States which repudiated their liabilities than to the British Islands, where a respect for mutual agreements and vested rights has always characterised our legislation."

These strong declarations furnish a convenient instrument for measuring the work done by the League in sowing new opinions; for Mr. Chichester Fortescue is now Lord Carlingford, having been sent to the Upper House by Mr. Gladstone for the specific purpose of defending a Land Bill which embodied, and has since carried into law, the precise principles which he so unreservedly condemned.

The Durham letter was in all men's minds, and Mr. Girdwood, on behalf of Ulster, took his stand against it on the moment. He warned the meeting that this stroke was probably devised and would certainly be employed by the landlords, to sow dissension between North and South. To create division was probably Lord John Russell's motive, and the Grand Orange Lodge had already seconded this purpose. In an address on their behalf, signed by Lord Enniskillen, as Right Worshipful Grand Master, there was no allusion to the kicks and cuffs given by Russell and his colleagues to the Orange body. On the contrary, true to his class interest, he hastened to confederate with the Whig Minister in his attempt to disunite the Irish people.[1]

The Rev. Julius M'Cullagh, P.M., cited the admonitions of Luther to the German aristocracy as very suitable to the existing condition of Ireland—Luther, who, it might be presumed, was a better Protestant than Lord John Russell—

"Ye princes, ye men of power (Luther says), you lavish in fine clothes, fine castles, fine eating and drinking, the peasant's hard-won produce, and what you must do first and foremost is, to put a stop to all this vain luxury of yours, to close up the holes through which this money runs, so that you may leave some little part in the peasant's pocket."

The Rev. Mr. Lennon, a priest of wide popular influence, warned the men of Louth that it was a known and proved enemy did this thing, and for an evil purpose—

"Let no Whig Minister cajole the people into the belief that it is about their faith or religion he is concerned. He has heard of your organisation in this great question, and he would like to disunite you according to the accursed policy of our rulers, 'Divide and govern.' But the advocates of the Tenant League are quite wide awake, and will not be caught in the net. Union is strength—division is weakness and ruin."

[1] The suspicion that the pious zeal of the Whigs concealed some political aim was greatly strengthened by a declaration of Joseph Hume that its true object was to turn away the attention of the people from indispensable political and financial reforms.

Mr. Duffy reminded them how much the League had accomplished, and how important it was to their enemies to break up the organisation which stood like a guardian angel between the people and their oppressors. The great Catholic Association had made little progress for the first year of its existence. The Anti-Corn-law League, as one of its leaders assured him, had lost two years in making mistakes. He trusted the Tenant League had not made any serious mistakes; it certainly had not lost any time—

"Its progress looked like necromancy; it looked like a miracle; it looked like—and was it not?—the special providence of God to unite the North and South. Swift, Grattan, and O'Connell had tried it in vain; but, in the fulness of time, and by infinitely weaker hands, the work was done. Before a month from the foundation of the League every journal in the British dominions was debating the Land question in Ireland. The League had effected a great union—the Union with the North; but a greater remained to be accomplished—a union with the manufacturers of Manchester and the artisans of Birmingham; a union with the Free Church party in Scotland, plundered by landlords; a union with the Colonial interest in the British Parliament, who are steadily forming an organised power in the House of Commons. But if all this were done, the crowning work still remained—to create a Parliamentary Party pledged to disregard all party considerations in the pursuit of tenant-right."

The general meeting of the League, which was attended by the same representative men from North and South, encountered the risk of sectarian quarrels with courage and frankness. They adopted a resolution declaring that no artifices or intrigue of our enemies should be allowed to interrupt that long-desired union of creeds and classes which the present movement had induced, and on which its ultimate success so mainly depended. The Rev. Mr. Cahill illustrated the need of union in a spirit of passionate conviction. Lord John Russell's remedy for landlord wrongs was to renew the cry of "Down with the Pope!"—

"Down with the Pope (he said), but will that revive the six hundred victims that were flung coffinless into one monster grave at Skibbereen? Yes, down with the Pope! but will that raise up from their crumbled ruins the 17,865 houses which the exterminators in two short years have levelled in the dust? Down with the Pope! but will that give food or drink or raiment to those wretched outcasts of landlord barbarism who are sucking subsistence from the rotten turnip—who are burning with fever in some roofless shed—without a drop to cool their parched lips, or who are wet with the dew and rains of Heaven—as they crouch without shelter or covering amid the scattered fragments of their once loved homes? Down with the Pope! but will that clear our roadstead of those ships which are sweeping away the strength, and bone, and wealth of our country, or bring back those hapless exiles who roam by the stagnant swamps, and over the horrid plains and desolate prairies of a distant land, cursing the laws that drove them from the green fields they never again will see?"

He warned the Whig intriguers that their device would fail—

"We have drawn around it the circle of charity which discord cannot enter. In this blessed union we have found our cure and our remedy. It will force you and your successors to treat us with respect and govern us with justice—it will muzzle the bloody jaws of ravening landlords. It will not revive the dead, but it will save the living; and in the words of Davis, by its magic influence, in spite of landlords and Government, we will win the rights which we seek—

"Landlords fooled us,
England ruled us,
Hounding us on to make us their prey;
But in their despite the Irish unite,
And Orange and Green
Will carry the day."

The landlords held a No-Popery meeting in the Rotunda, led by the Earl of Enniskillen and a following of the smaller gentry; and their journals enumerated the dangers by which the Church of the Empire was menaced by the intrigues of Rome. But they made little real progress; a League meeting was held in Armagh, the seat of the Primacy, with a Presbyterian Minister in the chair,[1] and an attempt to induce the local Orangemen to break it up altogether failed.

The Northern leaders continued on the alert, and gave forth no uncertain sound—

"In the present state of public matters (Dr. M'Knight wrote), when sectarian bitterness is organised and

[1] Rev. Gunn Browne. While this volume is passing through the press I read with satisfaction a declaration of Mr. Browne in favour of Home Rule as proposed by Mr. Gladstone.

encouraged under the auspices of Her Majesty's Government itself, I felt anxious, as a Northern Presbyterian, to prove to my Roman Catholic fellow-countrymen of the South that this most contemptible, wretched policy has in no degree affected the right-hearted tenant-right men of the North, who are as earnest and as cordial as ever in the maintenance of fraternal union with the South."

Mr. Bell was equally emphatic—

"No man (he said) could condemn more than he did the letter of Lord John Russell; as an Irishman, as an Ulsterman, as a friend to civil and religious liberty, he repudiated and denounced it."

The danger of Ireland being diverted from her real and urgent business seemed effectually overcome.

But when Parliament met, a new peril disclosed itself. The Ecclesiastical Titles Bill, introduced by the Whig Government, extended not merely to England, but to Ireland, where no ground of complaint had been given. If public acts and professions were any security for public conduct, no party were more committed against such a policy than the Whigs. They had recently appointed Irish Catholic Bishops to honorary offices by their titles, and gave them precedence in official documents over secular peers. And in India, Canada, and the West Indies bishops appointed by the Pope were recognised in Acts of Parliament and by the practice of the courts of law. But it was now proposed to make penal the assumption of the title of archbishop,

bishop, or dean of any existing diocese in the United Kingdom, or of any city, town, place, territory or district whatever within the United Kingdom, even though the same were not the title of an existing Protestant bishopric or deanery. And any deed executed by a Catholic bishop, or under his authority, was declared void if the name of his see should be used in the signature or the body of the instrument; and any bequest of real or personal property devised to a bishop or dean, or for the maintenance of any bishopric or deanery; and also any property for charitable or other purposes devised in trust to a bishop or dean by the title of his see or deanery, or by any deed in which he was referred to " as claiming to be, or being called or known, or reputed to be bishop or dean," or devised to any " chaplain or any subordinate of the person so designated," was ordered to pass to the Crown, to be disposed of at the Queen's pleasure, either for the purpose of the devisor or any other purpose.

The suspicion was widespread that this extension of the measure was designed to break up the union of parties in Ireland, but with so direct and wanton an attack on Catholic rights in the country it was no longer possible to avoid a Catholic agitation. All that the friends of the League could hope for was to prevent it becoming offensive to Protestants. Defence meetings were held in various southern counties, and the bishops met in conference and petitioned Parliament against the proposed measure, as one contrary to the essential discipline of the Catholic Church and to the spirit of divine laws which they were obliged to obey.

While the religious trouble was still new one of the seats for the County Limerick fell vacant by the death of the sitting member. To contest it in the interest of the League was a duty not to be evaded. Seats are now easily won in the same interest, and those who recognise in the fact the superior skill and strategy of the leaders of to-day may study the Limerick election of 1850 with advantage.

The first question was of a candidate. Dr. Croke[1] wrote to me to suggest an intelligent miller, Michael Ryan, of Bruree. He was a Tenant Leaguer, he said, and an honourable, honest, and independent man, and twenty such as he would give a good guarantee of success for the cause. I submitted the proposal to the Council, and he was adopted. A strong deputation was despatched to the constituency, and an appeal made to the country for funds to fight effectually. Lucas and Lalor went from Dublin, Mr. Rogers and Mr. Bell from the North, and Father Tom O'Shea from Ossory. Many influential local men proffered their assistance. Archdeacon Fitzgerald, Robert Potter (afterwards

[1] The present Archbishop of Cashel.

member for the city), Dr. Griffin and John O'Donnell, men of '48, and Dr. Croke, who was responsible for the selection of the candidate. A county meeting was summoned, which adopted the principles of the League and promised to support its candidate. A vigorous canvass was commenced through local meetings, and Mr. Ryan was everywhere well received. It was said that he would go to the House of Commons dressed in frieze woven in his own looms as a typical representative of the interests and opinions of the people. The deputation made their duties very plain to the constituency—

"Give me (said Dr. Croke) but twenty such as he. Let them oppose every Government hostile to Tenant Right. Let such opposition be continuous and unrelenting, and then I, for one, relieved from doubts which still, I must say, press heavily upon me with regard to the successful issue of this great movement, would account defeat almost impossible, victory all but certain."

This doctrine, which had been first taught by the Confederates in 1847, and again by the journals friendly to the League since its foundation, was now for the first time brought home to the minds of the people. The road to success they were told lay through Independent Opposition in Parliament.

The contest excited the keenest interest; it rivalled the Durham letter for a time as the inevitable topic in clubs and over dinner tables. The landlords knew how much they had at stake in preventing the League from grasping the great political weapon—a Parliamentary Party. But after surveying their resources, they were so confident of success that they brought two candidates into the field, a Whig and a Tory.[1]

On the day of nomination a company of carbineers, a large body of infantry, and 300 armed constabulary made a garrison of the city. The polling under the law then in operation lasted three days, and at its close the Whig landlord was elected by a majority of forty over the Tory landlord, and of eleven over the candidate of the League.

The circumstances which produced this result all belong to a past time. The constituency which even under the franchise then existing ought to have reached ten thousand, had been permitted by apathy to fall under six hundred; and among this small number there was a considerable proportion of £50 freeholders manufactured at will by the landlords. The Catholic Bishop, under the influence of the senior member, Mr. Monsell, it was said, supported the Whig candidate, and many electors who were still unprotected by the ballot found the landlords and the bishop too strong a combination to be resisted. Perhaps it counted for something, too, that the little handful of partisans who adhered to

[1] Mr. Wyndham Gould and Captain Dickson.

Mr. John O'Connell made themselves disagreeable. Mr. Rogers stated at a public meeting that in supporting the Tenant-Right candidate he must not be taken as approving of his declaration in favour of the Repeal of the Union. Such a statement he was clearly entitled to make, for the very foundation on which the League rested, without which it could never have come into existence, and wanting which it would immediately die, was that members joining it were bound to nothing but its fundamental principles. Two priests [1] wrote a public letter to ask the advice of their leader how they were to act under these alarming circumstances. "Here it is implied," said these skilful logicians, "that the principles of the League and the Repeal Association are diametrically opposed, and therefore either must be illegal!"

To utilise this fatuous controversy the local paper containing it was sent from Limerick to Belfast, and distributed among the ill-wishers of the League. The Northern leaders found themselves described among their neighbours as abettors of Repeal and allies of sedition. At the outset M'Knight wrote to me in grave alarm for the cause—

"I wish that Cardinal Wiseman and Lord John Russell had been both in Heaven three months ago, as they have thrown

---

[1] Rev. John Madden, P.P., and Rev. John Meagher, C.C. Kilteely.

national progress a whole quarter of a century back, and Omniscience alone can tell what is to be the issue. I have been doing all in my power to divert this cursed excitement into a neutral channel, but Dr. Cooke is now coming out, and he will gather around him all the old bigotry of Orange Toryism, while it must be confessed that the grandiloquent bombast, with which the new Hierarchy was originally ushered into publicity, was too well calculated to provoke the reaction which has taken place. Fortunately, Cooke has been so long in coming out that I have 'taken the wind out of his sails' to a considerable extent, though I am still very uneasy about his movements. Considerable numbers of the *Limerick and Clare Examiner* have been circulated here within the last few days, and there is some danger of a new element of mischief being got up, if prudential measures be not taken to stop it. The Address of Ryan to the electors of Limerick is a furious Repeal manifesto, while that of the Tenant League Deputation, in the very same paper, adopts him as the League Candidate, without the slightest hint or qualification; so that, so far as outward appearances go, the League in this case is formally and openly identified with Repeal, as well as with several other matters contained in Ryan's Address. Now, in the North, any impression of this kind would destroy us, and you will consequently see the necessity of getting the League out of this predicament."

The "Young Liberator," as Mr. John O'Connell was sometimes called in scorn, found another befitting topic. It was understood that the motive pleaded by the bishop, and some of the priests who followed him, for supporting the Whig candidate was that Mr. Monsell and his friend Lord Dunraven were about to become Catholics; and Lucas, the most devoted of Catholics, scoffed at the preference of two aristocratic converts over the interests of thousands of the faithful people.

Mr. John O'Connell seized on the fact to invite the universe to note the spectacle of an "English newspaper speculator, a man who had come to Ireland merely to sell his newspaper, presuming to criticise the bishop and venerated clergy of Limerick." Unfortunately for the appellant, the most upright and public-spirited of the clergy were of quite a different opinion from the venerated bishop, both as to the cause and its exponents. It seemed like the moral of this sad story that when the election was over 190 ejectments were served on a single estate in the county which had flinched from its duty.

Immediately after the lost election the county meetings were resumed. The great county of Down, where the population in a former generation had met in fratricidal conflict at Dollysbrae, now met in cordial union. One division assembled at Newtownards, where Archdeacon Fitzgerald, Father O'Shea, and Mr. Lucas represented the Council, sustained by leading Ulstermen. Dr. M'Knight addressed himself directly to the danger of the hour. He feared that to break up the League was one of the objects of the No-Popery movement—

"I freely confess (he said) that in matters of a purely religious character I would not give much for that man's moral integrity who would compromise the smallest religious obligation for any merely secular object; but, on the other hand, I have no language sufficiently strong to convey my reprobation and contempt for that policy which, under the hypocrisy of theological profession, degrades Christianity into an engine of State intrigue, and which, if it cannot directly employ the sanctity of Heaven in the work of Heaven's first enemy, at all events makes it subordinate to the interests of the second—namely, to the 'World' and its unprincipled debasements. Whether high personages intended it or not I may not affirm, but humbler parties have tried to break us up by arraying Protestants against Roman Catholics, and Orangemen against the industrial rights of both classes of their countrymen, in order that rackrenting and oppression and the extermination of the universal people may be still carried on through the agency of the people's own criminal divisions. In the North this base policy has been utterly unsuccessful, and the present glorious meeting in one of the most Presbyterian districts of Ulster is a triumphant demonstration of its failure."

Mr. Rogers spoke in the same spirit—

"Does my Presbyterianism (he demanded) forbid me to be a patriot? Is it because I am a follower of John Calvin that I am not to be a Christian? Will the farmers of Ireland—because they may conscientiously differ in their religious opinions—look on one another with distrust, and jealousy, and hatred, while landlords and the legislature, that differ in religion as widely as you do, are combined, heart and soul, to carry on against you the old familiar work of robbery, extermination, and death?

"'While your tyrants join in hate,
Will you not join in love?'

"In this matter I beseech you
  "'Leave points of belief
  To simpleton sages and reasoning fools.'"

The deputation from Dublin echoed these wise counsels. The second division of Down met at Downpatrick. The requisition was signed by upwards of twelve hundred persons of all creeds and parties in the county, and the meeting was on the same scale. The county Antrim met immediately afterwards at Broughshane, attended by the same deputation which had visited Down. Lucas taught the doctrines of the League with fresh illustrations. He cited the comparatively recent case of Ecclesiastical lands, in which the holdings were converted by Act of Parliament into free tenures, and the rent fixed by valuation. He specified a class of tenants, very numerous in almost all the English counties, whose tenancy was, strictly speaking, at will; but the English judges without a statute, and by the mere force of their decisions, had prevented the landlord from rendering the tenure of no value by the imposition of heavy fines, which would deprive tenants of the fruits of their industry. Hence it would be seen that there was nothing new, nothing unjust, nothing anarchical, as was alleged, in what the League demanded.

Archdeacon Fitzgerald renewed the always welcome theme of union. He reminded the county Antrim Presbyterians that they were descendants of the men who made a solemn League and Covenant against the arbitrary and cruel tyranny of the Stuart kings, and succeeded in establishing the religion which they loved. He trusted that the covenant which had been entered into between North and South would never be broken; that common sufferings and a common hope would cement that union still closer; and that as landlords united to crush and to oppress, so tenants would bind themselves together for self-defence, in a bond which would be indissoluble.

It was fortunate, doubtless, for the League that the contest was not one between Geneva and Rome, but between Prelacy and Popery, for the Presbyterians of Ulster had as little sympathy at bottom with the lawn sleeves and silk apron of the episcopacy in possession in England as with the biretta and pectoral cross of the new bishops.

The League was now nearly five months in existence, and the first general meeting was summoned. It was preceded by a long conference from which Select Committees on Organisation and Finance, and one to consider the bill which the Council desired to submit to Parliament, were appointed, reported and had their proposals taken into consideration. The election of League guardians instead of Landlord guardians in the Poor-law Unions was recommended, and arrangements for the general election commenced. It was at most eighteen months distant, and it might come much sooner. To get trustworthy candidates possessing a legal estate of £600 or £300 a year in land, or its equivalent in chattels, to assail and revise the Land Code, was a hard problem, but Patrick M'Mahon, a barrister, living in London by the daily labour of his profession, solved it effectually. He advised a course which will be described later when it came to be contested before a Parliamentary Committee. The Council recommended that the selection of candidates should take place in the district to be represented, in order that local opinion might be fully expressed; and that it should take place also in the presence and with the assistance of delegates from the Council, in order that the body charged with the heavy responsibility of conducting the cause to success might be ensured against having all their labour lost by the selection of incompetent or untrustworthy men.

The people sitting in sober council discharging their own business was an inspiring sight. Their opponents were conferring together at the Carlton Club, at the Stephen's-green and Kildare-street Clubs, in every Foxhunting Club in Ireland; and perhaps in the Cabinet in London. But here it might be hoped was a counterpoise. Some of the Free Trade leaders assured me that while they made speeches alone they made no calculable progress; it was when they sat down to their work round a table, like the directors of a public company, that they began to prosper, for success in such designs is never the birth of accident or blind chance, but the growth of busy days and anxious nights.

It was in the House of Commons the contest had to be conducted, and the Irish members never were more discredited and distrusted than at this time. The few honest men among them were too feeble to count for much; the majority were habitual jobbers, and some were accused of selling for hard cash the petty local patronage placed at their disposal by the Treasury. It was confidently believed that the League might replace the bulk of them at the General Election. But one of them, a man of remarkable ability, and embarrassed by no scruples, saw in these religious troubles an opportunity of winning political influence and popularity. William Keogh, member for Athlone, had bought his way into Parliament at the expense of Mr. Attwood, a Birmingham banker with a financial craze for which he recruited supporters at his personal cost. At the Irish bar Mr. Keogh was known as a man of considerable brains and no knowledge of law, but who had unbounded reliance on his resources as a political strategist to win the prizes of his profession, without the ordinary equipment or service. He was a ready and vigorous speaker, and Parliament estimated his ability and his character at their respective value.' He was by birth a Catholic, but had scoffed so systematically at Catholic feeling that his new zeal for the Church was a marvel of audacity. From an early period he had formed an alliance with a person never heard in debate, but who was extremely skilful in the wiles and devices by which weak men are governed. John Sadleir had been a prosperous attorney in Ireland, and since his admission to Parliament had become a banker and speculator in London, and was supposed to be prodigiously rich. The jobbers naturally gathered round Messrs. Sadleir and Keogh, and the honest men, who scarcely understood how competent a leader they had of their own class, fell into the rear. George Henry Moore was an Irish proprietor of fine intellect, which was highly cultivated, rhetorical gifts, little inferior to those which had made Richard Sheil a Parliamentary personage, and had a gentleman's disdain of shabbiness and subserviency. But he was abrupt and impatient, had an intellectual contempt for dulness which he did not always conceal, and was somewhat soured by having missed in Parliament the recognition he deserved. Under these leaders the bulk of the Irish members organised themselves into a party of defence. As the Peelites, of whom Sir James Graham and Mr. Gladstone were the most conspicuous representatives, and the

Manchester party, under Messrs. Cobden and Bright, disapproved of the new penal law, there was promise of a protracted, if not an effectual resistance. The danger to Ireland was that she would forget her nearest and dearest interests in this new contest. To me the question of questions was the protection of the people. They were dying out at the rate of a hundred a week in the sweltering wards of workhouses, in the poisonous emigrant ship, in the crowded jail, in the cellars and garrets of our cities, and in the dykes and ditches adjoining their ruined homesteads. The Irish Question and the Catholic Question was how to save them from destruction.

The chance that the dishonest members would reinstate themselves in popular favour was greatly aided by the circumstance that the Primate of the Catholic Church at this time was a man ignorant of their antecedents, ill-informed on Irish affairs, and disposed to regard them at best as altogether secondary to ecclesiastical interests. Half a year earlier, the Archbishopric of Armagh having fallen vacant was conferred by the Pope, with the added power of Apostolic Delegate, on Dr. Cullen, President of the Irish College at Rome. The new Primate bore no resemblance in manners, demeanour, or capacity, to the great ecclesiastics to whom Rome has ordinarily entrusted national missions. He was plain, clumsy, slow of

THE COUNCIL AND ITS FIRST TROUBLES. 137

speech, and intellectually narrow, and ill-informed. But he was a devoted churchman and a man of prodigious zeal and steadfastness of purpose. He paid no regard to the character or aim of the Irish members; they were fighting the battle of the Church, and he gave them his whole sympathy. Those who knew them better were confident that sooner or later they would use any power conferred upon them for their own advantage alone; and perhaps the more experienced foresaw that in the end they would avenge the bitter slavery of professing opinions which they did not hold, by running into unexampled extremes of hostility and treachery; which in due time occurred.

This trouble did not leave the League quite unshaken. Lucas's difficulties were trying. He was essentially a Catholic journalist, and it was in that character rather than as leader of opinion in Ireland that he was best known. He comprehended as clearly as any one the danger of setting two conflicting ideas before the country, and the primary importance of saving the lives of the people. But it had become the habit of his life to act with the Episcopacy. When the claims of the Church conflicted with secular interests he did not admit that there was any choice. The Church spoke to him with the same authority from the Vatican as from Mount Sinai. But he was persuaded that it was a mistaken policy of Irish bishops to endanger the success of the League by ignoring its interests and claims in favour of the new movement. He used his influence in private counsels and, perhaps, expostulations, but in his journal he kept in as close relation with their public action as his judgment and conscience permitted. My position was different. I was not a theologian. I had no taste for studies in this field, and consequently no solid knowledge of them. I hoped to aid in winning back for Ireland the right of self-government; and was willing to apply myself to any honourable task likely to promote this end. To save the Irish peasantry from imminent danger of destruction was an indispensable preliminary to such a hope; and I would not for any end whatever have jeopardised the chance of their safety. I escaped the dilemma which embarrassed Lucas by standing aloof from the new movement. In all that concerned the discipline of the Catholic Church I listened to the bishops with deference and submission, but in politics I must follow my own judgment and conscience, and I declined to seek counsel which I might not be able to follow. These sentiments found expression in the *Tablet* and *Nation*, but we made allowance for the exigencies of individual opinion, and preserved our personal relations undisturbed. His task was to keep the bishops and clergy, mine to keep the Northerns and the Nationalists, from taking undue offence or break-

THE COUNCIL AND ITS FIRST TROUBLES. 139

ing away from the Union. It was not always an easy task; Dr. M'Knight was pained, and finally exasperated, by Lucas's articles at this time, and sent his complaints to me. But there was no immediate remedy possible.

The contest over the Ecclesiastical Titles Bill in Parliament was stubborn, and the leader of the Opposition, though the prejudice of his supporters forbade him to resist the measure, was ready to take advantage of the discord which it occasioned in the Liberal ranks. In the thick of the battle Mr. Disraeli, by a well-directed motion on Colonial policy, supported by the Irish members, put Lord John Russell in a minority, and the Government resigned. Here was the penal law effectually destroyed if a government could be constituted from the majority. During the interregnum, while the country was in anxious suspense, the division list was published, and the weak policy, which, out of gratitude to O'Connell, had allowed his incapable and untrustworthy sons to nominate candidates for Parliament in 1846, was followed by the inexorable Nemesis. Two of his sons, his nephew, and the men they had taken most pains to impose on the people, voted to maintain Lord John Russell in power at the very crisis of the contest for religious liberty. It afterwards became public, by the evidence of Dr. Gray before a Parliamentary Committee, that he and others had employed earnest personal remonstrance to keep Mr. John O'Connell from committing this mean action, but utterly in vain. The public indignation at this discovery was intense. The Corporation of Limerick, the city which he represented, promptly censured him; a blow under which he staggered, and which brought his mischievous career to a sudden collapse.

Lord Derby, who was sent for in the first instance, failed to form a Government, and the Whigs, conscious of their weakness and unpopularity, sought the assistance of the Peelites, to obtain which they proposed to modify the Penal measure. Lord Aberdeen and Sir James Graham replied that no modification would be sufficient; it must be abandoned altogether, as it reversed the policy of the last thirty years. Agreement proved impossible, and in the end the old Government was recalled without any coalition, but with the bill which they were willing to modify fatally damaged by their proposed compromise.

We have now reached a point in the narrative when the League of North and South was assailed by dangers, not from without but from within. The camp-followers of both parties, and sometimes their pledged adherents, committed offences which would have produced certain disruption if the leaders had not been determined to allow nothing to divide them which did not violate honour or conscience. The fidelity of the Northerns, which had outlived the No Popery agitation, was put to a more disheartening test.

Early in April the county Longford became vacant by the appointment of Major Blackhall to a Colonial Governorship. It was only a month since the county had met and declared for the principles of the League. As the Council had not been able to send a deputation, Major Blackhall on that occasion had taken courage to assail the principle of valuation; but it was immediately vindicated by local men and adopted by the meeting. Here was an occasion to redeem and reverse the defeat at Limerick. The County Club opened communications with Sergeant Shee, who was first on the list of League candidates. He was willing to stand, but desired to limit the election expenses to a fixed sum. Before the negotiations had closed, as he conceived, the club suddenly adopted another candidate, as bad in every respect as it is possible to conceive. It was Mr. More O'Farrell, a landlord who might be assumed, in the absence of evidence, to be opposed to the League principles, an ancient colleague of Lord John Russell's, just returning from an office to which he had nominated him, and unlikely to go into embarrassing opposition. And a man who distributed among his former constituents the employments and donations which corrupt the people and their leaders. The County Club consisted in a large degree of the clergy of the diocese of Ardagh. The bishop was Dr. Higgins, who was a fierce agitator in 1843, but in 1846 applauded O'Connell's compact with the Whigs, and made against the Young Irelanders, who opposed that compact, the shamefully unjust charge that they were enemies of religion, and there was no doubt that he was chiefly responsible for the result.

All the sacrifices of the people, all the labours of the League, the hopes and the lives of the peasant were bartered away in a private cabal by a handful of men who thought only of their own interest. It was worse than Limerick, for there was no contest; the club candidate had a walk over. Major Blackhall, selected in the same fashion, had just sold his seat for a Colonial Governorship, and one party hack was replaced by another more experienced in the arts of intrigue and corruption. Longford, in the language of the time, had "sold the pass," and if this was an example of what might be expected in future elections the cause was lost beyond hope. The worst motives were ascribed to the transaction by those who were best informed. In the penal times the Irish priests had performed their duty with the fidelity of martyrs; in the long struggle for religious liberty they were leaders as generous and self-sacrificing as any nation has produced; but since 1834, when O'Connell's first compact with the Whigs brought them into relation with English political parties, some of them had learnt the evil lesson of employing their public influence no longer for public ends, but in huxtering bargains for personal advantages for themselves or their kin. This was the way the Longford surrender was interpreted. The League priests spoke on the subject with scorn and indignation which was pleasant to hear. Father Bernard Daly wrote to the *Nation* that the conduct of the clerical club was enough to disgust and crimson with shame all men of their own creed and politics, and to tear up from the heart of Presbyterians every fibre of confidence in the union so lately cemented. They seized the opportunity from which so much was expected to hand back again to their old taskmasters the poor people who had begun to hope once more, to smite them down before they were quite erect; and to close, so far as the political infamy of one county could do so, every vista of expectation of good which God, through the instrumentality of the Tenant League, had opened up—

"Well indeed (he said) might we hang our heads in the presence of the Northern members, if we dissembled the sentiments with which we regard so disastrous and fatal a proceeding, or if we failed to denounce it to the country with all our might, and in language not to be mistaken, as not only offensive to the League, but intrinsically vicious and scandalous."

The League sent a deputation to the first Northern meeting which occurred, and it was a peculiarly fit occasion, as it met in the capital of the North, to justify themselves. Rev. Dr. Kearney, P.P., declared that the Longford transactions must be ascribed to corruption or treachery. He was almost ashamed to go to Belfast after that foul surrender; but the people were true; the disaster sprung from want of courage and honesty in those who ought to be their teachers. The Longford Club, he feared, had tasted some of the crumbs of the Treasury. If corruption did not exist there was plainly treachery, because, instead of giving the county to the men to whom they had pledged themselves to give it, they had handed it over to a rejected implement of the Whigs.

Father Daly said shame affected men differently; for his part he would have been ashamed to stay away from Belfast. He bade the North remember that the traitors were few—

"There are about three thousand priests in Ireland (he said); of those it must be a small section that belong to the Longford Club, and depend upon it that the indignation and the shame felt by the remainder of that body at the result of the late election in Longford was as strong and as little concealed as it possibly could have been in the very heart of Ulster."

In conclusion, he quoted from a recent number of the *Times* a notice to quit to the whole Irish race, which was a significant comment on these transactions.

"The abstraction of the Celtic race at the rate of a quarter of a million a year is a surer remedy for the inveterate Irish disease than any human wit could have imagined."[1]

The League journals North and South dealt frankly with the disaster. The *Derry Standard* declared that if the corruption could not be checked it would be fatal to the union of parties and to the public cause.

"For our own part (the Editor[2] wrote) we will cleave to the union—the last hope of Ireland—while a wreck of it remains; till the Northern and Southern priests have, as a body, approved of the Limerick and Longford treachery; till the Roman Catholic laity have acquiesced slavishly in this base and cruel betrayal of the country; till the Roman Catholic Press becomes the apologist of sacerdotal recreancy; till a general election, under the new constituency, shall have proved that Longford venality was the first-fruits of a harvest of ecclesiastical treason. Then, indeed, we shall begin to think that the sooner the Irish race transfers itself to another land, where there are no 'old holy wells,' the better for the honour of humanity."

The *Tablet* and *Nation* named the offending priests, and held them up to public scorn; and at the monthly meeting of the Council, Father O'Shea moved a resolution calling on the electors to reject these untrustworthy counsellors and take the business into their own hands at the approaching general election.

[1] *Times*, Feb. 15, 1851. [2] Rev. Mr. Godkin, I.M.

While this transaction was still recent, another followed more lamentable and disastrous. Mr. Fagan, one of the members for the City of Cork, had incurred the censure of his constituents by not voting against Lord John Russell on Mr. Disraeli's motion, and promptly resigned his seat. Here, surely, it seemed was at last the opportunity which the League had awaited. Cork could dispose of the seat at the absolute discretion of the popular party; a man of respectable character had been ejected for subserviency to the Whig Government, and his successor, it might be assumed, would be a model of independence and public spirit. What tribune, glowing with holy zeal against the damnable system under which the country perished, did the capital of Munster select to speak in its name to the English Parliament? There is a predominant family of Catholic merchants in Cork who had won wide influence by the integrity and liberality of their commercial career. To found charities, to build churches, to augment the O'Connell tribute, their purses were always open; but patriotism in any large or national sense was little known among them. Of all the connection the least Irish was a barrister in London, who was skilled to write squibs in the periodicals and to enliven supper-tables by his drollery; a man about town who cared no more for Ireland than for Ultima Thule. This was the candidate chosen,

THE COUNCIL AND ITS FIRST TROUBLES 147

and Mr. Sergeant Murphy re-entered Parliament, where he had already sat for a short period, unpledged to the principles of the League, unpledged to resist the Government for supporting which his predecessor had been displaced; free to dispose of his talents and his votes to the best bidder, and in good time to exchange his seat for a pleasant commissionership within hail of Pall Mall; which he duly did. He made no pretence of serving Ireland, and soon after, when on some fall from duty, he was threatened by his constituents, he replied, as he was well entitled to do, that "he did not care a —— for his constituents." The treachery of Cork was worse than the treachery of Longford. Cork was the capital of Celtic Ireland; it was the centre of the bitterest wrongs and sufferings which the League was created to arrest. The graves of Skull and Skibbereen sweltered within the bounds of the county: the desolate wastes of Bantry lay close beyond it. Ennistymon and Kilrush, murdering their hundred paupers a week with strange and fearful diseases, were not far away; and the emigrant ships that packed up the strong men of the country for foreign consumption lay at Cove. The annihilation of Ireland was going on visibly day by day under its eyes. If Cork were not moved to resistance, where would resistance come from?

The disaster fell on the public mind like the news of a great battle lost by the surrender of a trusted citadel.

But the leaders of the League did not despair or flinch. The courage which they maintained among the stricken people, and their merciless exposure of the treason, laid the basis for a great victory near at hand, and helped to create the public opinion which makes treason hide its head in later times. If Longford, Limerick, and Cork are no longer difficult to win for independent candidates, to what is the change attributable? To wiser and abler leaders? Not altogether, perhaps. Many of the priests who were then Leaguers are now bishops, deans, archdeacons, or canons, and have not forgotten their old principles; the voters are sheltered by the ballot, and can vote without risk of consequences; the League journals and leaders, at their personal risk and peril, exposed the motives of these repeated betrayals, and finally the Fenian organisation, which rose on the ruins of the League, whatever were its errors and shortcomings, taught the peasantry the essential lesson not to permit their interests to be jobbed away by any leader, lay or clerical.[1]

The agitation against the Penal Law grew in force; the requisition for a meeting in Dublin was signed by

---

[1] The most unshrinking and merciless of all the exposures to which the transactions of 1851 were subjected was made somewhat later in a Státement submitted to the Pope by Lucas. He detailed many cases of the most painful treachery not touched on in this narrative. Large extracts are given in the second volume of his *Life* by his brother; but the worst cases are omitted.

the Catholic gentry of all political opinions. The entire body of Catholic Queen's Counsel, for example, with two exceptions, were among the requisitionists, and the meeting was remarkable for rank, authority, and popular enthusiasm. The resistance in Parliament was continued; it wearied and embarrassed the Government, and helped to bring the measure into contempt, but there was no probability of directly defeating it. But another opportunity of indirectly defeating it offered. The Government were again endangered by a hostile motion on their financial scheme, the resistance this time being led by Joseph Hume, one of their ordinary supporters; but when the division came, the latest members sent from Ireland went into the ministerial lobby. A little later another vote on the policy of the Government in Ceylon commanded the sympathy of generous men outside party connections. The House of Commons was asked to declare that the execution of eighteen persons and the transportation or corporal punishment of a hundred and forty others, which had been ordered in local troubles, were excessive; but the new members for Cork, Longford, and Limerick, and with them Morgan John O'Connell, O'Gorman Mahon, Mr. Fox, the second member for Longford, and other representatives of Irish constituencies, came to their succour and sanctioned these excesses.

To brace up public opinion in face of these damaging

transactions, the League determined to hold public meetings weekly in Dublin up to the period of the general election. Lucas seized the occasion to teach townsmen the special interest they had in the cause.

"There was in Ireland (he said) a million of agricultural families, and if in each of those families only one more shirt was got in the year, it would be an increased custom to the shopkeepers of Ireland of £100,000. Was trade in this country in such a prosperous condition that the expenditure of £100,000 was of no consequence? Suppose these families were able to get each a hat, a pair of trousers, or pair of shoes in the year more, or a gown, or petticoat, that little addition would give an expenditure of two millions a year to the tradesmen and shopkeepers of Ireland. He reminded his audience that in Prussia, within the last century, tenant farmers were in the same condition as in Ireland at present. In England sixteen to twenty out of every hundred individuals on the face of the soil were paupers; in Ireland twenty to twenty-five out of every hundred were paupers; but in Prussia, since the great change had taken place, only three and a half out of every hundred of the population were in a state of pauperism."

But there was a pause of consternation and despair, and the attendance of country members at the weekly meetings was not satisfactory. At the Catholic meetings which still continued there was a prodigious quantity of what is called "tall talk," which had ceased to have any definite meaning. One priest announced that for his part he was prepared to raise a battalion of two thousand men to resist any further aggressions on religious liberty. Archdeacon Fitzgerald advised him instead of levying an army for an imaginary service, in which no one had the least notion of taking the field, to consider whether he could fight the battle of the perishing people at the hustings to somewhat more purpose than had been done at Limerick and Longford. For his own part, he confessed he was disabled from heroic enterprises by the fact that one-half of his congregation had perished by famine or fled into exile. The public attention was monopolised by a measure which was a dead-letter, and which, whether dead or alive, would not withdraw a single member from the Church or a single soul from Heaven. It was time to turn from wailing over the Ecclesiastical Titles Act to the more serious business of saving the people.

Mr. Keogh's Irish party were voting as the country desired, and were gradually gaining a confidence which they ill deserved. To improve the occasion they resolved to found a Catholic Defence Association as soon as Parliament rose, which might, among other duties, recommend candidates at the general election; and, as they were little trusted by the popular Press, to found an organ of their own. They had recourse to the further device of employing T. M. Ray, who as the "dear Ray" of O'Connell's public correspondence was a familiar name to the people, as one of their agents. These were not cheerful tidings for the

League, and we soon learned that Mr. Sharman Crawford, probably under the influence of men he met daily in Parliament, complained that the League was not promoting his opinions, but opinions of their own, one of which—Perpetuity of Tenure—he could not support. Mr. Crawford was an honest and unselfish man, and the League could not afford to lose him. A deputation[1] was sent to London to communicate with him, and to ascertain at the same time what length the best of the existing members would go on the Land question if a bill were introduced in the coming session.

To me it seemed that founding a Catholic Defence Association after the penal act had become law, was in the popular language locking the stable door when the steed was stolen. That a second agitation would distract and divide the popular mind, and that it was cruel to talk of defending from future problematical attacks a people who at that moment were flying from every port, hunted from their shelter like wild beasts, or starved like vermin at home, nearly three millions out of the six millions being candidates for outdoor relief, and half a million already paupers in the workhouse. The worthlessness of a standing Association which had no specific work to do was illustrated at the moment by a significant incident.

[1] The deputation consisted of Mr. Lucas and Mr. Duffy.

THE COUNCIL AND ITS FIRST TROUBLES. 153

The Repeal Association was originally founded to enrol all Nationalists of whatever creed or class, and its sole business was to promote the Repeal of the Union. But Mr. John O'Connell had been able to induce his father, in failing health and waning intellect, to turn it into a sectarian organisation, to the complete ruin of its original purpose. No secular interest, he insisted, could be permitted to interfere with the constant guardianship of Catholic rights. And now, when Catholic rights had been at last seriously assailed, Mr. John O'Connell, stricken by the remonstrance of his constituents against his Whig votes, suddenly dissolved the Repeal Association, and retired from public life. He had kept the pretence of an army on foot till the day of battle arrived, and then precipitately disbanded it. Were the people to be permitted to enrol themselves anew under another pretender, of more brains, indeed, but whose integrity and fidelity were still more doubtful? But distracting the popular attention by two agitations was a trifle compared to the danger of committing the selection of condidates at the general election to dishonest counsellors. Mr. Sadleir was still little known, but that Mr. Keogh or Mr. John Reynolds would be safely entrusted with such a duty I entirely disbelieved. They had obtained the support of a great body of bishops, however, and if an Association having authority with the country was created, the constituencies, it might be feared, would be delivered over to them. I naturally wrote in this spirit, but with the caution and reserve which a great danger justified. Lucas was by this time of a different opinion. He insisted that the two movements need not seriously interfere with each other, that we must not separate from the bishops, and that as twenty Irish members had broken loose from English parties, they ought to be accepted as the nucleus of a League party. I knew these men better than he did, having seen them tested by previous experiments, and I told him that however many constituencies declared for them, whatever support they might receive from bishops, I could not recognise them as men in whom it was safe to put any confidence. We must endure them if we had no choice, but to accept and acknowledge them was to share the responsibility. When men are expressing their sincere convictions, difference of opinion need not interfere with their cordial relations; but on each side we had numerous friends to satisfy, and the controversy slipped into the newspapers. That Lucas was connected with the League was an offence to some of his ecclesiastical supporters, who thought his sole mission was to defend Catholic interests at home and abroad, and many of them were still full of rage at the exposure of the Longford priests. He was pressed, I have no doubt, from many sides to break openly from such unpractical and temerarious opinions.[1] He wrote a still stronger article in defence of the proposed organisation, and complained that I was throwing cold water on a necessary and salutary project which had been determined upon with the assent of many prelates and members of Parliament, and could not be abandoned. I replied that there was no public evidence that it had been considered by any one else than certain distrusted politicians in London, that only three or four bishops were cited as having approved, that its having "been determined" had been received as the justification of too many follies in Ireland within my own experience to make that formula an authority with me, and that if there were not better reasons forthcoming I would not spare cold water or hot.[2]

[1] "He (Dr. Cullen) always tried to set me against Moore and Duffy, while he set every one against me himself."—Lucas to Dr. MacHale.

[2] "If we are not to throw cold water upon a proposal calculated to imperil the most serious interests, we must be satisfied either that it tends to practical good (which in this case we entirely disbelieve), or that it was adopted by men entitled by personal fitness and public confidence to decide for the country. Otherwise we shall spare neither cold water nor hot. Ireland has had a warning already, as memorable as if a prophet cried out on the highways. Another Catholic organisation which professed the most boisterous zeal—which undertook to determine, on behalf of the Church and the country, on all possible occasions, and to cry down, in their name, whoever interposed a word of commonsense in the path of its figments—has left us an example which it is too soon to forget."—*Nation*, June 28.

He returned to the question fiercely and offensively. The deduction from Lucas's fine character was that in controversy he was sometimes passionately and blindly unreasonable; and fought for his own will, or what was worse, for opinions accepted from some one in ecclesiastical authority, as determinedly as for truth and justice. I liked and trusted him too well, and had too long acted in strict friendship with him to let a single incident interrupt our relations, and I treated it as being what I entirely believed it to be —the inspiration of some bishop or priest to whom the *Nation* was a stumbling-block.[1] But the Northern

---

[1] "The *Tablet* has fallen into an alarming fit of epilepsy over our paragraph on the Catholic movement last week. The cause of these unaccountable convulsions escapes our most careful diagnosis. It is true *we* think a second aggregate meeting in Dublin an impolitic method of inaugurating the Catholic Defence Association, and the *Tablet* thinks otherwise; but if you differ from a man on the shortest road to a given point, he does not commonly bellow like a bull of Bashan, or foam in the mouth on the occasion. If he does, you are compelled to cast about for the motive of such superfluous gymnastics—to inquire who bespoke them, or what design on the credulity of the bystanders they are intended to cover. As we are not inclined to raise such nice issues, we leave this part of the case as a riddle for the curious:—

'Riddle me, riddle me, ree,
Was it a Connaught D.D.,
Or only a Longford P.P.,
Bespoke us this beautiful spree?'"

—*Nation*, July 5.

["*Riddle me, riddle me, ree*, settled that business well (wrote a

members were not edified by the encouragement of a second agitation, and one which was certain to disturb uneasy spirits whom they laboured to keep in check, and they were wroth with Lucas.[1]

Early in July a League meeting was held on the banks of the Boyne on the anniversary of the historical battle, to re-animate the spirit of the country and renew the pledges of union. The sitting of the General Assembly of the Presbyterian Church, which was unexpectedly protracted, kept away the leading ministers. Lucas was in London on the deputation to Sharman Crawford, on which he and I had been sent, but Dr. M'Knight, Mr. Underwood, and Archdeacon Fitzgerald, John Francis Maguire, and Father

Leaguer). There is nothing like a flash of truth after all—stage thunder being a very small substitute."]

[1] "Protestants are universally enraged at the style in which their faith is habitually spoken of, and this, too, without excuse or necessity, while liberal Roman Catholics are ashamed and vexed to see all their liberal professions falsified on a sort of organic authority. Between ourselves the advocacy of the *Tablet* is utterly ruining the Roman Catholic cause amongst all classes of the community here, and if the clergy do not either disclaim it or put an end to this insane rant and gasconade nothing can save them from its destructive consequences. You took the right course in the last *Nation* by recalling public attention to the *legal consequences* of the late act, and you ought to press it, as the public are forgetting the injuries inflicted upon the Roman Catholic community amidst the outcry that is raised against the extravagances of the *Tablet*."—*Nation* Correspondence, Dr. M'Knight to Duffy.

O'Shea represented North and South; and the Moderator of the General Assembly; and the Catholic Primate sent good wishes and sympathy. The meeting, which was held on a hill overlooking the battlefield, was a suitable site for the proclamation of social peace; and, though the weather was tempestuous, the attendance was considerable. It was announced that the deputation to London had come to an understanding with Mr. Crawford on a bill to be introduced next session, and that a conference between him and the League to settle details would take place immediately in Dublin. As the Boyne meeting was contemporaneous with the Orange commemoration of the battle, it was recognised as one of its results that in this year there were no Orange riots in the North.[1]

Mr. Keogh also pushed on his policy vigorously. The meeting to found the Defence Association was skilfully managed. The concurrence of Cardinal Wiseman and the new English bishops had been obtained, the great bulk of the Irish bishops were zealous supporters, and a committee was appointed to organise and govern the movement, which left nothing

[1] Another result may be noticed. At the Synod of Armagh some ministers took exception to the conduct of their brethren who had joined the League. But in the face of this protest, Mr. Bell was chosen Moderator, and it was a fact which could not be misunderstood as a gauge of public opinion, that every Elder, without exception, voted for him.

to be desired on the part of the projectors. It consisted of certain English bishops who could never attend, certain Irish bishops who could rarely attend, and Mr. Keogh and his aides-de-camp, who would be always on the spot. Not one man connected with the Tenant League, not even Frederick Lucas, who had been so vehement for the project, was admitted into this committee.

Immediately after the Catholic meeting the conference between Mr. Crawford and the League took place. Mr. Keogh scored another success. To oust the dishonest members from control of the elections we needed the Northerns; and the Northerns could not separate from Mr. Crawford. That gentleman went to the conference, attended by John Sadleir, William Keogh, John Reynolds, and their ordinary tail, and made their acceptance along with him inevitable. After four hours anxious debate the basis of a bill to be introduced in the coming Session was agreed upon. But he had imposed a gang of shameless jobbers on the people by allying himself with them, and to this mistake the loss of a whole generation in the progress of the principles he represented may be traced. It may seem marvellous that an honest man not deficient in judgment and insight should commit such a mistake; but they were the chosen representatives of popular constituencies, supported by eminent ecclesiastics, and the Leaguers were in his eyes simply agitators for extreme measures.

Mr. Crawford attended a League meeting the same evening, and he was again accompanied by the Brigadiers, as they came to be called from having assumed the title of the Irish Brigade, who were whitewashed in the face of the people by this alliance. The bill agreed on was not the bill of the League, as it did not include perpetuity of tenure; but we had not one man in Parliament to introduce our own bill, and we had been beaten at every election in which we endeavoured to obtain such a representative. We did all that was possible. We reserved the right to submit our measure to the constituencies at the general election, and to obtain, if it proved possible, a League party in Parliament. It was a painful choice, but

> "if we refused
> The means so limited, the tools so rude,
> To execute our purpose, life would fleet,
> And we should fade, and nothing would be done."

There is one more election to record to complete a history of shameful treason to the interests of the suffering people. The resignation of Mr. John O'Connell gave the electors of Limerick City an opportunity of retrieving the disastrous error committed in the county. But their leaders were not disposed to avail themselves of it. To mark distinctly that it was a Catholic contest rather than an agrarian or national one which concerned them, an English Catholic, the Marquis of Arundel, heir of the Duke of Norfolk, was selected as their candidate. At the nomination Father Kenyon, of Templederry, proposed General O'Donnell, an Irishman, as a protest against this policy, and was with difficulty saved from being torn to pieces by a furious mob. The result was pronounced to be another great day for Ireland, and the new member was invited to a banquet to celebrate his triumph. There was a large attendance of ecclesiastics and Brigade members, but the hero of the day did not make his appearance, and after a little time he announced his intention to accept the Chiltern Hundreds, and retire from Parliament.[1]

If this painful story be worth telling, it is primarily as a lesson in conduct. The people have gained courage and public spirit since that time; but the kindred virtues of prudence, foresight, tolerance, and judgment only come from the practice of thinking and acting for themselves; never from the most beneficent state of pupilage. It is worth telling moreover as an evidence

---

[1] One of the League priests celebrated the event in the *Nation* by a parody on "O'Rourke's Noble Feast," beginning—

"The Arundel feast will never be forgot
By the priests who were there, or the peer—who was not."

that North and South can trust each other, for these defections raised no doubt in Ulster of the fidelity of the men who had founded the League.[1]

[1] Mr. Fitzgibbon was not a Northern, but he was an intense Protestant, and he stood firm in this crisis. An extract from a letter to me on the occasion will illustrate the great need there was that the *Nation* should not go with the fury of the hour, if the union with Protestants was to be preserved—

"I agree with Rogers in thinking that the Anti-papist cry will fail in the North, and I also think it will fail everywhere else. It would indeed be a prodigy if it had not some curs to yelp for it in the old haunts of religious and factious intolerance, but the fact I now believe is beyond doubt that intelligence is too much diffused amongst the middle class to suffer it to gain a victory or to fling the honest workers into conflict and strife again. They will not battle now except against their wily plunderers, be they Papist or Protestant, and their true friends must do all they can to keep them in their right ranks, facing their hereditary oppressors and not turning aside to skirmish with each other. I heartily congratulate and thank you for the good work you are doing in the *Nation* in guarding against this danger, and I rejoice to see the sound views and honest independence of our excellent friends in the North, whose talents and noble bearing are above all praise."

CHAPTER V.—(CONTINUED.)

THE LEAGUE COUNCIL AND ITS TROUBLES.

WHEN the Defence Association was organised and its standing committees named, John Francis Maguire and Maurice Leyne, representing important organs of opinion, were looked for there, and to shut out Frederick Lucas seemed a moral impossibility. But the Brigadiers did not lack courage, and they caused a resolution to be passed excluding all newspaper proprietors and editors together. It gave a sardonic character to the device that Messrs. Keogh, Sadleir, and Ousley Higgins were at the moment engaged in bringing out a newspaper of their own, intended to be the organ of the Association. As I was not a member

---

[1] They founded a newspaper called the *Telegraph*, and proposed to sell it at half the ordinary price—a rate which, as the newspaper stamp and paper duty were still unrepealed, experts declared could not pay the cost. But it might pay politically by influencing the constituencies. It was announced in the prospectus that "it was called into existence mainly at the desire of the founder of

of the Association, and had no personal ground of complaint, I was free to point out how ignorant and calamitous a mistake such a prohibition was in a country like Ireland, which had to depend upon journalists for the defence of its interests—

"After the Battle of the Boyne the first resistance offered to England was by Swift, who united Catholic and Protestant against their common enemy. What raised the Irish vicar to be the associate of Cabinet Ministers—the maker of peers and bishops, and to be himself a new power in the State? Notoriously his writings as editor of the *Political Examiner*. The successor of Swift was Charles Lucas, whose statue stands between those of Grattan and O'Connell in the Royal Exchange, and he was founder of the *Freeman's Journal*. Henry Grattan, who succeeded him, was not properly a journalist, but what Irish scholar had not placed in his library the *Barratariana*, containing his newspaper contributions? A little later Arthur O'Connor abandoned the succession to a peerage to become a journalist and leader of the people, and Daniel O'Connell's most efficient colleagues in the Catholic struggle were journalists. Richard Shiel commenced his career as a reporter in the office of the *Morning Chronicle*. Dr. England, the great enemy of the *Veto*, and afterwards the distinguished Bishop of Charleston, was editor of the *Cork Chronicle*. The Irish Confederation and the Tenant League furnished later instances when the battle of the people was fought by journalists."

the Catholic Defence Association," but as some of the bishops objected to the responsibility involved this passage had to be cancelled.

Mr. Keogh was warned that his stroke was at any rate premature—

"It is a familiar truth that great men do not like the Press. Cromwell set it in the pillory and clipped off its ears. Louis le Grand sent it to the Bastile; Napoleon put a gag between its teeth, and, where it could not be gagged, banished it. Pitt proffered a pension or a prison, and compelled it to choose. Even O'Connell occasionally denounced it to the people, and cut off the supplies. The tradition is to remain unbroken, it seems, but the forthcoming great man has made a blunder in point of time; he should have waited till he actually grasped the rod of empire before employing it to bar the passage. At present he is, perhaps (in the language of the national proverb), bolting the door with a boiled carrot." [1]

But an unexpected difficulty interrupted the prosperous course of the Brigadiers. A Secretary was required for the general committee, and they had a

[1] It is proper to place on record that Mr. Keogh, in a private note to me, declared that in the committee he had opposed the exclusion of journalists—a statement which I leave to the reader's judgment. "Although nothing is more grateful to my mind than the applause of my fellow-countrymen (he wrote), yet no power on earth could induce me to purchase it by unworthy compliance. You will understand, therefore, that I have no motive of a personal or political nature to accomplish when I inform you that I raised my voice and gave my opinion from first to last against the proposal to exclude newspaper proprietors and editors from the committee of the Defence Association. I don't think that you are capable of representing that I was in favour of this proposition after you are informed that I was against it. This infamy has been monopolised by the editor of a journal who is well aware of the truth."—*Nation* Correspondence, Keogh to Duffy.

young Connaughtman ready who could be relied on for obedience and discretion. He was recommended by the Archbishop of Tuam, who, it was afterwards announced, would regard the selection of a foreigner as fatal. But the Primate, who thought selections of this character belonged to him, quietly recommended an English convert, Mr. Henry Wilberforce, son of the famous anti-slavery leader, and brother of the Bishop of Oxford, who was elected accordingly. The Brigadiers were incensed at having the chief executive office given to a man not devoted to their interests, and they rashly appealed from the committee to the community. As the Catholic congregation issued from church on Sunday morning they were amazed to read a placard on the walls signed by Keogh, Sadleir, and their adherents, which announced that in opposition to five bishops who were present, and to the almost unanimous wish of the faithful Irish members, a stranger, wholly ignorant of the opinions and wishes of the people, had been chosen Secretary of the Defence Association. On the eve of a general election they regarded such a choice as an act of ignoble folly and national degradation, and it was made, they declared, in open defiance of the noble nationality which had hitherto been the life and inspiration of the Irish cause.[1]

---

[1] The most prominent of the Irish members, it was said, sustained by the most Irish of bishops, directly raised the question

THE LEAGUE COUNCIL AND ITS TROUBLES. 167

After a pause of wonder at the rashness and unwisdom of the appeal, the controversy was taken up warmly by Catholics outside the Association.

Lucas, who by this time had lost confidence in the new organisation, vehemently condemned the proceeding. He scoffed at their affectation of patriotism, and quoted a pamphlet of Mr. Keogh's written before he entered Parliament, in which he had turned Irish nationality into contempt.[1] The allegations in the Address were contradicted *seriatim;* one of the five bishops present had declined to vote, not approving of any of the candidates, and some of the others supported Mr. Wilberforce. The Brigadiers, he insisted, wanted a creature of their own, a totally incompetent person, and would not consent to postpone their appeal for a single day, as they had been entreated to do, that some accommodation might be arrived at.

I took a different view of the transaction. I had

---

whether Ireland is to be offered as a sacrifice to the interests and feelings of a handful of English Catholics, who, but for their connection with this country, would be "an enslaved sect, without rank, privilege, or position in the State, and subjects only in their subjection."—Address of the Irish Members on the election of Mr. Wilberforce. The document was written by G. H. Moore.

[1] Mr. Keogh's pamphlet was entitled *Ireland Imperialised*, and was an appeal to Lord Clarendon to efface the National party by a judicious distribution of places among safe men—like himself.

no confidence in the Irish members, but I thought there were good grounds to disapprove of the choice made. "Ireland for the English" had been the rule in too many places already to welcome it in the Catholic Defence Association. An illustrious Englishman was to be Rector of the Catholic University, and would have the training of the next generation of our young men, and Mr. Lucas would teach them through a powerful journal. These were justifiable and even salutary circumstances; but there were others which suggested the necessity of caution. Limerick had recently selected Lord Arundel to represent it in a great national emergency, and several English candidates were notoriously negotiating for Irish constituencies; an English squire had, it was alleged, found the capital for a journal to teach the Irish people their public duties, and English ecclesiastics, educated at Oxford, were giving a tone to Catholic society in Ireland which assuredly was not national. The Court of Wards had been the most successful stroke of policy in denationalising the ancient Irish families, and education was so powerful a solvent of opinions that the new policy might prove as disastrous.[1]

[1] "The bitterest enemies of Ireland for eight generations have been Anglicised Irishmen. Some Anglo-Irish Earl of Antrim some Anglo-Irish Clanricarde or Preston, some Anglo-Irish

The Primate, who had taken no public part in the election, at length interfered with a letter insisting that, as the Defence Association represented the Catholics of the United Kingdom, the choice of Mr. Wilberforce was reasonable and proper. To placate the Archbishop of Tuam the committee selected an Irish Assistant-Secretary in the person of Mr. Martin Crean, and the struggle ended in a compromise. During this controversy Mr. Keogh was entertained at a public dinner in Athlone, at which Dr. MacHale attended. The committee sent an invitation to Lucas, who committed the mistake of accepting it after his recent exposure of the guest of the evening. No toast was assigned to him, but when "the Press" was proposed, his friends called upon him and he rose to reply. Mr. Keogh's partisans shouted him down, and insisted on hearing the editor of a local newspaper in preference to one of the greatest publicists in Europe. When he was at length heard, Lucas, in the course of his speech, suggested that if the Opposition came into office Mr. Keogh would be offered the post of Solicitor-General, and one of the dangers to be foreseen was

Kenmare or Bellew, some Anglo-Irish Wyse or More O'Farrell, some Castle bishop or Castle hack who had learned to lisp like a Cockney and reason like a Jacobite, is always the man to betray the Irish interest in its last emergency. This is the history of Ireland since the Reformation."—*Nation*, on Mr. Wilberforce's appointment.

that he might accept it. Keogh, in a rage, replied that his assailant was a person who would plant a dagger in a man's back if he found a convenient opportunity. Next morning the Archbishop attempted to make peace where peace was impossible, and even disastrous, because the confidence on which it must rest was wholly wanting. He told Lucas that Mr. Keogh was the appointed Catholic leader, and that it was his duty to support him; and, in the end, he caused honesty and dishonesty to clasp hands. Here was a man who stood nearly alone in grasp of intellect and devotion to Catholic interests, and in the supreme gift of judging men, and the melancholy use the Archbishop made of his influence over him was to force him to embrace a person whom his conscience and judgment repudiated as a dishonest schemer. Dr. MacHale afterwards made such amends as were possible, but taking sides decisively at a later period; many of the bishops continued to uphold Mr. Keogh till half a generation later, when, from the safe asylum of the judicial bench, he covered them and all he had pretended to love with his scorn and contumely. One of the commonest errors committed in Irish affairs down to this day is the desire to hide away difference of opinion in a pretence of unanimity. Absolute unanimity is impossible among men who use their judgment and conscience; reasonable and honest difference of opinion is a public gain, as it helps to discipline opinion; and a popular leader has no more reason to fear a legitimate opposition than the leader of the House of Commons. But this is a truth which Ireland has never learned.

At this time a circumstance happened which proved to be of signal importance to the League. Dr. Murray, the Catholic Archbishop of Dublin, died, and the duty fell on the clergy of the ecclesiastical province to recommend three persons to Rome from whom a successor might be selected. It was intimated that the Propaganda desired to transfer the Primate from Armagh to the metropolis, and he obtained a majority of votes, and was declared *dignissimus*. The Archbishopric of Dublin had always been a post of political importance. Between the Invasion and the Reformation it had habitually been conferred on an Englishman. After the ecclesiastical property got transferred to the new Establishment by Henry VIII. and Elizabeth, there were two archbishops, an Englishman sent to watch over the King's interest, and an Irishman nominated by the Holy See. At the time of the Union, when the Catholic prelacy first got a grudging recognition from the Castle, the Archbishop was more of a courtier and diplomatist than any of his class in Ireland, and his successor had followed in his footsteps. In the long list of metropolitans, indeed, there is but one who has left a name cherished by the nation, Laurence O'Toole, properly Lorcan Tuatheill, and since canonised as St. Lorcan, held the office in the era of Strongbow, and died in exile contending for the rights of his race against the invader. It was hoped that the Propaganda, in transferring the Primate to Dublin, meant to give Ireland a successor to the patriot prelate of the twelfth century. While he remained at Armagh all parties regarded Dr. Cullen as a Nationalist,[1] but in truth no man ever held the office who was

[1] A private letter from the Lord-Lieutenant, Lord Clarendon, to Lord Shrewsbury, a Catholic peer, got published at this time, and sufficiently exhibits the opinion which the Government held of the Archbishop of Armagh—

"All good men in Ireland, of whatever creed or politics, are agreed in reverencing Dr. Murray as the *beau idéal* of a Christian pastor, and yet your Lordship found his Holiness irritated against him alone. All agree in considering Dr. MacHale as an ill-disposed demagogue, who does nothing but afford an example of all that a bishop ought not to do ; and yet when your Lordship blamed him you were told that you had a strange animosity to the Irish. Dr. Cullen, moreover, published a synodical address, in which he did not stop at condemning the colleges, but sought to set class against class, and to represent every poor man as a martyr, and every rich man as a tyrant. There is more rank communism in that address than could be chemically distilled from M. de Vericour's whole book. Mr. Lucas, editor of the *Tablet*—one of the most virulent and offensive newspapers in Europe—was in constant communication with Dr. Cullen, and is, moreover, the chief instigator, as his paper is the organ of the Tenant League, the object of which is to abolish the rights of property, and to shake to its very foundation everything on which society depends. He is ably assisted in this work of regeneration by the priests, who,

more essentially a foreigner. He was not an Englishman, but an Italian, who only regarded Ireland as a convenient fulcrum for the foreign policy of the Vatican. Shortly after his arrival at Armagh a keen observer who saw him close at hand, wrote to me:—" He has *not* genius, but he has great acquirements in divinity, great shrewdness, considerable knowledge of men and their motives, and great graces from God." It may be that he was a good bishop, but assuredly he was a bad Irishman. His ideal, as we can now discern it in his action, was to transfer the government of Ireland to bishops, and a few laymen prepared to accept their lead without question or criticism. It was a narrow and impossible policy; and after more than a generation has passed away, we can safely pronounce that it has proved in the end a disastrous failure. His fundamental fault was that he mistook his own imperfect acquaintance with facts for profound knowledge, and acted on his prejudices as if they were inspiration. The leaders of the Italian Nationalists (Mazzini and Garibaldi) mingled with their laudable desire to drive the Austrians out of Italy a fanatical

with this end in view, have fraternised with the Presbyterian clergy. But not a word of counsel or reprimand has been uttered by the Primate. On the contrary, his journal applauds, and the editor acts in the League with Mr. Duffy, of the *Nation*, who would have been at this hour a deported felon if one of the jury had not perjured himself."

antipathy to the Catholic Church, and Dr. Cullen saw in the Nationalists of Ireland only a reproduction of the Italian party. But in Ireland the Church had been the ally and confederate of the Nationalists, and religion was one of the main sources of the fidelity of the people to their public duties. The Irish Repealers no more represented the Carbonari than the Irish priests who were successively Repealers, Confederates, and Tenant-Righters, resembled the ecclesiastics who were allies of the House of Hapsburg. Some of the Meath Leaguers whispered that his original prejudice was fomented by bad advisers. His relatives in that county were graziers and "bull farmers" who had no sympathy with the struggling peasantry, and had no hesitation in adding field to field at the cost of their neighbours. His uncle, Father Maher, was a servile Whig, and party hack, and when the transfer to Dublin took place the Whig Catholics who had formed Dr. Murray's cabinet soon surrounded his successor.

After a time I discovered that he regarded me with particular disfavour as an "Irish Mazzini"—that was his phrase. Whenever I met him, which was rarely, and only at the table of some priest or layman of his diocese, he smiled affably, and I had no sort of notice of his real sentiments. But subterranean murmurs reached me from time to time through friendly

THE LEAGUE COUNCIL AND ITS TROUBLES. 175

ecclesiastics, and at length Lucas assured me that he urged him to separate from so dangerous a connection. Lucas was not the man to be ear-wigged into a policy which his judgment rejected, but to retain our alliance unbroken was not always easy. He was reminded from time to time by ecclesiastics of various ranks who had adhered to O'Connell in 1846, that the Young Irelanders had been accused by bishops of want of Catholic faith and zeal, and when he rejoined that the bishops who assailed the Young Irelanders in 1846 were the identical men who now supported Messrs. Sadleir and Keogh, the answer was pronounced insufficient.

On my side I was warned that while we were seeking concessions from the English Parliament which would never be obtained, the national spirit was dying out. My friends were suspicious of certain London Irishmen who were posing as candidates, and whom they insisted on regarding as *protégés* of Lucas. Maurice Leyne, at the League Council, one day in Lucas's presence, cited the case of one of these gentlemen who had been ostentatiously praying at O'Connell's grave, and inquired whether he was praying for a county constituency? The Catholic Colleges, the Press, the Pulpit, he insisted, were falling under English influence, and even the constituencies. An English nobleman, notable for nothing but, like Beaumarchais's hero, " having taken the trouble to be born," met with a reception in Limerick which rivalled O'Connell's at the Clare election. "We know and do not fear," he said, "the English who came in with Strongbow, the English who came in with Cromwell, the English who came in with William of Nassau; but how are we to guard against the new invaders to whom our strong places are given up—the English who came in with Lucas?"

When Parliament met, Sharman Crawford introduced his bill, and the value of the new alliance was tested. The Brigade supported the measure feebly, the Government opposed it, and it was lost by a majority of three to one. Mr. Crawford was of opinion that his measure was lost by the additions which were made to it at the Conference; but his most moderate proposals had never been better received. Happily the hope of aid through a general election visibly increased. Lord John Russell, who seems never to have understood what fidelity to a colleague meant, pushed Lord Palmerston out of the Government to satisfy a punctilio of Prince Albert; and those who knew the parties to the transaction predicted that the *coup* would be speedily avenged. In a few weeks the Whigs fell, on the motion of their late colleague, and Lord Derby was called to office, with a Cabinet of new men, of whom the most conspicuous was Mr. Disraeli. The fall of the Whigs was received with universal satisfaction in Ireland. Their weak and cruel policy during the famine, their Ecclesiastical Titles Bill, and a recent exposure before the courts of law of Lord Clarendon's connection, in 1848, with an infamous newspaper called the *World*, rendered them odious and detestable.

The Whigs, before turning out, had rewarded one of the Cork members—Dr. Power—for a long career of subserviency by the governorship of a Crown Colony. Several candidates more or less suitable were named for the vacancy, but the Brigadiers wanted Vincent Scully, a barrister without practice, but a landholder and a director of John Sadleir's Tipperary Bank. The *Tablet* and *Nation* warned the constituency that he was a confederate and relative of Sadleir's, and that it was dangerous to create a family party. Mr. Keogh attended the nomination in his character of leader of the Irish Brigade, and made a remarkable demonstration. The County Club, in the first instance, selected Mr. Alexander M'Carthy, but the leader induced the Bishop of Cloyne, Dr. Murphy, to support Mr. Scully, and he overcame resistance at the Club by pledges so plain and specific that it seemed captious and unreasonable to doubt them. He repudiated the idea of place-begging with scorn, and sealed his fidelity with an oath—

"I declared myself (Mr. Keogh said) in the presence of the bishops of Ireland and of my colleagues in Parliament, that let the Minister of the day be whom he may—let him be the Earl of Derby, let him be Sir James Graham, or Lord John Russell—it was all the same to us; and, SO HELP ME GOD, no matter who the Minister may be, no matter who the party in power may be, I will neither support that Minister nor that party unless he comes into power prepared to carry the measures which universal popular Ireland demands."[1]

Mr. Sadleir answered for the honour and patriotism of his relation, as for his own.[2] The Rev. Mr. Corcoran proposed Mr. Scully, he said, "because of his thorough and perfect identification with the Tenant League, and opposition to any Government not favourable to Irish rights." But the candidate sustained this *rôle* imperfectly. He had to admit that he had made a lease enabling him to distrain for rent three days after

[1] He described his intentions more specifically on a further occasion—"If all the Peelites in the House joined the Whig Administration, I would be their unmitigated, their untiring, their indefatigable opponent till we got justice. And what is that justice? I can state the terms of it well. I will not support any party which will not make it the first ingredient of their political existence to repeal the Ecclesiastical Titles Bill. I will have nothing to do with any party which, without interfering with the religious belief of the Protestant population, will not consent to remove from off the Catholics of this country the burthen of sustaining a Church Establishment with which they are not in communion."

[2] "His mother's brother (we'll ax no other),
    Tis he'll go bail for his father's son."
—Squib in the *Nation*, by a young Cork Priest.

it was due. He would vote for the second reading of Mr. Crawford's bill, but not pledge himself to details. With this manifest sham the great county of Cork was content, and Mr. Scully was elected.

The *Times* was confident, after the fate of Crawford's bill and the issue of the contested election, that the Irish Question was not likely to be a further embarrassment. It announced, with cynical plainness, that what was odious in Ireland—its population—would be got rid of, but what was pleasant and convenient for the employment of English capital still remained—

"Ireland's fertile soil, its rivers and lakes, its water-power, its minerals, and other materials for the wants and luxuries of man, may one day be developed; but all appearances are against the belief that this will ever happen in the days of the Celt. That tribe will soon fulfil the great law of Providence, which seems to enjoin and reward the union of races. It will mix with the Anglo-American, and be known no more as a jealous and separate people."

The *Nation* announced a counter-project, which, after a generation, has, under God's mercy to a struggling people, had a larger measure of success—

"To colonise Ireland, not with strangers, but with the Irish race; to plant the people, who are flying away in a panic, among their kith and kin; to substitute the industry and integrity of the country as owners of the soil, in lieu of bankruptcy and profligacy; to create a small proprietary, constituted of the best of the existing farmers, of the most skilful workmen, whom Mr. Dargan and his colleagues, the Board of Works and the Ordnance Survey, have trained in Ireland; of the picked teetotallers, who have learned thrift and foresight as well as temperance; and of the most enterprising and successful of the Irish in England; and to stop the growth of pauperism by giving the people a motive for exertion."

That the incidents narrated in this chapter should have left the League unbroken is creditable to the Northern leaders, who were sorely tried. But is it not creditable to the Catholic leaders also, a confidence in whose fidelity and integrity was the essential condition of its existence?

CHAPTER VI.

THE GENERAL ELECTION.

FROM the beginning, the hopes of the League had been set on the enthusiasm and *élan* of a general election, and now this coveted opportunity was near at hand. If it were wasted, all would be lost.

Those who saw the organisation from the outside could imperfectly estimate the difficulties which beset its leaders. The funds had fallen low, the attendance of country members slackened, and as the general election approached, the ambition of wealthy nincompoops, who had joined the League in the vague hope of getting into Parliament, became troublesome. The promise of contributions to the ten thousand pounds fund had been imperfectly fulfilled. Leinster contributed £810; Ulster, £132; Munster, £117; and Connaught nothing. A systematic canvass of towns was commenced by deputations, and of rural districts by the local societies, and the means were with difficulty obtained of continuing the agitation with the strictest economy. The office of Secretary had been performed in turn by various members of the Council, owing to the difficulty of finding a man acceptable both to North and South as a permanent officer. The Southerns were willing and anxious to accept an Ulsterman, but the Ulstermen who offered themselves were not approved of by the Northern leaders; at length Mr. Biudon, a Munster Protestant, was selected as a compromise. A weekly periodical, entitled the *Irish Tenant League*, was established, not only for the purpose of spreading the League principles but as a measure of economy. The printing and postage of the circulars summoning the Council amounted to nearly £20 a month, for which a notice in the periodical might be substituted; and in another direction it might be made equivalent to a monthly tract without incurring new expenditure.

The first Conference and the unexampled union of North and South were not gains more marvellous than the success now won against a legion of impediments and discouragements. Since Catholic Emancipation only one dissolution of Parliament had been turned to adequate account in Ireland. A fatal weakness had uniformly betrayed the Irish cause; the people and their trusted counsellors, whenever they were offered the choice between integrity and plausible dishonesty, did not know how to choose. They could struggle and suffer for a just cause, but they could not, it seemed, protect it from systematic betrayal. That fatal weakness was as plain to the Leaguers then as it is to the mass of Irishmen at this hour; and they pressed upon the people in every tone of sympathy and remonstrance the supreme duty of contending only for honest men and honest principles. Lucas stated once more the wrongs and the remedy in language of singular vigour and clearness. Several of the League priests exhorted their own districts to set an example of vigilant preparation; and Archdeacon Fitzgerald, with all the authority derived from his age and his office, appealed directly to the bishops, who had been the chief offenders hitherto, to take a lead in this work. He bade them remember the examples of sainted prelates of old who came to the rescue of their faithful people to save them from pillage and extirpation; though there was not a single instance where the calamity sought to be averted could bear comparison with the wholesale devastation inflicted on Ireland by the landlords. St. Leo went forth to arrest the destroying hand of Attila. St. Flavian, of Antioch, travelled eight hundred miles to protect his people from impending destruction. The Bishop of Chiappa (Las Casas) crossed the Atlantic, to and from Spain, at six different times to save his unhappy flock from the murderous oppression inflicted under the pretence of rights of property.

He warned them not to permit the exterminator to assume religious zeal as a cloak for greed and malice; nor under any pretence to countenance any man who killed, banished, or shut up in workhouse dungeons those who would not pay impossible rents. "The man who made a desert around him—who looked from his hall-door on ruins of farmhouses, once the scenes of peace, innocence, and honest toil; who made of Ireland an anticipated hell, should not find in the favour of an abused and deluded people a sort of game licence to hunt them down like wolves or hares!" Let the candidate be an Irish Brigademan, but let it be also a *sine quâ non* that he shall be pledged to support a Land Bill which, while it inflicts no real wrong upon any human being, would keep our people at home, and perhaps reclaim those who were banished.

"A Tipperary Priest" painted the desolation of the country in language of plain sense and natural feeling—

"Two-thirds of my own congregation (he said) have departed to the workhouse or gone to America. I was, God help me, very proud of my flock seven or eight years ago. I rejoiced—I felt, perhaps, an unbecoming pride—when they crowded around my chapel in their holiday finery on a Sunday, and I used to point to them as the decentest and best conducted people in the country. My chapel always overflowed. There is hardly a third of it occupied at present—and the showy gowns and ribbons, and the bright kerchiefs have almost disappeared. There is instead squalor and rags, tottering old age, and no children."

The same theme was expanded in the *Nation*—

"Ireland was fast dissolving before the landlord, as the Jewish nation dissolved before the curse of God, as the Carthagenian nation dissolved before the sword of Rome, as the Red Indian silently dissolved before the face of the white man. A hospitable and pious people, whose doors were wide open to the stranger—an industrious and thrifty race who produced abundantly and lived frugally, were given over to slow extinction. They perish cruelly, shivering in rags, cowering under dripping roofs, fed on chance alms, rotting in workhouses or stifling in emigrant ships, and flung out of them to mix with the polluted dregs of great cities, and forget the God that made them and the country that bore them. And the landlord comes behind, and plucks down their dwellings as the ratcatcher destroys the nests to stop the propagation of the vermin."

Another writer in the same journal described, in words of penetrating force, the sham policy presented for the support of the people by the Brigadiers—

"Priests and people, wakening from the ecstatic excitement of a religious war, look round the country to see the tenant-farmers trooping out of it in thousands, and what remedy did the Brigade propose? Read their answer in Mr. Moore's speech at Ballina. Tenant-right will be proposed, but it is quite impossible to carry it next session, or in a cycle of sessions. So Mr. Moore says boldly and bluntly. It is quite possible, nevertheless, we are assured, to repeal the Ecclesiastical Titles Bill, get vote by ballot, create a score of new Irish constituencies, turn out the Whigs, and turn in any party else! Oh, good and all seeing God! the mortal blindness of this most unhappy and sore-stricken people!"

Father Daly detailed the method and agencies by which an honest Parliamentary Party might be created. At present unsound members were selected by local prejudice or by private negotiation with influential persons, and when they were chosen it was next to impossible to get rid of them. By aid of the League, candidates might be obtained who would not flinch from their duty.

Mr. Underwood exhorted the Northern electors to put aside party feeling during this struggle; they might hate the Pope, but let them remember that *his* name was never seen in a process of ejectment; and George Henry Moore recommended, as pledges were everywhere in England exacted from candidates to vote for the abolition of the Maynooth grant, that Irish candidates should be pledged to the disestablishment of the Protestant Church in Ireland.

In the *Nation* I strove to familiarise the people with the policy by which alone the cause might be carried to success—the policy of Independent Opposition; a policy which meant union with no English party, and hostility to none which was prepared to advance our cause. It is necessary to quote the language employed, that it may be understood, if the people were foully betrayed in the end, they were fully forewarned of the danger.

The balance of English parties, it was said, afforded

a rare opportunity to an Independent Irish minority. Free Trade and Protection were going to fight their last battle; the Anti-Corn Law League was already revived, and Protection was in force in Downing Street—

"Ireland held the key of the position. She was able to say to them—'Debate and divide, gentlemen, it is your right; but Ireland must decide who shall have the majority.' This was the talismanic sentence which would open the ears of English parties to the Irish question."

If Ireland must support the party which proved most friendly, it was necessary to have plain evidence which party answered this description. Neither showed such a disposition at present—

"The Free Traders had a fanatical hatred to the principles of the League, and a cold immovable contempt for everything beyond the narrow range of their circumscribed horizon. They were not men of imagination or sympathy. The slaughter of Skibbereen affected them no more than the murder of the Innocents. It was cast into the perspective of vast distance by their little scientific spyglasses. Moral indignation that kindles at injustice, instinctive sympathies with a chivalrous people, were little known in Manchester. They had, indeed, a desire to do what they considered reasonable and just. But what was reasonable and just in their eyes? They would sacrifice an Irish province to a theory if it had the Manchester stamp on it."

The *modus operandi* was described over and over again—

"Whatever party can attain the control of the House of Commons rules the empire. For ten years no

English Minister has had an effective working majority of more than a hundred for an entire session. More than a third of his majority was always Irish. Deducting the Irish, it has never exceeded sixty. Whenever the League can send into the House of Commons fifty members prepared to insist upon the tenants' charter in supreme disregard of party interests, it will be carried. They will be able to overturn any Minister by walking across the floor of the house."

But this result was to be attained only by men who to integrity and capacity added the strictest discipline—

"Against a Government bound together with ribs of iron, against a disciplined aristocracy accustomed from boyhood to command and obey, the naked people had to fight this battle. It was fatuity to hope they would do it by choosing an indiscriminate herd of members, and leaving each to follow his individual will and pleasure. The people must establish a discipline and erect an authority of their own equal to those of their antagonists. What discipline and what authority, the League must determine."

This was the position Ireland would hold in the new Parliament, and its value would altogether depend on the class of men to whom the duty was intrusted—

"If the leaders of English parties had to consider not what they must yield to Ireland, but what they must offer to individual ambitions and cupidities to secure Irish votes, the opportunity would be fatally lost. Mr. A would be supplied by the Treasury with a purse to pay his 'debts of honour,' Mr. B promised a colonia appointment; Mr. C, who has money, would get a baronetcy; and Messrs. E and F, who managed the business,[1]

---

[1] The men who "managed the business," Messrs. Keogh and Sadleir, strictly fulfilled this prediction.

might aspire to become Irish Secretary and Solicitor-General respectively. 'Ireland's opportunity' would be bought and paid for by a mess of pottage."

One of these exhortations closed with language which proved prophetic—

"God sends opportunities; it is man's privilege to use or abuse them. Another opportunity is sent to Ireland; let Irishmen bethink themselves in time whether it will be wisely used, idly lost, or treacherously sold to the enemy. The men they send to the next Parliament will determine the result."[1]

General expostulation was followed by specific action. In the counties where the League principles were strongest the selection of candidates immediately commenced. The Council advised that the choice should be made by a conference representing the constituency, and be afterwards confirmed or rejected by the people in public assembly. To transform opinion from a protoplasm to a vertebrate and sinewy power, it must act for itself; there is no other method under heaven for turning serfs into citizens. To find in a country so poor and so derided as Ireland fifty or sixty candidates able to live six months of the year in London and willing to maintain a constant struggle for a cause disparaged even by the middle class was not easy. But the Council sought them assiduously. Their aim was to create a party not of their own adherents, but in the first instance of men who would impress Parliament by their

[1] *Nation*, March 6, 1852.

character and ability. In the *Autobiography of John Stuart Mill*, and the *Selected Speeches of Lord O'Hagan*, evidence will be found that both these distinguished persons were applied to to become candidates of the League, with whose principles they were in substantial harmony.[1] The Leaguers of Meath desired to choose Lucas and Sergeant Shee; but the project met a strong opponent in the bishop, who was unwilling to displace Mr. Corbally, a Catholic squire—personally respectable and politically a nonentity. Finally Lucas and Corbally were selected. But the Brigadiers were determined to keep Lucas out of Parliament; and the Parliamentary Committee of the Defence Association promptly passed a resolution declaring that they would see a contest in Meath with great pain, and exhorting the constituency not to turn their back on representatives who had served them faithfully. Mr. Grattan, in

---

[1] In his *Autobiography* Mr. Mill states that fourteen years before Westminster sent him to Parliament, Mr. Lucas and Mr. Duffy were authorised by the Tenant League to offer him a county constituency in Ireland; which, concurring with the fundamental principles of the League, he would have accepted but for his relations to the East India Company at that time. Lord O'Hagan, who afterwards defended the League principles in the House of Lords as embodied in the Land Act of 1880, was also invited to become a candidate. In a note on the recently published volume of his *Select Speeches* (p. 520) he says—"In 1882 Frederick Lucas intreated me to accept a constituency without adopting the peculiar views of the party of which he and my friend Sir Charles Duffy were the most influential leaders."

whose interest this declaration was made, had hereditary claims on Irish sympathy, till he had effaced them by his own conduct. In the contest between O'Connell and the Young Irelanders he had not taken a side, but sheltered himself in abject silence. During the famine he had voted for Coercion when relief was denied; and he now repudiated the principles by which it was hoped the people might be saved. He was a man not indisposed to act generously if he found generous sentiments acceptable to his ordinary associates; but he was not strong enough to stand alone, and in Parliament he had drifted with the current. It is strange that in an association of which eminent prelates of the three nations were members no one repudiated this intrigue against a man who had served them so faithfully as Frederick Lucas. But the priests and people of Meath could take care of themselves. They replied to this exhortation by a resolution declaring that some of the Committee (of the Catholic Defence Association) which undertook to recommend candidates to Irish constituencies were exterminating landlords, and other untrustworthy politicians, and that they disdained their guidance. The *Nation* welcomed their nomination in terms which time amply justified—

"Meath has chosen wisely for its own interests; Lucas will be an incomparable Leaguer and a whole Catholic Defence Association in himself. It is surprising that Parliament was not opened to him long ago, for his capacity is peculiarly adapted for that field. He is an eminent journalist, but he will be a more eminent debater. His success, we are convinced, will be immediate and remarkable. After a few sessions he will hold a place in the House as individual and notable as any man's who has not sat in a Cabinet Council. His impregnable coolness and masculine vigour, his resources, and the reserve of vehement passion which great occasions call out, will make him a master of that practical eloquence which sways the House of Commons."

In Kilkenny the bishop desired no change, but the League priests were of a different mind, and in the end Sergeant Shee and Captain Greene, one of the sitting members, were nominated as the popular candidates. Louth selected Tristram Kennedy, a barrister, who had been agent for the Marquis of Bath's property in an adjoining county, and had distinguished himself by fair and considerate dealing with the tenantry. In Sligo and Leitrim it was necessary to have candidates who would spend largely to bring up voters to the poll, and probably for local churches and charities, which the constituency had grown accustomed to expect; as if a seat in Parliament, instead of being a public trust, was a personal prize. The League recommended two Irishmen resident in London, Mr. Swift, recently sheriff of Middlesex, and Dr. Brady, a medical man in good practice.

In Ireland the boroughs were much more under the influence of patrons and cabals than the counties, and it was considered a great gain when Dungannon nominated John Francis Maguire, and New Ross requested the League to name one or more candidates for the consideration of a local committee. The story of the contest in the latter borough is worthy, on several grounds, chiefly from the universal interest it excited and the example it set, of being told in detail.

The Council named three candidates—Charles Gavan Duffy, Patrick Lalor of Tinakill, and Patrick M'Mahon, of the Temple, London, who were immediately communicated with. A deputation, consisting of Father Tom O'Shea and Mr. Bindon, the secretary, was appointed to visit the constituency, and I was requested to accompany them as the first candidate on the list. On a dull morning in spring, the sky overcast and threatening, and rain falling at intervals, Mr. Bindon and I arrived at Callan, and made our way to the Curates' cottage. We found Father O'Shea disabled by bronchitis, which had kept him indoors for several days. When we told our errand Father Keefe shook his head at the rash project of an invalid facing the unfriendly sky, and suggested an appeal to the doctor. But the indomitable Leaguer would listen to no remonstrance where public duty and private friendship were concerned, and before an hour we were on the road to New Ross. Many a time since there has risen to my memory the picture of the stalwart priest on an open car, and muffled to the chin, but constantly forgetful of his temporary ailment in eager debate on the mission he had undertaken. When we reached New Ross he set out alone for a personal visit to his fellow-student in former days, Father Doyle, the senior curate, who was understood to exercise a decisive influence over the election committee. After considerable delay he returned to announce that his mission had failed. Father Doyle expressed personal respect and sympathy with the candidate, but he was confident from the feeling of the committee, who were most vehement Old Irelanders, that they would not accept him, and he declined to moot a project which must necessarily fail. I determined on the instant to see Father Doyle personally, and we all set out for his residence. He received us courteously, and while we were sharing his evening meal, repeated what he had already said to Father O'Shea. I requested him to summon the committee for next morning, and allow me to face their prejudice, and see how far it could justify itself in my presence. He thought the attempt useless for any practical end, but at length consented, as a courtesy, to issue the necessary summons. He required, however, as a preliminary condition, that we should consult the wishes of his parish priest; without whose concurrence he would not move a step. We called upon that gentleman, who made no objection to the experiment. He was not a politician, he said, and was prepared to accept the decision of the people, whatever it might be. Next morning the committee, which consisted of about two dozen persons, mustered eighteen or twenty, and Father Doyle, who was suffering from influenza, arrived, wrapped in a heavy cloak and muffler, to look on, he said, but not prepared to take part in the proceedings. Three or four members who would not consent to pay me the courtesy of listening to me came to the door and stared in for a minute or two as at some strange animal, and then took their departure. I had formed a resolution during a sleepless night to make that day a cardinal one in my life; it might be one of discomfiture and disaster; but at any rate it should be signal and decisive. I told the committee I had been forewarned of their prejudice against me because I was associated with men whom I believed to be the most enlightened and disinterested whom Ireland had known in this century, but they had probably only heard one side of the case, and should now hear the other. A committee who were all Irishmen, who were probably all Repealers, and who had the additional ground of sympathy that they were all Catholics, afforded as fair a tribunal as I could ever hope to appeal to on my past career and my present designs, and I had come to the fixed resolution of accepting their verdict as final, whatever it might be. If after hearing my defence of the conduct of the Young

Irelanders, and my aims in entering Parliament, they declared that I was not a fit candidate for New Ross, I would abandon my candidature, resign my seat on the Council of the League, discontinue the *Nation*, and retire from Irish affairs for ever. This was my fixed determination, and I spoke for an hour under the strong feeling created by the belief that it was perhaps my last appeal to an Irish audience.

I do not know, and I can never know, to what extent I won the sympathy of the committee, for a factor came into play which baffled all calculation. As soon as I sat down Father Doyle stripped off his cloak and muffler, and plunged into the business. He declared he would give me his unequivocal support, and made a passionate appeal for fair play, before which opposition seemed gradually to melt away. There were thrilling cheers, as he urged point after point, which were not for the orator solely, and when I withdrew I believed that a majority of the committee were prepared to support me.

But prejudice gives way slowly. After I had returned to Dublin a letter came from a friend in the committee,[1] informing me that either Mr. Lalor or Mr. M'Mahon would unite the whole committee, which

---

[1] Mr. William Power, who, with his brother, Mr. Michael Power, supported me from the outset. The latter was a man of remarkable ability and decision of character.

I should certainly not do, and recommending that I would allow the name of one of them to be substituted for mine, and select some other constituency. But in the meantime Mr. Lalor had answered to the communication of the Council, that he would not re-enter Parliament, but would gladly support me; and Mr. M'Mahon wrote to me that he would only become a candidate for any constituency if the men who had created the League were chosen before him, without whom he would be useless in Parliament.[1] The League felt that the contest was a decisive one; the more so that I was resolved to accept the verdict as final. An address to the electors of Ross, signed by fifty of the leading Leaguers, North and South, lay and clerical, was issued, and a deputation, consisting of Pat Lalor, Father Daly, Father O'Shea, Rev. David Bell, and others, set out to address the constituency in a public meeting.[2] Meantime two candidates with

[1] "You should know that unless you, and Lucas, and Pat Lalor, and Sergeant Shee and such men get in, I have not the remotest wish for a seat. It would be disheartening and disgusting to me to be thrust in among a mob of fools, knaves, cheats, sots, hypocrites, and cowards. With these notions you will therefore understand that I would not spend £5 to get in for any borough or county in the island, unless I was to go in as one of a party prepared honestly to stand by the people, and sufficiently numerous to serve them in some way."—*Nation* Correspondence, M'Mahon to Duffy, March 25, 1852.

[2] By this time Mr. Fitzgibbon had retired, discontented with

local connections entered the field—Sir Thomas Redington, late Under-Secretary for Ireland, whose father-in-law was the sitting member; and Mr. Henry Lambert, who had represented the county Wexford twenty years earlier. The parish priest, it was hinted, supported Redington, and Mr. Tottenham, the proprietor of the town, supported Mr. Lambert. With the parish priest the Bishop of Ferns was understood to sympathise, and there could be no doubt that the Archbishop of the Province, Dr. Cullen, the Apostolic Delegate, would not be sorry to see me defeated. The parish priest who had received me so graciously suddenly became hostile. On my second visit to the borough, I had the solace of hearing his estimate of the three candidates communicated to his congregation on a Sunday morning after Mass. Henry Lambert was objectionable, he said, as having been tried in Parliament already, and found wanting; whereas Sir Thomas Redington was a Catholic gentleman who had already served his country with distinction. As for the stranger from Dublin, he would not conceal his opinion that that gentleman was aiming at a position which

the *Tablet* articles, I think. He became secretary of a Native Manufacture movement, and, after a little time, died. Mr. Lalor had also left the League in disgust with the perversity of some of the Council, who were too critical, he considered, on his administration of affairs as hon. secretary.

neither God nor man had intended for him, or intended him for.

The landlord was equally decisive. His tenants were forewarned of the wrath with which he would regard the selection of an enemy of the rights of property as representative of his town. Against the ecclesiastical influence it would have been as impossible to prevail in Ross as it had proved elsewhere, but for the dauntless courage of Father Doyle. He had romised his support, he said, and he did not feel relieved from his pledge because his respected pastor had changed his mind. Those who know what are the relations of a curate to a parish priest—to a bishop—to an archbishop, will alone be able to estimate the fortitude of the stand he made. In a political contest, he declared, he had to consider political motives and consequences, and that no array of authorities on the other side could induce him to prefer Redington or Lambert as a representative of the people's interests to the other candidate. In face of this testimony the secret wishes of his ecclesiastical superiors counted for nothing in the minds of a people familiar with his daily life of unsleeping services to the poor. The territorial influence was counterbalanced, and in the end effaced, by the popular and national feeling which the contest speedily excited. It occupied the Press everywhere; it was the chief topic wherever political issues were debated, and the interest constantly increased.

I was fortunate in my antagonists; Mr. Lambert had been elected as a Repealer in O'Connell's first Repeal movement in 1832, but had deserted the party in the House of Commons, and was known to the people as "Luttrell Lambert."[1] Sir Thomas Redington had been Under-Secretary for Ireland when Lord John Russell was Premier. He and his colleagues had armed the Orangemen against the Repealers in '48, had packed juries against the political prisoners by excluding Catholics, had suborned Birch and Conway to malign the Young Irelanders, and he continued to serve under the Government which passed the Ecclesiastical Titles Act. As a landlord, he had expelled a hundred and eighty persons from his Galway property since the famine. It was felt throughout Ireland that in a contest between the Castle Catholic and the country Catholic—the jury-packer and the prisoner against whom juries were packed, it was impossible to be neutral. Mr. Keogh and his colleagues on the Committee of the Defence

---

[1] It may be necessary to tell English readers that Luttrell, the progenitor of the house of Carhampton, held a command at the battle of Aughrim under James II., and sold to the enemy a pass which exposed the flank of the Irish army; hence the phrase "sold the pass," to signify political treachery, and a "Luttrell" to signify a traitor.

Association said not a word in my favour, but the *Tablet* dared them to support the Catholic official who had been a party to the penal law against bishops.

Redington commenced to canvass the borough, and he was formidable in a military point of view, for his coming was preceded by a troop of dragoons, a company of infantry, and three detachments of police. But he made no way with the electors, and was only followed throughout the borough by a hired retinue of disorderly and disreputable persons. Intimidation and bribery were tried; prosperous shopkeepers were warned that they would lose the custom of the gentry, and more than one humble elector brought to Father Doyle the half notes given to secure his vote at a specific price. To restore the courage of the shopkeepers threatened with loss of custom we resolved to parade before their eyes the greater mass of customers on whom they could rely. A day was fixed for canvassing the borough on my behalf. New Ross is on the verge of Wexford and Kilkenny, and many thousand farmers from these counties attended to give their assistance, headed by teetotal bands. The young priests throughout the diocese of Ferns, some of whom had been Young Irelanders, and all of whom were friends of Father Doyle, came to Ross to aid the popular cause, and the result of two days' canvass was that a majority of the electors were pledged to support Duffy. The names were immediately printed, and it was declared that for all honest purposes the contest was at an end. But Redington's friends in Dublin insisted that when it came to voting he was still certain to be elected. "Sa' Thomas is pe'fectly secua" became one of the popular by-words of the day. In fact bribery and secret influence were so extensively employed that if the contest had not raised popular feeling to a fever height he might have been successful. There is an Augustinian monastery in Ross; the Prior went with Duffy, but all the friars were supporters of Redington, and with them half a score of shopkeepers or professional men to whom the county families allied with Redington were prodigious personages. If he had remained in office while the Penal Law was passed, these electors were of opinion that it was not for any personal profit or advantage but because he could be more useful, that he had adhered to the enemy. But to any one who recalled the price at which Catholic liberty was purchased in Ireland, how many victims went to the block to maintain it, how many left home and kindred to die in exile rather than relinquish an iota of it, and the noble sacrifices which poor electors in our own day had made, and the seductions they had often spurned to record a single vote on the right side, these excuses sounded mean and sordid.

The *Freeman's Journal* announced that the Reform Club in London had granted funds to tamper with New Ross, and then, as a counter move, a public fund was immediately opened to bear the entire expenses of the election. The design spread from Dublin to London, and from London to New York. Enough funds, and more than enough, were supplied for the long contest, and the election did not cost me a shilling. I have many times before and since refused to accept tribute or testimonial for public services to the Irish people, but to relieve a man from the necessity of buying a seat which he does not intend to sell is a wise national policy, and a good public investment. That the Council of the League should fight the battle stubbornly was natural, but it warms my heart still at this distant day to remember how many friends, who had no special duty, took part in it. John Dillon and Richard O'Gorman in New York, Colonel French and Michael O'Grady[1] in London, promoted the election fund. William O'Hara, uncle of Mrs. John Dillon, when my intention of entering Parliament became public, offered me a qualification by a rent-charge on his estate in the county Dublin; and when a report got abroad that Redington hoped to defeat me on some supposed informality in this

[1] Afterwards Minister of Public Works in the Colony of Victoria.

instrument, William Eliot Hudson, living apart from politics, engrossed in the cultivation of national art and literature, sent me a rent-charge on his estate in Cork to make assurance doubly sure.[1] Our opponents were equally active. Sir Thomas continued his canvass with limited success; but the only newspaper in the county at that time, existing by favour of the gentry, came to his aid by assailing my prominent supporters by name as revolutionists and Carbonari,

---

[1] It is pleasant to recall timely aid in such a fierce contest with ignorance and prejudice, and I cannot refrain from quoting one or two notable instances. Father Mathew interposed effectively in a letter to the popular candidate—

"New Ross shone as a gem of the brightest lustre in the temperance crown, therefore I exult in the prospect of such a consistent and faithful advocate of teetotalism as my friend, Charles Gavan Duffy, being the chosen representative in Parliament of New Ross. From my heart earnestly wishing the accomplishment of an event so honourable to them and to you, I am, my dearest friend, your ever affectionate
"THEOBALD MATHEW."

Another ecclesiastic, who was destined to stand in the front of the Irish Church in aftertime, in sending his contribution to the election fund, sent sympathy, which was more precious than material help—

"Of that man and his principles—his love of justice and his hatred of oppression—his eagerness to exalt the character while improving the social condition of our prostrated, yet not unpainstaking people, I have happily no need to speak. His name falls at length like a household word upon Irish ears; his repute becomes greater as he himself grows more mature; and the heroic devotion to the cause of nationality of which he has already given the most unequivocal proofs is his best security for future services, and his best title to the senatorial honours with which I hope to see him soon surrounded.
"T. W. CROKE, D.D."

and Mr. Francis Wyse, brother to the Whig official, wrote a pamphlet, in the character of an ardent Nationalist, denouncing me for postponing Repeal to the Land Question. The young priests, two of whom afterwards entered religious orders to devote themselves exclusively to good works, and a third who died on mission duty in Australia, met the assault gallantly by taking in sport the title of "Carbonari Curates." A farmer, indignant at Mr. Wyse's dissimulation, wrote to the *Nation* denouncing him as a bad landlord, who was only solicitous for the interest of his class.[1] The Castle journal, which lived on Secret Service money when the Whigs were in office, assailed me in every number. I am of a clan which had been memorable in Irish history before the landing of the first Englishman in the island; I had lived my whole life in public duties which were not at any rate obscure or discreditable; but the Castle critic was of opinion that I was an "adventurer," and when he remembered that I had been tried for treason-felony he proclaimed it

[1] Mr. Wyse rejoined by an action for libel against the *Nation*, and, after a fierce contest, obtained a farthing damages. One of my friends, who was present on the occasion, produced a halfpenny, and offered to settle his claim on the instant if he would favour him with the balance. But the jester made too little account of the tragic ingenuity of penal laws against the Press in Ireland. Though the jury assessed Mr. Wyse's damages at a farthing, the law levied his costs off the defendant, and they amounted to £120.

preposterous to compare my claims with those of the eminent official against whom I had the presumption to appear. I joined issue in a letter, not to the libellers, but to their employer—

"I am 'an adventurer' (it seems) 'without stake or fortune in the country.' Well, be it so. I have no more stake in the country than Henry Grattan had when he entered the Irish Parliament. I am not much richer than Andrew Marvell when he sat in the English Commons. But let it be noted that whatever I have, great or small, was honestly earned. Not a penny of it was won by denying the country or the creed of my fathers. There is no blood-money in it, Mr. Under-Secretary. Dublin Castle stood open for me also if I could walk in the miry footsteps of a Monahan or a Redington. The mart where Irish Catholics are 'bought, sold, or exchanged at the highest market-price' would not have refused even such humble capacities as mine, when it finds it answers to buy up squires from Galway, and 'fat cattle from the banks of the Barrow.' . . . I am 'an adventurer'! 'Thank Heaven, I am independent,' Robert Burns wrote, 'for I have learned to hold a plough.' If I may venture to parody so noble a sentiment, I would say, 'Thank Heaven, I am independent, for I have learned to hold a pen!'"

The contest, I reminded my adversary, had begun in the Court in Green-street. In their own dens of law I had defied him and his patron, Lord Clarendon, and now the case was set down for a re-hearing at New Ross.—

"There we shall have fair play at last. Mr. Justice Perrin shall not close the door against the people. Mr.

Sheriff French shall not pack the panel. Mr. Solicitor Hatchell shall not pick and choose the jury. Mr. Baron Lefroy shall not harangue the audience in 'double-barrelled' charges. We shall have untainted justice, and you shall remember it to your dying day."

The prediction was justified. In the end Redington withdrew from the contest in despair. Lambert, however, aided by the owner of the town, and a small, compact, Tory party, went to the poll. The night before the polling, the bulk of the electors assembled for the last time, and so high had the enthusiasm risen, that they resolved not to separate till the booths opened next morning. Father Doyle reminded them that to avoid the perils of an election petition they must be at the cost individually of whatever refreshments they required. In the morning they marched to the booths in tallies of three, and before ten o'clock all our doubtful votes were polled. By twelve the contest was over, and I had won by a majority of more than two to one. Even my bitterest Old Ireland opponents in the committee voted for me in the end. That night the town was illuminated, and the neighbouring hills blazed with bonfires to celebrate an event which a dozen weeks before seemed impossible. National enthusiasm, deputations of popular men from distant places, and the other agencies employed proved effective; but, in truth, they would have been in vain but for the indomitable courage of Father Doyle. If the constituency of New Ross made a bad choice on that occasion there is no freeing him from the main responsibility. The contest, indeed, rendered intelligible a perplexing difficulty in Irish affairs. It enabled us to understand that the Young Irelanders failed in '48 because they had so solid a mass of prejudice to encounter; but they did not hope vainly in hoping to overcome it if only there were time to make themselves known to the priests and people.

During the canvass in Ross, the county took fire from the borough. It seemed certain at first that two respectable Whigs would be elected, but the young priests, headed by Father Doyle, insisted on having a candidate on whom the tenants could rely for effectual help. As a testimony of goodwill to the North, they proposed to elect Sharman Crawford, or failing him, Dr. M'Knight. When I transmitted this proposal to Belfast, M'Knight replied that the Northerns considered it indispensable to win Down, and that it would only be won with Crawford's name and assistance; otherwise the tenants would not resist their landlords. As for himself, his duty as a journalist fixing him in Belfast, a career in Parliament was out of the question. Patrick M'Mahon, who had served the League efficiently from his chambers in the Temple, was invited to stand, but he replied that he could not afford the expense of a contest. It was agreed to renew the invitation, with an assurance that the election would cost him nothing. He was named candidate in his absence, and a vigorous canvass commenced. There was no pretence that he belonged to the class from whom Wexford had selected members up to that time; on the contrary, the plain fact was insisted upon as the sign of a beneficent revolution that he was merely an honest man, of good ability, who had no ties, except to the people from whom he sprang. "He has no estate (it was said), no aristocratic connections, no private fortune; but he is a man of known ability and known honour, who is gradually mounting the heights of his profession by honourable labour, and who at every step of his career found leisure to give silent and unostentatious help to the Irish cause." That such a man, without any personal solicitation, should be selected by a great county was the promise of a new era in Irish affairs. Even the Council of the League were alarmed at so strong a measure, and Lucas wrote to warn me that we were going too fast.[1] But the Carbonari Curates persisted, and carried him in at the head of the poll.

[1] "I take it for granted M'Mahon has about as much chance in Wexford as I have in the city of London, and the temptation is strong upon me to disconnect the *Tablet* altogether from an unwise move—as I, in my ignorance of the facts, imagine it to be—which will re-act perniciously upon the League and upon the country. Perhaps, if I knew more, I should think differently; but at present all my information is on one side, and I have no

For the second seat a Conservative defeated the Whigs by the narrow majority of five. When M'Mahon's success was certain, his friends offered to bring in one of the Whigs who was a good landlord, if the other would retire, but neither would give way, and they destroyed each other. The expenses incurred in a long contest did not reach £200, and the candidate's share was the price of a return ticket from London.

The county elections went largely in favour of the League. In Meath, Lucas defeated Grattan by nearly four to one, and was permitted to pay no part of the expenses. In Louth, Tristram Kennedy was elected at a moderate cost. And it is a fact of great significance that all these men justified exceptional treatment by remaining steadfast in their fidelity to the popular cause. In Leitrim and Sligo, the League candidates, Dr. Brady and Mr. Swift, were also elected; but after serious expenditure. They were wealthy men, however, and notwithstanding the penalty imposed on them, remained true to their pledges.[1] Everywhere

---

notion of appearing connected in Wexford with a hopeless defeat, which, if suffered at all, will be suffered against my judgment. Your own affairs, I imagine, go on well—so do mine."—Lucas to Duffy.

[1] Edward Butler, afterwards distinguished as Attorney-General for New South Wales, accompanied Dr. Brady on his canvass as representative of the League, and largely contributed to his success.

either the principles of the League or of Crawford's bill had been accepted by popular candidates, and more than half the members elected were pledged to a settlement of the Land Question on these bases. There were only two drawbacks to the national success. In the Clare contest a calamitous loss of life occurred at Sixmile Bridge. Six peasants were shot by the soldiers in an election riot, and it embittered this tragedy that they fell not in the defence of rights in which they had any interest, but to promote the election of two of the most selfish and worthless men sent to the new Parliament. The other was the success of the Brigadiers Mr. Keogh brought in several men of his own class, and Mr. Sadleir had succeeded in forming a family party. His brother, who was associated with him in the Tipperary Bank, and his cousin, Frank Scully, sat for Tipperary. Another cousin, Mr. Keating, sat for Waterford, and a third, Vincent Scully, for Cork County. The Queen's County elected a tenant-farmer supposed to represent the interests of his class, but he proved in the end to be a creature of Sadleir.[1]

[1] This farmer was named Michael Dunne. Vincent Scully was not without ability and information, but his manners were eccentric and his pronunciation ridiculous from a sort of puerile lisp. Francis Scully was merely feeble and commonplace. An English member asked Sergeant Murphy how he contrived to distinguish between the two wonderful Scullys. "Oh, easily," said the Sergeant; "we call Vincent Rum-Scully and Francis Num-Scully."

When the borough elections finished Maguire was member for Dungarvan, which in 1847 and in 1851 he had solicited in vain. In Limerick City, Robert Potter, a respectable local solicitor, was chosen. In Galway, Anthony O'Flaherty, who had a good reputation till he became the confidant of Mr. Keogh, defeated the son of the Whig magnate, Lord Clanricarde. In Cork City, Fagan was re-elected. In Youghal, Mr. Butt, who, though he was still a Conservative and a Protectionist, had Irish instincts, defeated the nominee of the Duke of Devonshire. In Waterford, Thomas Meagher, father of the Young Ireland orator, an honest, unobtrusive man, was re-elected. In Drogheda, Mr. James M'Cann, a respectable miller, replaced Sir William Somerville, the late Whig Chief Secretary. The City of Dublin fell to the Tories through the venal votes of freemen of the Old Corporation, but it was counted a full equivalent for the loss of the capital that John Reynolds was relegated to private life, and with him Patrick Somers and O'Gorman Mahon, Sir Henry Winston Barron and Morgan John O'Connell. Two English Catholics, Mr. Charles Townley and Sir George Bowyer, got in for Sligo and Dundalk under the wing of the Defence Association, and by definite pledges on the Land Question.

The Northerners had much to bear before the general election, in the defection of Southern constituencies, and they bore it well. It was now the turn of the Southerners to be magnanimous. Tenant-right had been successful everywhere except in the Tenant-right province. There it accomplished nothing. In the county Down, it was determined to elect Sharman Crawford free of expense, and he had such claims upon the tenant-farmers that it was not too much to expect; but he was defeated by over a thousand votes. He attributed the result to the systematic coercion of tenants; but if the prosperous farmers of Down had been willing to make the sacrifices common in the South his success was easy and certain. In Monaghan an immense rally was made for Dr. Gray. He got the support of the Catholic electors universally; but although he was a Protestant, and had connections in the county of orthodox Orange politics, the Presbyterian farmers voted with their landlords, and he was defeated. In Cavan, where the League was strong, a future Minister and a ministerialist were chosen; and every other constituency in Ulster elected enemies of the League, except Newry, which chose Mr. Kirk, a linen bleacher, whose professions promised well, though they proved of limited value in the end. The Northern leaders, I am persuaded, did their best, and in the day of defeat they proclaimed that they would try again and again till their object was accomplished; but their rout by the landlords was not the less decisive for the present. Not a murmur was heard in the League; their failure was recognised only as a national calamity. In the other provinces the result was unexampled—a majority of the members for Ireland for the first time since the Union were pledged to the interest of the people, and among them the only ultimate deceivers were some whose bad faith had been foreseen and predicted from the beginning. Nothing like this had ever been accomplished in Ireland before. Considering the difficulties to be encountered, it may be questioned if anything like it has been accomplished since. After Columbus had taught his audience how eggs can be made to stand on end that feat was no longer an exploit or a marvel.

⁎ See Note on p. 190.

CHAPTER VII.

THE LEAGUE IN PARLIAMENT.

WHEN the elections were over the Government and the Opposition each claimed a majority in the new Parliament. This was the precise result we had hoped and predicted; for now, plainly, Irish votes would prove decisive. The League had got the instrument it demanded—a Parliamentary Party, and, wisely and honestly employed, all the successes promised might be accomplished. While the public mind was elated by a sense of triumph and the new members were still under the spell of the hustings, a Conference of the friends of Tenant-right was summoned by the League, to which all the members pledged to Crawford's bill were invited. It met on September 8th in the City Assembly House at Dublin. Three Whig members elected for Munster counties excused themselves,[1] and Mr. Kirk, the

[1] Mr. Monsell and Mr. Gould, members for County Limerick, and Mr. Power, member for County Waterford. These gentlemen were supported by the respective local bishops.

sole Tenant-right member whom Ulster had sent to Parliament, refused to attend. Upwards of forty members of Parliament—a quorum of the House of Commons—about two hundred Catholics and Presbyterian clergymen, and gentlemen farmers, traders, and professional men from every district in the country, assembled in the virtual Irish Parliament, which undertook the future responsibility of the Tenant cause. Sharman Crawford presided; the Council deliberated from ten o'clock in the morning till ten o'clock at night, and the debates were conducted with uninterrupted temper and courtesy.

The object of the men who had founded the League and who in that day's proceedings might recognise a marvellous evidence of success, was to obtain the adhesion of the whole body of members to the principle of Independent Opposition. It was no longer the time for being hypercritical on the pretensions of this man or that; the people had chosen, and with the recruits they had furnished we must succeed or fail. Agenda prepared by the Council were submitted for the pleasure of the Conference as a convenient programme; and George Henry Moore, who, up to this time, never had been in good relations with the League, declared on behalf of himself and certain others that they had come to listen with attention and deference to any proposals submitted to the Conference, but they could not undertake to be bound by them. This was a procedure which would have rendered the meeting abortive, and Mr. Lucas, Dr. Gray, and Mr. Duffy contended that there were not two parties present, but only one. It was a Conference of the friends of Sharman Crawford's bill whether in or out of Parliament, and the ordinary practice of deliberative assemblies was that gentlemen should hold themselves bound by any proposition from which they did not publicly dissent. After debate this course was unanimously adopted.

Mr. Keogh grasped the situation, and made a vigorous attempt to become leader of the entire party. He proposed a resolution, which was first in the League agenda, declaring that no measure which fell short of the general principles of Crawford's bill would be satisfactory to the country. And he announced it to be the intention of the gentlemen with whom he acted to press these principles on the attention of the Legislature at every suitable opportunity. After a debate, in which the old and new members took part, the motion was unanimously adopted. Mr. Sadleir proposed another of the League resolutions, declaring that in case of a Land Bill being introduced into Parliament on which the country had not already pronounced, it would be the duty of the Irish members to cause the opinion of the people to be elicited upon it before determining to accept or reject it. Mr. Sadleir was as diplomatic as his leader. From what he had seen and heard at the Conference, he declared he could discern nothing to justify the assumption outside that there were two parties among the popular members. It seemed to him that they were all animated by the same spirit.

As Mr. Crawford had no longer a seat in Parliament it was necessary to provide for the management of the bill and of the party pledged to it, and it was directed by a unanimous vote that Mr. Sergeant Shee, Mr. Keogh, Mr. Lucas, and Mr. Gavan Duffy should be requested to place their names on the back of the bill and take charge of it. Mr. Potter, the newly-elected member for Limerick, proposed the testing resolution that the Irish members should hold themselves independent of, and in opposition to, any Government which did not make it a part of their policy, and a Cabinet question, to give the tenant-farmers of Ireland the measure of justice provided by Sharman Crawford's bill. Colonel Fulke Greville,[1] on the part of the new members, cordially assented to this proposal, and Mr. Moore, on behalf of the old members, admitted that it embodied the whole question of policy—

"If they were to go back to the old system of duly introducing certain bills, and getting them duly negatived, and then go on in support of the Ministry by whose

[1] Afterwards Lord Greville.

sanction these bills were lost, then such a conference or such a bill as Mr. Crawford's would be a delusion, a mockery, and a snare:"

but he considered the wording objectionable. He could not pledge himself to give a pertinacious opposition to every Government which did not include in a bill every syllable of a scheme of reform laid before them for the first time that day. Mr. J. D. Fitzgerald [1] agreed with Mr. Moore that to pledge the members to a policy of indiscriminate obstruction was in the highest degree injudicious.

"But at the same time he felt it to be his solemn duty to declare, in the presence of that vast and influential assemblage, that he should never be found supporting any Government which would not consent to make a Cabinet question—a question to be supported by the ministerial aid and influence—of a measure embodying provisions for the real and tangible relief of the outraged and injured land tenantry of this country—real and permanent relief in its fullest meaning, acceptance and extent."

After a considerable debate, the resolution was adopted in the following form:—

"That, in the unanimous opinion of this Conference, it is essential to the proper management of this cause that the members of Parliament who have been returned on Tenant-right principles should hold themselves perfectly independent of and in opposition to all Govern-

---

[1] The present Lord Fitzgerald.

ments which do not make it a part of their policy, and a Cabinet question, to give to the tenantry of Ireland a measure fully embodying the principles of Sharman Crawford's bill."

On a second day the Conference considered proposals for improving the efficiency of the League and for organising the Parliamentary Party. New adhesions raised the number of members of Parliament accepting the decisions of the Conference to upwards of fifty, and no opposition from any quarter disturbed its unanimity.[1] Since John Forster vacated the chair of the Irish Commons half a century before, so effectual and practical a work for Ireland was not accomplished as at these two sittings. A banquet to Sharman Crawford closed the proceedings, and the members separated to prepare for a winter's session in Parliament.[2]

---

[1] An exposition of the principles of the bill, written in plain, untechnical language, was adopted and issued for public information. It is only necessary to cite one important provision respecting arrears :—" That by the changes in the law already alluded to, the calamitous failure of the potato crop, and the increase of local taxation consequent on these and other causes, great ARREARS OF RENT have accumulated on tenants; which arrears discourage their industry and oppress their energies ; that from the peculiar causes which have led to the accumulation of these arrears, it is just and politic that tenants in this special case should be enabled to *compound for these arrears* by means of the same tribunals as may be provided for other cases arising under a tenant-right law."

[2] A little later another Conference was held, at the instance of Mr. Moore, on the question of Religious Equality. As many

THE LEAGUE IN PARLIAMENT. 221

The press which supported the Brigade saw in the unanimity of the Conference a prospect of the entire party being led by Mr. Keogh in whatever direction might suit him, and overflowed with compliments to the new members. But those who watched the signs of the times thought it a significant fact that in the list which these official organs published of "Members who might be relied on to vote for Religious Liberty" the names of Mr. Lucas and Mr. Duffy were omitted. They were persons, it might be assumed, who could not be relied on for this purpose. A little later the *Morning Chronicle*, the organ of the Peelites, with whom the Brigade were known to be more intimate than was safe for their political independence, assailed these members along with Mr. Maguire, as the probable allies in secret of the Tories.[1]

English members were pledged to refuse the Maynooth grant, it was resolved as a natural and justifiable retaliation to demand the abolition of the Irish Establishment.

[1] "Mr. Lucas, Mr. Duffy, and Mr. Maguire contrived to force down the throats of their colleagues the pledge of opposition to every Government and party which should withhold its support from all the principles of Mr. Crawford's bill." And again—"It may seem extravagant to suspect Mr. Lucas, Mr. Duffy, or Mr. Maguire of any good-will to Lord Derby; but when two parties have an obvious sinister motive in contracting a tacit alliance, it is impossible to disregard rumours *which assure us* that such a compact has been actually entered into."—*Morning Chronicle.*

Mr. Maguire's inclusion in this anathema was accounted for by knowing persons on the hypothesis that the writer in the

The *Nation* stated the principle of independent opposition, as it was understood by the new party :—

"The Irish members, we believe, will keep themselves apart as an independent party and a distinct power. Precisely as the Pitt party, the Peel party, and the Protectionist party did, when they were small minorities and in hopeless opposition. They will act together; and in order to do so submit individual opinion, within the limits of conscience, to the common sense of the majority. They will vote for every measure of benefit to Ireland, no matter from whom it may proceed. They will vote against Ministers opposed to the Irish measures, *not*, as the *Chronicle* alleges, on every question, but on any question (not involving the serious interest of Ireland) on which they can be turned out of office."[1]

These are the principles which in the end carried the Irish question to success.

Parliament met on the 4th November. The Queen's speech announced that her advisers meditated a liberal and generous policy towards Ireland; and at an unusually early period four bills, designed to regulate the Land question in all its branches, were submitted to the House of Commons. It was plain that the Irish party, mustering more than fifty votes, were worth conciliating. The new men arrived in London with an eager desire to begin work, there was so much to do, and such urgent

Chronicle was the Brigade Candidate for Dungarvan—whom Mr. Maguire had defeated—and a man who was Mr. Keogh's most efficient partisan in the press and in diplomacy.

[1] *Nation*, Oct. 2, 1852.

need that it should be done quickly; but they were reminded good humouredly that a sailor is of little use till he has learned to know the ropes, and that to succeed in Parliament they must study Parliamentary methods clinically. Some of the seniors were not indisposed to teach them the art of enjoying London, if that would content them; but as regards political action, they were o opinion that it must be left to men accustomed to the ways of the House. This diplomacy had probably often proved sufficient to bewilder and stifle new members, but to the Leaguers it was simply a subject of merriment. They understood how infinitely strength is multiplied by association, and what prodigious results a few resolute men bound together by love of a common cause have accomplished, and they insisted upon organisation and action. Mr. Keogh manifestly desired to keep them quiet till his personal plans were ripe for execution. But to the Leaguers a seat in Parliament was only valuable as furnishing an opportunity of pushing forward the business they had in hand, and before their determined will these impediments proved only cobwebs. A party consultation was held, attended by nearly all the members pledged to Crawford's bill. Unanimity and discipline are important, but there would have been slight value in a unanimity which was only an agreement to do nothing; and the business of the Session, after much debate and difficulty, got organised.

Sub-committees were appointed, charged with special duties, on which men who took little part in debate employed themselves. Parliamentary capacity does not necessarily mean the power of talking. Franklin and Jefferson rarely spoke in Congress, and Andrew Marvel never uttered a sentence in the House of Commons. But the Irish Party did not want capacity of any sort to be formidable or to accomplish anything within the range of Parliamentary action, on one condition—that they retained the support of the country. Sergeant Shee, who was regarded as the leader of both wings, had acquired by long practice at the Bar an easy and fluent elocution and an imperturbable temper. He had mastered the Land question like a brief in a leading case, and was well equipped for debate. He desired to help the League by all prudent and legitimate methods, but he was not overmastered by any great conviction or prepared to make any disagreeable sacrifice. He was what is called a man of the world, determined to stand well with Sergeants' Inn and Westminster Hall. But his reputation was extremely useful to the party at the outset, and his massive head and stately carriage made him a notable figure in the House. Mr. Keogh had more political ability, but far less weight. As he was an important agent in these transactions the reader should be able to form some picture of him at that period. He was a man of middle size, well made, and with a head and figure which his admirers were accustomed to tell him resembled those of the first Napoleon. His manners were so insinuating that it was hard to resist them if one did not start with a lively distrust, for he belonged to the gay, exuberant class of Irish adventurers, who are fatal to weak women and credulous men. Among his intimates, until fortune dazzled him with a chance of leadership, he scoffed at the belief that political professions were anything more than a convenient mask for ambition. But in later days he sometimes played the part of a patriot with considerable skill. On some public occasion he declared that his aim in life was "to raise himself and his country together." Practical people thought this was a very sensible formula of political faith, while men of more generous disposition condemned it as grovelling and sordid. But the controversy was a waste of time, for the proposition did not in the least represent his intentions. He was determined to raise himself, and was as profoundly indifferent to what became of his country as any adventurer on record. In his profession he had been a successful advocate, but he knew as little law as a man of vigorous capacity who had passed his life in circuit courts could manage to carry away.

Of the men who had no sinister ambition to promote, but went into Parliament purely for public ends, the most notable were Lucas and Moore. The one was a type of the bourgeoisie, refined by culture and a high sense of duty, the other a type of the gentry spiritualised by patriotism and courage. New men who desire to win sympathy for an unpopular cause in an assembly so cynical and critical as the House of Commons have need of much discretion. Lucas, who possessed self-control in an eminent degree in debate, though he was vehement and sometimes violent in his journal, was soon recognised as a skilled debater. He had serenity and temper, and was habitually deferential to the House, but under these graces there lay, as no one could fail to see, "genuine, solid, old Teutonic pluck." With time he would have become much more than a great debater: of the qualities which constitute an orator, he possessed profound conviction and wide knowledge. His lucid narrative arrested attention by the mesmeric feeling that he was uttering well-weighed convictions. He had mastered the case of Ireland not only with his intellect but with his sympathy, and his audience felt that he was telling them what he entirely believed to be true. It was usual to compare him with his kinsman, Mr. Bright, whom he resembled in appearance and in some of his most notable gifts. Whatever Mr. Bright has since accomplished I am persuaded Lucas might have done, if he had not sacrificed personal ambition to the claims of conscience. To sympathetic eyes he was then and always a figure of ideal dignity and worth.

He was poor because he devoted his great abilities to the interests of a suffering people instead of to his own advancement. He had English prejudice to face, because he had become a Catholic. All this was in the nature of things; but I do not doubt that if he had remained a Protestant, and hardened into a prosperous lawyer or manufacturer, he would have been a more important personage, not only in the eyes of England, but in the eyes of those for whom he made so many sacrifices. For there are few things the mass of mankind recognise so imperfectly as a man in whom there are no elements of the commonplace.[1]

Moore was more agile and lively than Lucas, had greater skill and address in social controversy, and understood the temper of the House better, for he belonged to the predominant class by birth, and had been their associate from an early age in studies and sports. It was a serious drawback to his usefulness that he was impatient of labour, impatient of dulness, and impatient of contradiction. Among men whom he esteemed and who were his intellectual peers, he was a charming companion — frank, cordial, and winning. In an Irish Parliament, or even in an

[1] Sergeant Murphy was credited with a *mot* which was hailed with the laughter that awaits a sarcasm if it be grotesquely untrue, almost as certainly as if it be apt and felicitous. "Mr. Lucas," said the Sergeant, " is *Lucus a non lucendo,* which I venture to translate Lucas—not Bright."

English one with a powerful party behind him, he would have uttered speeches almost as full of high passion and as glittering with brilliant conceits as Grattan's. But he was discontented; and the patience, moderation of statement, and dignity of character necessary to counterbalance prejudice, were wanting. He was entirely sincere in desiring the success of the Irish cause, but he had seen much of life on its seamy side, and had only limited confidence in its speedy attainment. His abilities were brilliant; he could condense opinion into axioms easy to be remembered almost as successfully as Mr. Disraeli, and, like that orator, possessed the art of constructing epigrams which stung too keenly to be forgiven. But he did not give the impression of a man who brings the force of a strong character to promote an end which he passionately desires; and though he pleased or provoked an audience almost at will, he rarely controlled or persuaded it in any considerable degree.

Colonel Greville was not an orator, scarcely a debater, but he was a man of good sense and honour, who never interposed in debate without producing a solid effect as the result of character and position. Patrick M'Mahon had none of the graces or arts by which a hostile audience is sometimes won. He could not arrest the attention of the indifferent, and his physical impediments were so many that he could scarcely retain the attention of the well-disposed. But he had a safe judgment, a penetrating intellect, indomitable industry, and so complete devotion to the interests of the Irish people, that he was of more value than a dozen men of more showy gifts. All these men were in the vigour of manhood; Keogh at five-and-thirty being the youngest by a year, and Shee, the eldest, by several years. Sergeant Murphy was the type of Irish member loved by political clubs in London. He never embarrassed them by inconvenient proposals or alarming theories, and was ready to jest upon all subjects, his own nation being no exception; and nothing is pleasanter to Cockney ears, than an Irishman who is ready to banter Irish patriotism or mock at Irish misery. The Sergeant was a Bohemian—a jolly good fellow, which nobody could deny, pleasant in smoking-rooms, and irresistible over a broiled bone at midnight. It was he who pronounced Bellamy's a better night house than Evans's, for he was always sure of a sympathetic audience up stairs. It would be injustice not to note that he was neither a hypocrite nor an impostor; he made no pretence of using his political position for any other purpose than his own advancement.

The League members did not permit the party Whips on either side to communicate with them, and did not ask even information from the Government, except across the House. Sergeant Shee was an exception, to a limited and justifiable extent. It was necessary to ask facilities for his bill, and, as he had no notion of making enemies unnecessarily, he took an early opportunity of telling Mr. Hayter that he would gladly support the Government when he agreed with them. "You are very obliging," rejoined the Whip, "but we want men who will be glad to support the Government when they don't agree with them."

Election petitions rained on the new Parliament. More than a fourth of the House had their seats called in question, so that it became doubtful if committees to try them could be constituted, as no member against whom a petition is lodged can sit on a committee. More than twenty of the Irish party were assailed in this way, including nearly all the leaders of both branches.

When political parties were carefully scrutinised, it became plain that the Government were in a minority, unless they could obtain support from some section of the Opposition. In the third week Mr. Villiers launched a party vote against them; but the immediate danger was postponed by an adroit amendment, framed by Lord Palmerston, who had not yet come to an understanding with his late colleagues, and was resolved that a political crisis should not precede that event. A little later Mr. Napier's bills came on for consideration, and proved better than we had expected, the vital principle of compensation for past improvement being distinctly recognised. Sergeant Shee obtained permission to introduce the League bill, and it was set down for reading as early as the Government measures. To dangle their bills before the eyes of Irish members, but not to press any of them to a division till the contest with the Free Traders had terminated, was the ministerial strategy. Mr. Disraeli, with easy nonchalance, announced that the whole question must stand over until after the Christmas recess. But the Irish party were present in force, and not disposed to be trifled with. They contended that the Government bills ought to be read a second time, and Sergeant Shee's also, and referred together to a select committee fairly chosen from the landlord and tenant parties. The Government gave no answer to this audacious proposal. The Whig party, the Peelite section, Cobden, Bright, and the Free Traders, even Joseph Hume, Sir Joshua Walmsley, and the small knot of Radicals, had left the Irishmen without aid or countenance; but they stood firm, and renewed their proposal again and again. As the Government were not prepared to yield, the Irishmen moved the adjournment of the debate, and were supported by Lord Godrich,[1] Lord Monck, the son of Lord Normanby,

[1] Lord Goderich is the present Marquis of Ripon, who maintained in India the wise and courageous policy of righting wrongs,

whose name was still popular in Ireland, the son of William Cobbett, and a few newly elected Radicals, and mustered fifty-nine votes. It was plain there would be a protracted and unflinching contest, and after much parley the Government gave way, and consented to read all the bills a second time, and send them to a committee of the character suggested. To the consternation of the Irish landlords, the measure which they had derided for twenty years as "Crawford's Craze" received the second reading, which affirms the leading principles of a bill, and was to be referred to a committee, nominated by Mr. Napier and Sergeant Shee, to settle the details. Next day the *Times* was furious and the Tory Press dumbfoundered by this concession.

Mr. Disraeli then introduced his first budget. It was not Protectionist after all, and the Whigs became alarmed with the idea that he would reconcile himself with the House. "Give Dizzy six months," they whispered, "and he'll wheedle a majority." A motion was privately handed about, sanctioned by Whigs, Peelites, and Free Traders, which must bring down the Government, and the Irish party were invited to support it. The Leaguers made anwser that the

with which he commenced public life. Lord Monck is the late Commissioner for the Irish Land Court, and the Marquis of Normanby is the late Governor of Victoria, Australia.

question which interested them was not Free Trade but Tenant Right, and that they had been deserted by Free Traders of all sections when they were pressing for a settlement of that question. To the Brigadiers, however, it was clear that they must support a motion which satisfied Mr. Sidney Herbert and Sir James Graham; and as Mr. Keogh had objected since Parliament met to place his name on the League Bill, the other gentlemen to whom it was entrusted had to consider the crisis for themselves. There were, we estimated, at least twenty members who would take whatever course was best for the interest of the Irish cause.

At this moment Sergeant Shee invited Lucas and me to a consultation at his chambers in Sergeants' Inn, on an overture which was private at the moment, but the lapse of a generation has rendered it historical. A Cabinet Minister still living requested him to ascertain on what conditions the independent Irish party would support the Government on the coming division. We set down in writing the concessions which would justify our support, of which the chief was that a Land Bill providing compensation for past improvements should be made a measure on which the Government would stake its existence. Others related to a Catholic University, and Catholic chaplains in the army and navy, prisons, and workhouses. We received back our paper after a day or two with the propositions noted. Some were rejected, others postponed for future consideration: but enough was conceded on the main question to justify us in taking the responsibility of advising our friends to vote against the Whig amendment. The Conservative party at that time distrusted nobody so rootedly as Mr. Disraeli. They were always ready to believe stories of Machiavellian subtlety and bad faith against their brilliant leader. The solemn and circumspect Peel had betrayed Conservative interests, and what was to be expected of a middle-aged dandy who wore a plum-coloured velvet waistcoat and a goatee, and had written tragedies and romances? Some official, to whom rent was dearer than office, whispered among the Irish peers that Dizzy had sold them for the League vote, and a deputation was immediately sent to Lord Derby to demand explanations and guarantees. Lord Roden, Grand Master of the Orangemen, was put forward in the House of Lords to question him on the subject. He inquired whether the fact of reading for the second time a bill identical with Mr. Sharman Crawford's indicated any intention of adopting the principles of that measure if they should be approved of by the select committee to whom it was about to be referred. Lord Derby assured him that whatever might be the decision of the committee, the Government would not under any circumstances accept the principles of Crawford's bill. The discontented landlords were appeased, but the Irish party, who were pledged to support no Government which did not accept these identical principles, could no longer vote with Mr. Disraeli without violating their pledges and setting a fatal example. On the division they voted against the Government, and it fell by a majority of nineteen in a very full House. Ten votes transferred from the "ayes" to the "noes" would have saved them, and they would have had twenty such votes but for Lord Derby's declaration. The peers obtained delay by this sudden *coup*, but they made the final settlement more stringent. All the principles which the landlords resisted at that time are now the law of the land, but a crop of new demands has sprung up from the exasperation of hope deferred.

The Derby Government resigned, and the main sections of the Opposition having coalesced, there was no difficulty in forming a new administration. The trouble between Lord John Russell and Lord Palmerston was composed, by reducing the former from the leadership of the Government to the leadership of the House. Lord Aberdeen became Prime Minister, supported by his political friends, Mr. Gladstone, Sir James Graham, Mr. Sidney Herbert, and Mr. Cardwell. The Whigs, in addition to the placated rivals, and Sir Charles Wood in the Commons, had the Duke of Argyll and Lord Granville in the other House. The Free

Traders were represented by Sir William Molesworth and Mr. Milner Gibson. If the Government was strong, it was only strong through the dangerous expedient of open questions. It included the authors of the Ecclesiastical Titles Bill, and its most pronounced opponents —the guardians of the Established Church in Ireland, and its vowed destroyers—the known champions of Radical Reform, and its habitual impugners—men who had rarely voted in the same lobby except to secure the vacancy which had made them Ministers. It was noted that the Peelites got the lion's share of power. A hundred Radicals had two places in the Cabinet, a hundred and fifty Whigs six offices, and thirty-five Peelites as many as the hundred and fifty Whigs, and three times as many as the hundred Radicals. Another incongruity much noted at the time was that the leaders got relegated to places for which they were peculiarly unfit. Lord John Russell, who, in the phrase of Peel, was a home-spun Minister, with experience ranging from Downing Street to the Isle of Wight, was made Foreign Secretary, with the supervision of two hemispheres. Lord Palmerston, who had long held the threads of foreign intrigue in his fingers, was restricted to the management of domestic police in the Home Office. Sir William Molesworth, who had made colonial affairs his special study, and was an authority upon them, as far as an amiable literary epicurean could be an authority on anything, was set over the making of roads and the draining of fens. And Mr. Gladstone, who had a pet theory in finance that the precarious incomes of professional men (liable to be ruined by sickness or death) ought to be taxed at the same annual rate as the fixed property of land-owners and fund-owners, was placed in the office where this unpopular doctrine could not be long put in abeyance.

But when the minor offices came to be filled all other criticism was swallowed up in the indignation they created. Mr. John Sadleir was a Lord of the Treasury, and Mr. William Keogh Solicitor-General. Up to the last minute, in the most express and emphatic manner, Messrs. Keogh and Sadleir had pledged themselves never to take office from, never to support, always to act in opposition to, any Ministry not pledged to repeal the Ecclesiastical Titles Bill, to abolish the Church Establishment, and to make a Land Bill, framed on the principles of Sharman Crawford's, a Cabinet question. And here was a Government to whom these things were plainly impossible. The Whigs had passed the obnoxious penal law, the Peelites were the bulwark of the Established Church, and Lord Palmerston was notoriously the enemy of Tenant-right. So open a disregard of honour and principle had never been seen even in the career of Castle politicians. The

Leaguers were not surprised at a perfidy which they had predicted, but they were outraged by its audacious cynicism and alarmed at its evil example. No one could tell how far the treason would spread. Mr. Anthony O'Flaherty was spoken of as Irish Secretary, and Mr. Vincent Scully for some legal sinecure. It was plain that the military law, which, to prevent desertion, prescribes the flogging of deserters, was applicable to the case, and the leaders and journals of the League applied it vigorously. The provincial Press put the new officials in a pillory, and George Henry Moore separated himself from them peremptorily, warning the country that a question which demanded instant attention from the constituencies was how many followers they could carry with them across the House? But though at the outset the desertion seemed to be condemned by a verdict that was universal, it soon became plain that under various decent disguises there were men ready to applaud and justify this "free trade in political profligacy."

At the beginning, the friends of the deserters hazarded a suggestion that they had got private assurances from the Cabinet which saved their honour. But before the adjournment for the ministerial elections Lord Aberdeen explained the policy and intentions of the Government, and did not say a syllable respecting Tenant-right or Religious Equality. Preparations to contest the Irish elections immediately commenced, but the League concentrated the contest on the seats of those who had violated their pledges.[1]

One of the Conferences by which the Council kept itself in harmony with the country was summoned to consider the crisis. It met early in January, and the attendance was large and representative. There seemed at first but one feeling of wrath and indignation. Every speaker denounced the treason. The policy was plain, and the facts lay in a nutshell. It was therefore with pain and astonishment that we found a different feeling prevail among the Northerns. Dr. M'Knight interposed to complain that the Council had condemned the new officials without waiting for a general meeting. Was it not, he asked, one of the grievances of the Irish people that so many offices were filled by their enemies? The evil in his opinion was not that two

[1] Their just wrath did not prevent them discriminating. Mr. Monsell, the present Lord Emly, accepted office under Lord Aberdeen; but as he had not attended the Conference, nor received the support of the League at his election, the *Nation* acquitted him of all breach of faith.

"Mr. William Monsell (it said) has broken no pledge, belied no antecedents, forfeited no principles, that we are aware of. His friends may feel hurt, and if his constituency have a spark of spirit they will reject him; but he has only done what he might be expected to do—what he never undertook not to do—and we may freely acquit him of any stain in the transaction. Not so Limerick, if it submit to be further misrepresented by her Majesty's Clerk of the Ordnance."

members had got places, but that twenty had not obtained that additional power of being useful. It was not certain what would be the land policy of the new Government, against whom it was proposed to go into opposition, and Messrs. Sadleir and Keogh were condemned upon evidence which would not satisfy an impartial tribunal.

He was asked by one of the League members [1] what impediment forbade the land policy of the Government being made public. They had disclosed their policy on Parliamentary Reform and Free Trade, why not on the Land question, if there was any policy to disclose? The new officials were addressing their constituents, and had the ordinary opportunity of justifying themselves. In truth, the issue which the Conference had to consider was, whether members elected at immense sacrifice, by an impoverished people, were to make conditions for the country or only conditions for themselves? Who would have the courage to counsel an unfortunate tenant to defy his task-master at the hustings, if the member elected might postpone the tenant's interest to his own? He asked the Conference to declare that it was an unpardonable sin to betray the trusting people. If not, he would like to receive instructions which should suffice for the future as well as for the past. When a Government was next in need

[1] Mr. Gavan Duffy.

of Irish votes, were the League members to say with Dr. M'Knight that the cause would be greatly advanced by having good men in office, and they would like something worth having for themselves? Or were they to say in the spirit of the Conference of 1852—You must introduce a Cabinet measure embodying the principles of Crawford's bill or you shall have no votes from us? If the League betrayed the confidence of the people, all hope of maintaining an Irish party was at an end. Though Grattan or O'Connell rose from the grave, the constituencies would not make a sacrifice for him if their present hopes were betrayed.

Rev. Mr. Rogers, P.M., admitted that the new officials were bound by the Conference pledge, but he was not yet clear that they had violated it. If they were proved guilty of baseness he was ready to condemn them, but he asked delay to ascertain the policy of the Government, and to request explanations from Mr. Keogh and Mr. Sadleir.

Mr. Lucas demanded how long this dilatory plea was to run. Must they delay till the deserters were re-elected, and the new Government and the people of England assured that the constituents approved of their conduct? If the Government could buy Irish support in Parliament by their distribution of places they would pay that easy price for it, and there would be an end to the hope of public concessions. In truth, there was no uncertainty about their land policy. He had himself attended a private meeting of electors at Carlow, to whom Mr. Sadleir admitted that he had got no terms from the Government, but he was confident that Lord Aberdeen must do something, the question was so advanced in Parliament.

Dr. Gray asked those who were doubtful of the intentions of the Government respecting Tenant-right to note that the Irish officials were silent in their public addresses on the subject. But at Cavan the Chief Secretary's[1] proposer was not silent. Archdeacon Beresford promised on his behalf and in his presence that he would uphold the Established Church and protect the landed interest from wild and visionary schemes of confiscation; the Church being the one which Messrs. Sadleir and Keogh were pledged to disestablish, and the visionary schemes being beyond question the principles of the League.

One of the Northern members, the Rev. Mr. Rintoul, P.M., considered that a damaging case had been made out against the new officials; and another, Mr. Thomas Montgomery, acquiesced in this view. Mr. Rogers then said that he had been warned at Belfast not to condemn men for accepting office at the instigation of others who had sought office themselves and were disappointed at

[1] Sir John Young, an Irish Peelite, was Chief Secretary of the new Government in Ireland.

not obtaining it. He was invited and pressed to name any one to whom this description would apply; after some difficulty he said that the report had no reference to Mr. Lucas or Mr. Duffy, but it was certainly circulated with respect to Mr. Moore. Moore promptly denied the imputation, and challenged the new officials, who must be acquainted with the facts, to state any circumstance which lent the smallest justification to it.[1] A Mr. Fitzpatrick, who was not a member of the League, and who was afterwards identified as a valuator in the employment of the Government, was permitted as a favour to address the Conference, and pronounced Messrs. Sadleir and Keogh impeccable. A division was finally taken on a motion condemning them, and was supported by the entire meeting excepting Mr. Michael Dunne, M.P., Dr. M'Knight, Mr. Rogers, and the Mr. Fitzpatrick aforesaid. Before the Conference separated a deputation, consisting of two members of Parliament and three Catholic clergymen, was despatched to Carlow to exhort the electors to reject Mr. Sadleir.

This controversy with the Northerners came on the Council as a profound surprise. Hitherto our unanimity had been cordial and unbroken. Nobody doubted that devotion to the cause was as strong in the North as in the South. There was sometimes difference of opinion

---

[1] This challenge never elicited any fact injurious to Mr. Moore and I have no doubt the story was entirely untrue.

respecting the best method and agencies for promoting our common purpose, but it was sincere and open, and left no bitterness behind. In this case we were confident that a week or two would convince our allies that we knew the deserters better than they did, and that we should be speedily in accord again.

The day after the League Conference, a meeting of the friends of Religious Equality reaffirmed the principles of Independent Opposition, and condemned the deserters. Here also they found a single defender—a Mr. Sharkey, an attorney, who was not a member of the association, and who turned out to be one of Mr. Keogh's election agents at Athlone.

The Archbishop of Tuam, who had given Mr. Keogh effective support while he believed in his honesty, was asked to express an opinion on his recent action, and in a public letter to Mr. Moore condemned it unequivocally as an undoubted breach of morality.

The deputation to Carlow produced a decisive effect. The election resulted in the rout of the deserters. Mr. Sadleir lost his seat by the refusal of the voters who had previously supported him to continue their confidence. It was a just and signal punishment, and was the more notable that the bishop of the diocese, Father Maher, uncle to the Archbishop of Dublin, and several priests resident in the borough, supported him enthusiastically. A further humiliation, almost equivalent to the loss of his seat, awaited him. During his canvass he ventured to suggest that Lord John Russell had proffered to the Brigadiers a practical retractation of the course he had taken on the Ecclesiastical Titles Bill; and when Lord John was questioned on the subject in Parliament he repudiated it with unconcealed scorn. No explanation, he affirmed, had been given, nor had any been asked.

But the chief offender remained to be dealt with. Mr. Keogh's seat having been the subject of an election petition, he could not under the law of Parliament go to a new election till the petition was tried, and when the House resumed its sittings, both the deserters were without seats. Mr. Anthony O'Flaherty had been spoken of for the Chief Secretaryship of Ireland, and later for the Under-Secretaryship; but the example of Carlow was not encouraging, and in the end he got nothing; in good time, however, his much abler brother, Mr. Edmond O'Flaherty, was inducted into public employment.

In Meath and Mayo the members of the Independent Opposition were entertained at public banquets, and the provincial press nearly universally pronounced for the opinions which they represented. But the battle was only begun. Dr. Cullen, whose office of Apostolic Delegate conferred on him an authority which could not be measured by any standard theretofore existing in Ireland, had gradually become more and more of what is known as a Castle bishop. By this time he was secretly at work on the side of the Government, and some of his suffragan bishops were ready, in concert with him, to discourage and repress priests who were zealous for the League. Father Doyle, of Ross, was the first victim. Before the Ross election was over he had been threatened by his enemies with removal to some penal parish, and now it was announced that he must quit the town, where for seven years he had performed apostolic labours, and betake himself to a country curacy. Nobody doubted that he was a victim to the intrigues of Whig Catholics who had the ear of the bishop and archbishop. The transaction raised a serious question for honest men in Parliament, whether a seat was worth the price exacted from the poor people, if, in addition, generous young priests who took the people's side must be subject to the penalty of banishment, and perhaps ruin. There was widespread indignation, which found vent in the newspapers. In Ross, the rage of the people threatened dangerous extremities. A deputation of the most respectable inhabitants went to the Bishop at Enniscorthy to urge the recall of Father Doyle: a deputation of Catholic ladies followed them next day on the same mission. When it was found that there was no present hope of his remaining among them, a public mourning was decreed by common consent, and on the day of his departure business was suspended, and the shops shut up as for an overwhelming public calamity. On Sunday he was already at his new mission, but the people would not be separated from him. The parish chapel of Ross was literally empty, and twenty cars started for Dungannon, ten miles off, with the principal parishioners, to attend *his* Mass. A multitude of the poor people, young and old, of both sexes, who could not afford this conveyance, walked the entire way. "It was a touching sight," says a correspondent of the *Nation*, "to see men and women, toilworn, on the winter day, and many of them in tears, flocking round the altar of their banished priest."

This transaction was only the first in a long series which had for their purpose to extinguish political independence among the priests.[1]

[1] No one bore the event with so much equanimity as the victim. "My removal," he wrote to me, "to any mission on the face of the globe would cause me no pain beyond that of being separated from a people, the most unselfish and affectionate within the four seas which encompass us. I am quite ashamed and confounded at the simple unstudied manifestations of gratitude and love which surround me on every side, and of which I feel myself totally unworthy. My dear friend, what torture or death is too cruel for the traitors who would betray such a people, and barter their interests for a mess of Government pottage, or some paltry personal advantage! After all, his Lordship—though one would not suspect him of it—has played a great trick on the Whigs—ten miles from Ross! just a convenient distance to drive in to one of our evening meetings at the Tolsel."

When Parliament re-assembled in February the first point to be considered was how many members would remain true to the pledge and party of Independent Opposition. A meeting was called in one of the committee-rooms of the House to consider the question. Thirty-eight members attended, and in the debate which ensued one-and-twenty expressed themselves prepared to sit and act as before the appointment of Keogh and Sadleir. The others were determined to support the Government, and in the House the party was divided in this proportion.

An Election Committee having considered the petition against Mr. Keogh, and declared him duly elected, his acceptance of office vacated his seat, and a contest for Athlone commenced. Mr. Norton, an ex-judge, from British Guiana, who had opposed Mr. Keogh on a former occasion, stood again, and to prevent division, was accepted by all the opponents of the Solicitor-General. At the same time Mr. Keogh was able to announce that the Catholic bishop expressed the most anxious wishes for his success. This bishop was the celebrated "Dove of Elphin," who went to Conciliation Hall to denounce the Young Irelanders as bad Catholics; but he had at last, it seemed, found a Catholic to his mind in the person of Mr. Keogh. As the contest proceeded one of Mr. Norton's agents was detected in a case of palpable bribery; so that if the electors chose him he was made a harmless opponent. But the majority, under the exhortation of the bishop and local clergy, supported Mr. Keogh; and it was long afterwards before it was discovered that Mr. Norton was his ally in secret, and had been brought on the scene by a stroke of subtle strategy to prevent the appearance of a genuine opponent.

It was now possible to estimate more exactly the results of the treason. So loud a clamour over the lapse of one or two apostates was declared by some respectable blockheads to be quite extravagant and incommensurate. But the new Government had bought more than a brace of deserters. They had bought the power of lowering fatally the position and influence of the Irish party; they had driven a wedge right through it, dividing it into two sections, and English opinion scarcely took the pains of discriminating between them.[1] In the House which is reputed to be

---

"It was a subject of eager curiosity in the House (and, I presume, will be none the less so in Ireland) to ascertain where each newcomer would take up his place. In their accustomed seats below the gangway of the Opposition benches I observed Colonel Greville, Mr. Moore, Sergeant Shee, Mr. Tristram Kennedy, Mr. Lucas, Mr. Swift, Dr. Brady, Captain Bellew, Mr. Urquhart, Mr. Bowyer, Mr. Fitzstephen French, Mr. O'Connor Henchy, Mr. Potter, Mr. Sullivan, Mr. M'Mahon, Captain Greene, Mr. Heard (Kinsale), Mr. Duffy, and perhaps one or two more. On the Ministerial benches, in addition to Mr. Monsell, I observed Sergeant Murphy, Mr. Townely (Sligo), Sir John J. Fitzgerald (representative of Sixmile Bridge), Mr. Anthony O'Flaherty, Mr. Kirk, Mr. J. D. Fitzgerald, and Mr. William Fagan. There were nearly a dozen other members about the House who avoided taking

the first assembly of gentlemen in the world, the men who had violated their pledged honour, and some of them their plighted oaths, did not meet visible contempt or repudiation. There have always been men of high aims and a keen sense of duty in the House of Commons; but it is far from being a select school of patriotism or probity. It consists in a large degree of men who are *blasé* from experience of the worst side of life, of aged and wealthy capitalists who have made money by stringent competition, and of younger sons in the army and navy, who no more ask a reason for their side on a division than in a battle. But above all, the transaction was in Ireland. Had English members been guilty of desertion so cynical, they would have been punished, if only by party zeal; but with respect to Ireland, if the result were convenient and satisfactory, no troublesome questions were asked.

When one section coalesced with the Whigs and Peelites, it was assumed, indeed, as a necessary sequence, that the other would coalesce with the Tories. The House did not in the least understand, and would have treated with scorn the suggestion, that these men had no personal aims, did not expect office or profit of

their side; and a meeting of the Irish party has been called by requisition for Monday next—mainly, I am told, on the motion of these gentlemen—to consider its future course—to consider, in fact, whether it will keep or violate the pledge taken in the City Assembly House in last September."—Parliamentary Correspondence of the *Nation*.

any sort, and had no alliance or understanding with either of the only parties whom it recognised.

The earliest labour of the Leaguers was to get the select committee appointed to whom the late Government had consented to refer all the Land Bills. After much negotiation a committee of twenty-nine members was chosen, which was a nearer approximation to a fair one than ever had been before granted on an Irish question.[1]

[1] In the *Nation* of the period the members of it are thus discriminated, with much too favourable an estimate of some of the members—

FRIENDS OF THE IRISH TENANTS.	FRIENDS OF THE IRISH LANDLORDS.
Sergeant Shee	Sir John Young
Mr. Lucas	Lord Palmerston
Mr. Kirk (the only Ulster Tenant-righter in Parliament)	Lord Naas
	Sir R. Ferguson
Mr. J. D. Fitzgerald	Mr. Herbert
Mr. Fagan	Lord Monck
Mr. James Sadleir (brother to the Lord of the Treasury)	Mr. Walpole
	Mr. Napier
Colonel Greville	Mr. Davison
Mr. Gavan Duffy	Mr. Chichester Fortescue
Mr. Urquhart	Mr. Hamilton
	Mr. Whiteside
ENGLISH LIBERALS.	Mr. Grogan
Mr. Bright	
Mr. Phillimore, Q.C.	ENGLISH TORIES.
Mr. Dunlop (Law Adviser to Free Church of Scotland)	Mr. Henry Drummond
	Mr. Mackenzie
Mr. Bouverie (Chairman of the Committee)	Mr. Vernon

But a Parliamentary party has rarely had to maintain itself against circumstances so discouraging as surrounded the Leaguers. The work was incessant and exhausting. On days when the Select Committee sat they attended the House at noon and only left it after midnight. Every Irish or Catholic interest in any part of the empire was referred to some of them; and most of them had to work at their profession as barristers or journalists on penalty of personal disaster. When they took their seats in the House they were surrounded by enemies. Not only the stolid squires and military dandies who constituted the bulk of the Tory party, but a section of the Irish Tories, the agents of the landlords, who outnumbered the small and diminishing group who represented the sufferings and wants of the people. And if they looked across the chamber, they saw not alone the Whig majority, led by Palmerston, who scoffed at their claims, and Russell, to whom no cause was sacred if it was not strong in votes; but a third Irish party, elected by the suffrage, and sometimes purchased by the blood, of the suffering people, who were more numerous than they, who represented larger constituencies, and who were supported by an undoubted majority of the Irish bishops. And as the session proceeded, whenever a candidate went to the hustings in the name of Independent Opposition his fate was to be hamstrung from behind by the crosier of some Whig prelate. If there were no English members in the House they were overwhelmed by the representatives of Tenant-right constituencies, North and South; and to many honest English members it seemed certain that we needs must be making unreasonable demands, since we were not supported at the hustings by the class on whose behalf they were made.

It was no wonder that a feeling of despair began to spring up anew in the mind of the people who had been so often defeated and betrayed. But the League journals reminded them that success in the English Parliament comes slowly at best. Plunket spent half a lifetime making bootless motions on the Catholic question; Grey and Brougham saw a generation pass while they agitated for Reform in Parliament. The battle of the Corn Laws was twice as long as the war of Troy; the rapidest success in the annals of Parliament—Peel's creation of a Conservative party to resist the Whigs after the Reform Bill—cost three or four years. The Irish party had not been quite five months in the House of Commons, and in these five months the question they had charge of gained more ground than in the previous twenty years.

In March and April the Election Committees were at work, and had made havoc with members old and new. A dozen Englishmen were unseated for bribery, and as many Irishmen were menaced with the same fate, either for intimidation, rioting, or want of qualification. Mr. Keogh had escaped from this ordeal by giving evidence concerning his landed possessions, which was a marvel and a bye-word in Dublin. The next Irish petition tried was the one against the member for New Ross. It was charged that I was incapable of sitting, being subject to a prosecution for high treason at the suit of her Majesty the Queen; that I had interrupted the free exercise of the franchise by violence and intimidation; that certain of the electors, the night before the polling, were treated with meat, drink, and entertainment to secure their votes, and that at the time of the election I was not duly qualified pursuant to the provisions of 1 and 2 Vic. chap. 48. The committee was constituted in the usual manner, of two Whigs, two Tories, and a chairman of moderate politics. The first allegation, that I was under a prosecution for high treason, was inserted to prejudice the committee against me. It was untrue in point of fact: and if it had been true did not constitute a disqualification. The charge that a popular constituency had been intimidated into voting for a candidate whom they supported with passionate enthusiasm against their personal interest was absurd on the face of it; and after hearing Mr. Lambert's witnesses the committee declared the charge frivolous and vexatious, and ordered him to pay the costs of the sitting member on this allegation. The charge of treating the night before the polling was merely a guess, and through the precaution which Father Doyle had insisted upon it proved to be an ill-founded one. But the question of qualification remained, and it was to be tried for the first time on the naked facts of the case, without any of the fictitious pretences commonly employed to mislead an Election Committee. I instructed my counsel to withhold nothing and extenuate nothing.[1]

My first witness was Mr. O'Hara, a retired solicitor, of capacity and experience. After stating that he had offered me, and that I had accepted, a rent-charge of £300 a year on his landed property, he was cross-examined. "I presume Mr. Duffy paid at least a dozen years' purchase for this annuity, or was it twenty years?" said the counsel for the petitioner, in the tone of badinage usual on such occasions. "No," replied Mr. O'Hara, "he did not pay a penny." "Did not pay a penny!" echoed the learned counsel, with uplifted hands and eyebrows, and a triumphant glance at the committee. "The annuity (he continued) was receivable quarterly; no doubt Mr. Duffy collected it punctually?" "No," replied Mr. O'Hara, "he has not collected it at all."

[1] My counsel were Mr. O'Malley, Q.C., and Mr. Huddleston, the present Baron Huddleston. They expressed great satisfaction and relief at the frank character of the case relied upon; which sentiment Baron Huddleston has publicly repeated in the present year, 1886

"Pray tell us, Mr. O'Hara, were you surprised at this neglect in realising his property?" "Certainly not; I granted the annuity for the purpose of a Parliamentary qualification, and I never expected him to enforce it." "So, sir, you created this charge on your estate without receiving any price for it? the grantee never asked you to pay a single instalment, and you admit that you never expected that he would? In point of fact, was not the arrangement a mere pretence and delusion?" "Not at all," rejoined Mr. O'Hara, with admirable coolness, "the law requires that a borough member shall have a legal estate of £300 a year, and I granted Mr. Duffy such an estate as effectually as if he had paid ten thousand pounds for it; he had the right and power to enforce it at his discretion; if he had judgment creditors they might enter on the land, seize my cattle, and sell them to satisfy their claims. I have given him all I could give. The price to be received in return is, I conceive, a question affecting me alone."

Mr. Hudson was in attendance to prove a second rent-charge; but it was not necessary to produce him, as the intrinsic value of Mr. O'Hara's was not disputed. The committee retired to deliberate on the case submitted to them. M'Mahon, from the beginning, had advised that the legal estate was all the law required; and when the room was cleared he was still confident in this view. But my friends generally were apprehensive that the committee would be of a different opinion. Some of them urged me to stand again if the decision should be unfavourable. "Folly," I replied somewhat impatiently; "if the decision be unfavourable it is because my qualification is invalid, and there will be an end to my Parliamentary career." Dr. Brady, the League member for Leitrim, had been taught the value of money by early struggles gallantly surmounted, and this is an experience which prosperity seldom completely counteracts. But he had at bottom a generous Irish nature, easily kindled into a flame. "Certainly not," he rejoined. "Stock or dividends constitute an unassailable qualification, and I will transfer £10,000 to your credit to-morrow morning if the necessity arises." The necessity did not arise, for after a few minutes we were called into the committee-room to be informed that my qualification was valid. This decision, in a case where nothing was coloured or withheld, contributed to bring the practice of requiring a property qualification to an end. In the next Parliament it was abolished. The petition against Moore in Mayo had an equally favourable issue for the sitting member; and in the cases of Lucas and Kennedy the petitions were withdrawn.[1]

[1] The receipts and expenditure of the New Ross election fund and the New Ross petition fund were, at my request, audited and published in detail. The former, after paying all the costs of the

The Ulster Tenant-right party sent Dr. M'Knight and Mr. Rogers to London to watch the progress of the Select Committee, and we saw with surprise and pain that they relied on the deserters and their colleagues more than on the members of the League. In the committee, Mr. Kirk from the North, and the nominees of Mr. Keogh, proved lukewarm friends of the tenant-farmer, but the deputation could not be persuaded to recognise facts which time has placed beyond controversy. To break with the North was to throw away a moiety of our strength; but to condone the treason of the deserters was to throw it away altogether. Alliances between Irish members and the English Government, whether under O'Connell or his sons, or under Mr. Keogh's Brigade, had only one result; a few men got places or promotion, and the claims of the people were ignored or derided. The Southerns had gone through this bitter experience more than once, but the Northerns recalled the fact with the languid memory of spectators who had no interest at stake.

---

election, left a balance which was appropriated to the costs of an action for bribery, arising out of the election. The expenses of the petition amounted to £400. Mr. Lambert had been compelled to pay £128 as costs incurred in refuting his unfounded charge of intimidation; after furnishing the balance up to £400, the trustees had a surplus of £155, of which £72 were remitted to New Ross for local purposes, and the balance applied to paying a portion of the costs of Mr. Wyse's action arising out of the election.

But the most important deserter from the principles which had carried Crawford's bill to a second reading remains to be mentioned. It was Mr. Crawford himself. He published a letter advising the tenant-farmers to accept and be thankful for a measure more moderate than his bill. He described the policy by which the Irish party had won so signal a success in the current session, and described it accurately as a policy of "acting on their pledges." But though two members had just forfeited theirs, he was not disposed to complain. He found it impossible to doubt that they would use the position they had obtained to promote public ends.[1]

[1] "I believe I may say that I adhered with a desperate fidelity to this question, and I do not abandon a single principle or detail of the Tenant-right Bill as being inconsistent with justice. But still, when I think there is a great amount of good within your reach, I will not take the selfish course of counselling an adhesion to my own measures or my own views, to obstruct useful progress, and to impede national benefit, or to encourage delusive agitation for any object which I do not believe to be attainable; such a course I would consider one among the greatest political crimes a man possessing any share of public confidence can commit."—Mr. Sharman Crawford's Address to the Tenant-farmers and People of Ireland, Nov., 1853.

"By what means was success to be sought? It was obtained by Irish members acting faithfully on their pledges. This power will continue and increase if the same bond of action still hold the body together: and still more so when two of its most distinguished members have accepted office; and we cannot doubt that such acceptance of office by them is accompanied by an expected power to advance this particular question to which they are so strongly pledged."—*Ibid.*

Though we all now know that he might as reasonably have given credit for good intentions to Titus Oates as to John Sadleir, it would be cruel to triumph over the mistakes of an honourable man. But it is less easy to forgive him having disparaged and misrepresented the policy of Independent Opposition. As the Derby Budget was, he conceived, injurious to British interests (by augmenting the house tax, which did not extend to Ireland), he affirmed that Irish members would not have been justified in supporting it in order to save a Government which had in hand a land code beneficial to Ireland. Such a policy, he insisted, would not promote, but defeat, the tenants' claims. As he had been twenty years in Parliament without getting his bill read a second time, while the men whom he lectured carried it to a second reading in a single session, it would have been modest to recognise that they were better judges of Parliamentary policy than he. We now know that the aid which he lent the traitors at this crisis marred the cause with which his name is honourably identified more than his life-long labours had advanced it. And that the policy of Independent Opposition, which he rejected, and which Mr. Butt, when he became an Irish leader, equally rejected, is the only one which has advanced the Irish cause, and which, revived in the present day, promises to carry it to complete success.

The motives of the Northern delegates in falling

away from their old colleagues were as much mixed as human motives commonly are. The example of Crawford counted for much. An unjust prejudice against Lucas as a furious bigot (which he was not), prevailed from an early period, and some of them were persuaded that it is only men in office who can carry questions successfully through the House of Commons. But Negro Slavery had been abolished by Wilberforce, Religious Equality established by O'Connell, and Free Trade by Cobden, without any of them having held office under the Crown. There were lower motives also at work. The Prime Minister was a Presbyterian, and the Duke of Argyll and two other colleagues belonged to the same Church. If there were four Catholics in the Cabinet it could not be doubted that the Catholics, who had imperilled the League on the Ecclesiastical Titles Bill, would have been found hoorahing at their backs, and we were patient with this sympathy. But when the *Banner of Ulster* announced as certain that patronage would reward complacency in lower places, it became plain that Whig agents were at work in Ulster.[1] The most active intriguer was said to be a Mr. Wilson Kennedy, an influential elder of the

---

[1] "If Ulster had in Parliament Liberal Presbyterian representatives, *every one of these men* who might be qualified for official duties would have a place in the Irish administration. This is *not* a mere hypothesis."—*Banner of Ulster*, quoted in *Nation*.

General Assembly, who had been Presbyterian candidate for Coleraine against Lord Naas, and who was an intimate friend and ally of Mr. John Sadleir, and managing director of the Tipperary Joint Stock Bank. Dr. M'Knight had lately been on a visit with him, and unfriendly inferences were drawn from the fact. No one had done so much to organise the tenant cause in the North as M'Knight; no one had done as much to confirm the Union of North and South; but against these services must be set the fact that he helped to the best of his ability the men who betrayed and ruined for an entire generation the cause he served so well. And as he had been forward in ascribing personal motives to Moore and others, it was inevitable that his own motives for favouring the dispensers of patronage should be unfavourably judged.

As the Derby government had been overthrown on their financial proposals the Budget of the new Government was awaited with keen interest. When it was submitted by Mr. Gladstone it was found to contain a number of salutary proposals. A hundred domestic commodities were to be relieved from duties, certain oppressive taxes were to be repealed, and the advertisement duty abolished. But to recoup the Treasury for this sacrifice it was proposed to extend the income-tax to Ireland, which had been exempt hitherto in consideration of its poverty. This new impost was estimated to yield half a million sterling. To impose such a burthen on Ireland at a period of great distress in order to confer a boon upon England, which was overflowing with prosperity, was a startling proposal. The late administration had refrained from this measure on the specific ground that the direct taxes already paid in Ireland were heavier than those paid in England in proportion to the resources of the country. No people rejoices in additional burthens, and the state of Ireland at the time justified the universal resistance with which the proposal was encountered. But success was essential to the existence of the Government, and their Irish supporters did not shrink from this new test. On the second reading, so absorbing was the interest that only one Irish member was absent, seventy-two voted against the Budget, and thirty-two supported it.[1] In committee the Leaguers fought it in detail, and one of those "scenes" which the House loves better than grave debate sprang out of their resistance. An Irish member[2] had the audacity to tell the Government that they obtained their majority by arts as base as

---

[1] Colonel Dunne proposed a preliminary inquiry to ascertain whether the system of imperial finance did not press with undue weight upon Ireland, before imposing the new tax; among the majority who refused inquiry were Maurice O'Connell, William Kirk, Fox of Longford, and the ordinary tail of Mr. Keogh.

[2] Mr. Duffy.

those which enabled Walpole and the Pelhams to recruit supporters two generations earlier. His words were taken down, and he was directed to attend in his place the next day that he might withdraw them, or suffer the penalty of refusal. When the House reassembled he declined to withdraw them, and undertook, if a committee were granted, to prove that the career of Messrs. Keogh, Sadleir, and some of their associates justified them. The leader of the House objected to this investigation, on the ground that his colleagues had not been corrupted, but only converted to better opinions, and the deserters sat dumb and gloomy amidst the jeers of the Opposition. But a bribe is not less a bribe because it is paid quarterly at the Treasury; and the infamy of the transaction was for the first time made plain to Englishmen.

The resistance of the Irish members to the income-tax was not mere impatience of taxation, but rather a well-grounded fear that the same injustice which marked other branches of the connection between the two countries would prevail in this department. Irish gentlemen not unfriendly to Mr. Gladstone, and who are competent witnesses on the subject, affirm that from that time to the present he has increased our burthens by an amount exceeding fifty millions sterling, and that the wise concessions which he has made in reforming the Land Code and disestablishing the Church are scarcely a set-off for the exhausting drain created by his financial policy.[1]

As soon as their vote on the income-tax made it

[1] Mr. Gladstone based his infliction of the income-tax on Ireland on the article of the Union which provided that whenever the debt of Ireland, which in 1801 was less than a sixteenth part of the British debt, should have reached the much higher proportion of 1 Irish to 7½ British, it should then be competent for the United Parliament to abolish separate Irish and British quotas of taxation, and to tax both countries indiscriminately. The figures are as follows, according to a Parliamentary return (No. 35, year 1819) :—British debt on the 5th January, 1801, £450,504,984; Irish debt at the same date, £28,545,134. Now, when the liabilities of the two countries were so widely unequal —the British debt being 16½ times as large as the Irish—it is clear that it would have been unfair and dishonest to raise the taxation of Ireland to the British level without giving Ireland a substantial equivalent for the new burthen entailed upon her by the Union. But as the object of the authors of the Union was to bring Ireland under British burthens without giving her any equivalent, they adopted the device of getting Ireland into debt beyond her means to pay by deliberately over-estimating her relative taxable ability in the appointment of common expenses. The "Irish" debt was rapidly forced up to the prescribed proportion of 1 Irish to 7½ British by this fraudulent expedient. Instead of wealth the Union gave us debt—debt which was fictitious, so far as it originated in the initial overcharge—and this debt, thus forced upon Ireland, had been made by the 7th Article of the Union, the condition of consolidating the Irish and English Exchequers, and enabling the English Parliament to tax Ireland indiscriminately with Great Britain. The question is examined at some length by Mr. Daunt in an article entitled "How the Union Robs Ireland," in the *Dublin Review* for April, 1883.

plain that there was nothing to be feared from the bulk of the Irish members, Lord Palmerston told the select committee on the Land Bills, that for his part he saw no necessity for legislation on the question. Next day Crawford's bill was set aside by nineteen to nine, Mr. Kirk, the only tenant-righter sent from the North, voting in the majority. Mr. Napier's bills were next taken in hand and carefully pruned. The Tenants Compensation Bill, as it left the committee, ignored Ulster Tenant-right, and denied compensation for the class of improvements most commonly made in Ireland. The country had been rendered habitable by an industry like that which raised Venice on a quagmire or Holland on a sandbank; yet all improvements more than twenty years in existence were confiscated. Ireland is a moist country, spotted with bogs and wastes, for which draining and reclamation are beyond all things necessary; but compensation for drains or reclaimed waste and bog was omitted. Inordinate rents had as we know created habitual arrears; in former measures a landlord ejecting a tenant was enabled to set-off these arrears against any claims for compensation, but the modified bill went a step farther, and declared that if a tenant was ejected for non-payment of rent or arrears he should not be entitled to compensation for any improvements whatever. But the Northern farmers had not sent one member to Parliament, and their trusted spokesman had justified the policy by which their interest was betrayed.[1]

In the midst of this treason the question was carried from the House of Commons to the country. The members for Clare were unseated for intimidation. They had uniformly supported the Government, and revelled in patronage for their relatives and dependants. The member for Sligo, an Englishman, introduced by the Brigadiers, was unseated for bribery; and Maurice O'Connell, who had long been a moral wreck and a spectacle humiliating to Irishmen, rendered Tralee vacant by his death. Here were opportunities for the country to redeem itself. In the fervour of a general election, when districts caught fire from each other, great results were accomplished; but in solitary elections the odds in favour of the landlords were sometimes overwhelming. To the Government and the gentry there was now added the episcopacy, and some-

---

[1] When the bills came back from the committee the first division in the House was on the question of terminating the tenancy of agricultural labourers on a month's notice, as if there were not evictions enough already in Ireland. Mr. Kirk, Frank and Vincent Scully, Anthony O'Flaherty, and Cecil Lawless supported the proposal. Against another amendment, forbidding magistrates to act in cases connected with the estates they owned or managed, Maurice O'Connell, Fox, Grace, Kirk, and other Irish members voted.

times, under the influence of the bishops, the majority of the local clergy. There was always a group of patriotic priests in a constituency ready to face all consequences; but the world, the devil, and the flesh were often too strong for them. The people had many excuses for lethargy, but when all is said, they were fatally wrong; you can do little for a class who will do nothing for themselves. In Tralee Mr. Shine Lalor, a country gentleman of good character and capacity, presented himself on the principles of Independent Opposition, and was well received. Mr. Daniel O'Connell, the youngest son of O'Connell, was at this time out of Parliament. He had resigned his seat, it was said, in order to accept a foreign consulship, and the arrangement having fallen through he needed another seat to qualify him for another situation. The local clergy helped him against Mr. Lalor, and a furious mob howled at that gentleman for presuming to oppose the son of the Liberator. The young O'Connell was elected, and took his seat in time to support the Government on their land policy, and whenever they needed him throughout the session. In Clare the unseated members presented themselves for re-election. They had not voted once in the interests of their constituents when the Government needed their assistance, and they merited condign punishment. They were re-elected, the pretence being that their opponent was an exterminator; but their re-election pulled down more rooftrees in the future than Colonel Vandeleur had done in the past. In Sligo a singular farce was performed. Mr. Sadleir stood for the vacancy, and was proposed by the parish priests and supported by the Bishop of Kildare and Leighlin, who had previously helped him at Carlow. With him stood Mr. Somers, the late member, a *protégé* of Lord Palmerston. But a genuine candidate of the League was in the field. Father Feeny, the vicar-general of the diocese, proposed Mr. Cantwell, and Father Peter O'Connor supported him with vigour and enthusiasm. At the same time a Mr. Hanley, connected with a bigoted newspaper in London, came over to figure as an Exeter Hall candidate. His libels on Catholic men and opinions were so rabid that the Protestant electors disavowed him in a public meeting. But he served as a patent justification for supporting at all hazards a leader of the Catholic Defence Association. The mob, recruited from Lord Palmerston's estate, was more furious than the mobs at Limerick or Tralee. Half a dozen priests who supported Cantwell were threatened, hustled, and assailed whenever they appeared in the streets. "Hell broke loose," one of them declared, "could scarcely have exceeded the scenes they witnessed."

The Catholic champion was duly elected, and soon after it was discovered that Mr. Hanley had been brought over from London by Mr. Sadleir for this specific purpose—

"All that is now required (said Archdeacon Fitzgerald) to establish an Irish member as the very pink of patriot representatives is, not to vote against Maynooth College or the Nunneries, and the veriest runaway from his party or his pledges will give no such vote, for this very sufficient reason, that under existing circumstances such a vote has no marketable value."

Before this universal triumph of corruption national feeling became almost afraid to show itself. An Industrial Exhibition, opened at the expense of William Dargan, an eminent contractor, was held in connection with the Royal Dublin Society, and the Queen was brought over to witness the loyalty and satisfaction of the people. The Exhibition building was ornamented by all the flags of Europe except one: there was no Irish flag. All these disasters were like a cordial to the enemies of our race. The *Times* uttered another jubilant prediction that the Celt would disappear from Ireland as completely as the elk or the wolf—

"Both the Roman Catholics of Ireland and the race identified with that faith there are all leaving Ireland. Ere long there will be none left. At the present rate of emigration, which cannot be less than 200,000, chiefly Roman Catholics, in a year, our children will see the time when the Celts will be as obsolete in Ireland as the Phœnicians in Cornwall, and the Roman Catholic system as forgotten as the worship of Astarte. In fifty years Ireland will be Protestant to a man, and the Church Establishment will be no longer the 'flagrant injustice,' the 'one great anomaly,' the 'latent disorder,' the 'imperial danger,' which Mr. G. H. Moore describes it."

More than thirty of the fifty years have since elapsed, and the fell prophecy does not seem to be in course of fulfilment. But who can tell how largely it has contributed to the exasperation of the men whose flight to America it proclaimed so triumphantly? It contained perhaps the first seeds of the Dynamite and Invincible conspiracies, and is intrinsically as cruel and base as they.

In this era of disaster a new antagonist appeared against the men who were struggling to save a remnant of the Irish race. John Mitchel had escaped from Van Diemen's Land and established a newspaper in New York, and in that journal he vehemently exhorted Irish Nationalists to have nothing to do with the League. The principles it contended for—rent fixed by the State and permanent tenure—would never be accepted by the House of Commons. Never, never! But there was hope elsewhere; before twelve months had elapsed an expedition from America might be seen on the shores of Ireland. To this cruel rhodomontade many young men gave their joyful assent; they refrained from helping the work which could be accomplished, and had been accomplished, and wasted their lives dreaming of an expedition as fabulous as the sleeping warriors under the hill of Aileah.[1]

The estrangement of the Northern delegates, it will be noted, did not originate in any hereditary causes of quarrel existing between North and South. It sprang from such a difference of political opinion as constantly divides men in England, and in all countries where free institutions exist. The controversy primarily was whether certain persons in accepting office had acted with probity and good faith. No difference of creed was involved, for the men impeached were not Northern or Protestants, but Catholics, and those who impeached them were also Catholics. Still less did a provincial question arise, for none of the deserters were Ulster men. It may be confidently assumed, I think, that while four years of harmonious action justifies the conclusion that Irishmen of various races can sink

---

[1] Those who have read *Four Years of Irish History* will be at no loss to understand that it was at me Mr. Mitchel's enmity was aimed, or to recognise what was its origin. But they only half know the facts and factors in the case. To understand them fully see note on "John Mitchel, Gavan Duffy, and the League," in the Appendix to this volume.

their differences for public ends as well as Swiss or Hungarians of various races, the break in their friendly relations was one which must have happened wherever free controversy exists, and does not disturb that conclusion.

CHAPTER VIII.

ANOTHER RALLY OF THE LEAGUE.

IN the face of these disheartening difficulties the leaders did not despair; the harvest was a plentiful one, and there was still in every constituency a group of faithful priests and farmers ready to make another struggle. If the North returned to its place in the movement with its old zeal, all would still be well. A Conference had become the established agency for maintaining a steady connection with public opinion, and a Conference was called for the 5th October. It will be noted that the system of agitation which O'Connell had established—a weekly meeting, which was in effect a monologue by the leader on current affairs, and the collection of a weekly rent—had quite disappeared, and was replaced by a genuine consultation at headquarters, and local consultations from time to time at convenient places. Sharman Crawford, Sergeant Shee, about a dozen members of Parliament, a large number of Southern priests and farmers, and half a dozen delegates from Ulster attended. But there were now plainly two parties face to face—one which still upheld the fidelity of Messrs. Sadleir and Keogh, and another which saw in them the worst enemies of the cause.

The earliest business submitted was a table exhibiting the votes of Irish members of the past session. It led to angry controversy. Father Quaid undertook to defend the members for Clare, and Dr. M'Knight propounded the amazing thesis that to consider the votes of members of Parliament was no part of the business of the Conference. But though their conduct might not be scrutinised or censured, it was permissible, it seems, to applaud them at discretion, for the learned Doctor confidently affirmed that there was one member to whom the farmers owed more than to any other man in Parliament, and this was Mr. William Keogh.

Mr. Bowyer, an English Catholic, who sat for Dundalk, and who, though personally upright, had that tolerance for backsliding in others which characterises men who take only a languid interest in a public question, made a proposal which he thought all parties ought to accept. The pledge which bound members to oppose any Administration that did not make Crawford's bill a "Cabinet question" might be modified by substituting "Government question." The Administration must introduce such a bill, but need not stake its existence on it. Mr. Rogers gave this proposal his warmest support, but it was shown so conclusively in the debate which ensued that the change would enable an Administration to play with the question, without any serious purpose of legislating upon it, that Sharman Crawford supported the retention of the word "cabinet," and only two hands were held up in support of the amendment.

Dr. M'Knight, who had charged Moore with place-begging at the last Conference, now charged Lucas with treachery to the cause. He had privately advised the Chief Secretary for Ireland (so the Doctor declared) to lay aside his Land Bills and postpone legislation to another session. As Lucas pronounced the imputation to be wholly false, I have no doubt it was so; but had he desired to postpone or defeat a bill which denied compensation for the most usual and necessary improvements to be made hereafter, and for all past improvements more than twenty years in existence, who could blame him? At the Conference Sharman Crawford was silent on this subject, but a week later he published a letter adopting the charge. There were few things which the Northern delegates might not have done with impunity, so strong was the desire to retain them in the League, but to whitewash sordid traitors and disparage a man who was devoting his life to the

contest was past human endurance, and these proceedings excited general indignation. A vote of confidence in the Independent Party and of censure on the deserters was adopted. The Northern deputation did not attend on the subsequent days, and when they returned home Dr. M'Knight wrote of the Council with fierce hostility.

Looking back on that quarrel through the vista of years, I recognise that though Lucas was right in principle he was often precipitate and passionate in manner and unskilful in method. Assailed on all sides by mercenary and unscrupulous enemies—for since Mr. Keogh had the patronage of Ireland to dispense he had troops of adherents—he (and all of us perhaps) struck blows which not merely inflicted just punishment on traitors, but sometimes turned timid friends into active enemies. We did not under-estimate the value of Sharman Crawford's co-operation ; but how can you co-operate with a man who offers you a public and deliberate insult ? And this is what Crawford did in the case of Lucas. In a letter to Dr. M'Knight, written for publication, he affirmed that he had been compelled by various mis-statements and equivocations to decline personal communication with Mr. Lucas except in the presence of witnesses ![1]

[1] I desire to reproduce one fact in the controversy in a note at the end of the chapter, because the party to which I belonged

A strong man rarely escapes the aberrations to which strength has a tendency; and though Lucas was a calm and philosophical thinker, he easily became a passionate and fanatical controversialist, not consciously unjust to his adversaries, but harsh and unmeasured; and after this incredible imputation much may be forgiven him. It is proper to say that the Northerns from the beginning feared him as a furious bigot, mistaking for bigotry the devotion of a profoundly religious man to the faith which he had embraced at so many sacrifices; and Dr. M'Knight, from the foundation of the League, took as much pains to warn me against him as Dr. Cullen took to warn him against me. But a crisis had now come when the League had to choose—and I especially, who was most closely allied with the Northerns—had to choose between parties who no longer trusted each other, and we chose unhesitatingly the man of highest integrity and plainest disinterestedness. My judgment on the controversy, when all the parties to it are dead, is that Crawford was misled by shameless lying on the part of the new officials, and was grossly unjust to Lucas; and that Lucas, too indignant to rest on the solid ground of his character and services,

had suffered such shame and torture by the methods of dealing with public money in the Repeal Association, that they could not endure that suspicion should rest for a moment on any fund with which they were concerned.—See note "The Northerns and the League Funds."

which furnished ample protection, became an aggressor in turn, and was unjust to Crawford. In the height of his indignation he used language respecting him which it was hopeless that a cold, proud man would ever forgive.

On the two last days the business was less political. Mr. Lucas made a masterly statement on the revival of manufactures in Flanders. Mr. M'Mahon brought forward a scheme to develop Irish fisheries, and Mr. Kennedy, who had planted industrial schools in Farney, explained the method which had been adopted with a view to its extension. Mr. Duffy submitted a plan of a Small Proprietors' Society, for enabling farmers to buy their own farms whenever they came under the hammer of the Encumbered Estates Court, to which a number of practical men had given a warm approval, notably Mr. Cobden and Mr. Bright. The price of freehold land was abnormally low, and the proposal was to form a joint-stock company which would resell to the tenants at wholesale prices. The Irish capital which hides itself annually in stocks, mortgages, and savings banks, it was estimated would be sufficient for the purpose. When the project was first mooted, eighteen months earlier, it had the misfortune to attract the attention of Mr. John Sadleir, who was unknown to me at that time. Had I known him, I would have understood that his object was probably to make a humane enterprise a milch cow for his firm of attorneys and land-jobbers. "There are men," says Richelieu, "who, if you saw them praying on the Mount of Olives, you would understand that they were about to build an oil-mill up there."

Before the recess terminated two more elections occurred of the fatal character already described. Early in November Clonmel fell vacant by the death of Cecil Lawless; a local committee was appointed to prepare for the event, and commenced its labours by a declaration that entire independence of party must characterise their future representative. The Rev. Dr. Burke, the senior parish priest, was reported to have said that he would be influenced neither by favour nor by affection, and that if he carried the key of the borough, as was alleged, he would use it to lock out traitors; but his action proved strangely at variance with his professions. A Tipperary constituency was not easy to win. The county was represented by a brother and a cousin of John Sadleir; the Tipperary Bank, which the family controlled, exercised wide influence over farmers and shopkeepers. But the League was bound to take the field, and a strong deputation was despatched to the constituency.[1] The

[1] The deputation consisted of Moore, Lucas, Duffy, Dr. Gray, and Father O'Shea. We had a candidate in reserve who promised to be a popular one. He had written to me from Paris offering

local committee received the deputation with great favour, and it seemed for a time that Clonmel would do its duty. The town is distributed into two parishes; in one of them the bulk of the electors and all the clergy were adherents of the League, in the other the parish priest announced as candidate Mr. John O'Connell, who would stand on the principles of Daniel O'Connell. It was but a year since Mr. John O'Connell had resigned Limerick, and shrunk into private life, and the deputation understood perfectly well that the only Daniel O'Connell whose principles he would adopt was the young gentleman whose election for Tralee had given another servile adherent to the Government. The zeal of an aged priest for the son of the Liberator would be respectable, and even admirable, if it was his own interest he was sacrificing to the sentiment. But the cause of the people was not his private property, and,

to stand on League principles; and, having made confidential inquiries, as I was bound to do, he seemed peculiarly suitable. A well-informed friend assured me that "he was a young man just emerging from his minority; of promising abilities and striking appearance, possessing a moderate hereditary estate, tribunitial blood as a kinsman of O'Connell's and a Celtic title—an excellent equipment for public usefulness in Ireland. But" my friend added, "*Per contra* his nearest relatives are Whigs; and it is a fact not to be overlooked that among O'Connell's immense family connection scarcely one has been distinguished by public spirit or unselfish aims." This candidate was The O'Donoghue, but circumstances in the end forbade our putting any person in nomination.

as it was quite impossible to believe that an intelligent man misunderstood the motives of the candidate, he must be held guilty of a cruel wrong to his race and his country. The deputation said plainly that the pretence of O'Connell's son was idle. In truth, O'Connell had no son, and never had a son, in the sense of an inheritor of his courage and patriotism. It was a sad retrospect to look back on the career of the men of his blood, whom the people had trusted for the sake of his illustrious name and services. One son abandoned Meath for a situation from the Whigs; another abandoned Waterford for the same purpose; a namesake and son-in-law abandoned Kerry; and a second son-in-law Dublin on a like temptation; and the constituencies so abandoned had all but one fallen into the hands of Tories or Castle hacks.

The committee heard Mr. O'Connell and the League deputation in succession. The latter made the National policy so plain that the committee declared by a large majority they would accept no candidate not pledged to sit and act with the party of Independent Opposition. A public meeting of electors exhibited a similar spirit. But the Whigs were advised by men who were skilful and experienced in intrigue, and in the end the committee were induced to accept a ridiculous compromise. Mr. John O'Connell, they affirmed, undertook to act on the principles of Independent Opposition, if he were excused from sitting with men who distrusted him, and on this understanding they accepted him. In the end he explained away or repudiated the stringent conditions of the contract; but the exact terms were of no importance, for it was a pledge which no one expected him to keep. He went into Parliament to support a Government from whom he expected a personal favour, and he supported them servilely till it was obtained. There was a bitter sting in the summing up of his career by Father O'Shea, standing on the same balcony with him, in face of the electors of Clonmel. "Alas for Ireland!

"Unprized are her sons till they've learned to betray,
Undistinguished they live *if they shame not their sires*."

Before Parliament re-assembled the chief Leaguers were entertained at public dinners by their constituents. If the support they received from the country gradually diminished in area it increased in intensity. They used these occasions to enforce on the people the melancholy truth that the disasters which had befallen their cause was nobody's fault but their own; they had preferred evil to good, and the natural consequences followed—

"Of the five-and-twenty deserters who have gone over to the enemy (said one Leaguer) there are three-and-twenty of whom I could have told with as much certainty twelve months ago as at this hour that they would betray the country on the first opportunity. If constituencies will elect men notoriously corrupt or notoriously allied with the Whigs, it is too absurd to pretend that an experiment has failed because they have done what any man might have foretold they would do. If you were going to fight, and selected poltroons for officers, of course you would lose the battle. If you were going to try a case at law, and selected blockheads for counsel, of course you would lose the case. But does that prove that with brave men and wise men you would fail? Look at the candidates recommended or assisted by the Tenant League; not one single man of them has proved untrue."

The gradual substitution of private aims for public ones was illustrated by individual instances familiar at that time to the whole country—

"A learned member for a midland county recently declared that he meant to preserve his independence most jealously, but he would feel at liberty to recommend his constituents to Government for local distinctions, such as the magistracy. A learned member for the largest county in Ireland went a step further, and declared that he would feel it his duty to recommend deserving persons for public offices in Ireland on all fitting opportunities. Another said that for his part he had promised his own constituents to get them situations as often as he could, and he meant to keep his promise. But a learned Sergeant capped the climax. He affirmed that promotion for himself in his profession was his right, that he hoped it would come soon, and that he would very gladly accept it."[1]

The Sadleirite Press retorted by a steady fire of misrepresentation. As the Leaguers had relinquished all personal aims in politics, they were, of course, charged with sordid baseness, and, as Lucas was a Catholic of

---

[1] Speech of Mr. Duffy at Dundalk.

antique type, he was naturally proclaimed to be merely a selfish pervert and a "whitewashed Quaker."[1]

Against all these reverses fortune supplied one signal set-off. In Mr. Sadleir's contest for Carlow he had struck an audaciously foul blow, for which he was unexpectedly made responsible. Mr. Dowling, an elector who refused to support him, and threatened to canvass his tenants against him, was arrested by one of Sadleir's election agents on his way to the hustings and carried to the local office of the Tipperary Bank. There were bills of his in the bank which had not come to maturity, and he had given to a friend who endorsed them a bond as a counter security. On this bond he was arrested. As no attorney could sign the certificate in such a transaction without risk of being struck off the rolls, the name of a dying attorney was forged to the instrument. In these proceedings it was proved that Mr. Sadleir had intervened, not merely through relatives and agents, but personally by direction and assistance. When he came to be examined, however, he denied everything and repudiated everybody. He swore that the manager of the bank, whose guest he was during the election, acted without his knowledge; and that though Dowling was

[1] A number of priests, of whom Father Redmond, of Arklow, was the most notable, attacked Lucas in the newspapers, one of them employing the phrase quoted above. By this time Lucas was persuaded that they had the sanction and encouragement of Dr. Cullen for attacking him.

arrested in his presence and conveyed to his bank, he was not aware of either fact. But a spectator described him as having quite lost his accustomed dash and pluck in the witness-box. The jury disbelieved the Lord of the Treasury and gave a verdict for Dowling. When the news was flashed throughout the Empire the sensation was intense. One of the Queen's Government directing a fraudulent arrest, supported by deliberate forgery, was an unheard-of scandal; but it was still worse to have such an official disbelieved on oath by a respectable jury. He was compelled to resign his office and quit Downing-street for ever. The humiliation of his fall can only be estimated by measuring the height to which he had hoped to climb. It was understood that he was confident of becoming a peer and marrying into a family of European repute as financiers. And it might have been so; he had faculties which with better fortune would have made him a Law or a Hudson.

The first reverse was followed by a second. Mr. Dowling took an action for false imprisonment, and obtained signal damages. In most civilised countries this exposure would have ruined and scattered the political connection which he had created; but in Ireland it ruined no one but Mr. Sadleir. His most intimate confederates still held up their heads, and not one bishop or ecclesiastic of any rank abandoned the party. Mr.

Chichester Fortescue[1] accepted the office which Mr. Sadleir was forced to relinquish, and his seat for Louth became vacant. The League determined to contest it, and Mr. M'Namara Cantwell was put in nomination. Mr. Cantwell was one of the proprietors of the *Freeman's Journal*, and a member of the Committee of the Defence Association, as well as of the League Council; but his chief claim at the moment was that in his professional capacity as an attorney, he had conducted the Dowling case to a successful issue. The County Club approved of his candidature, and he commenced a canvass, accompanied by Mr. Moore and Mr. Cashel Hoey, and a little later by Dr. Gray and Father O'Shea. Thirty priests, half of them curates, welcomed him cordially; but Mr. Fortescue was not left without clerical supporters. Fifteen priests, of whom it was noticed as a significant fact that only one was a curate, declared for the new Lord of the Treasury. He had much more effectual clerical backing, however, for which we were not prepared. Dr. Cullen, who had gradually become more and more associated with Whig politics, now for the first time threw his whole weight openly on the side of the Government. The fearless spirit and great popularity of Father O'Shea had proved important forces in the contest, and when it was at its height Dr. Cullen sent a private note to the Bishop of Ossory advising his recall

[1] The present Lord Carlingford.

from Louth, and recommending, if he had gone without regular leave of absence, that he should be suspended, and in any case that he should be prohibited from leaving the diocese or parish for any public purpose whatever. The feelings which this arbitrary stroke of authority excited, the dangers it created, the action it provoked, have all been described by Lucas[1] with a vigour and plainness which relieve me from the necessity of telling the story in detail. The immediate effect was to lose the election. Backed by the Apostolic Delegate the Whig priests set no limit to their hardihood, and at the polling the new Lord of the Treasury obtained a decided majority.

The session opened at the beginning of February, and the first Irish business was an unequivocal charge which had been made against certain Irish members of trafficking in Government offices for their personal profit. At a League banquet in Tuam Dr. Gray and Mr. Christopher Kelly specified cases of gross corruption which had fallen within their own knowledge. Mr. Butt, on behalf of the members implicated, demanded inquiry, and a select committee was appointed for the purpose. After minute investigation a multitude of unpleasant facts were established, on which it is needless to return.[2] But it came out incidentally that the

[1] In his "Statement" for the Pope.
[2] Dr. Gray's statement was that a young man was negotiating

Duke of Newcastle and certain of the Peelites had subscribed money for Mr. Keogh's election. Mr. Lucas, who was examined before the committee, told them that there was a class of corruptionists in Ireland worse than those who sold petty places for money, or trucked them against election accounts. These were men who got into Parliament by specific pledges, sometimes confirmed by solemn oaths, and then repudiated them for their personal profit. While this committee was still sitting, a meeting was held in Dublin to protest against the inspection of nunneries. Mr. John Reynolds, against whom it had just been proved that he accepted money extracted from officers for whom he had procured compensation in Parliament, appeared as a Catholic champion. The main purpose of his speech, however, was not a vindication of nunneries, but an attack on the editor of the *Tablet*. It was with immense difficulty a hearing was obtained for Lucas to defend himself. He was serving the Irish people with a consummate ability which

the purchase of a vice-guardianship from a member of Parliament for £300 when the office of vice-guardian was abolished. He produced the young man, who reluctantly admitted the fact. Mr. Kelly's statement was that a stipendiary magistracy was sold for £1,000, of which only £500 were paid, the magistrate, when secure in office, having refused the second instalment. The stipendiary magistrate was produced, and denied the bargain. But he was compelled to admit that immediately after his appointment he lent £400 to Mr. Somers, of which he never was repa principal or interest, though fourteen years had elapsed.

U

commanded the attention of the House of Commons, and in Dublin he was shouted down at the bidding of a demagogue just detected in corrupt practices. And Lucas was confident that in assailing him the demagogue had the secret support and encouragement of Dr. Cullen.[1]

In the programme of the Government the principal measure for the session was a Reform Bill, but before it got beyond the second reading a war with Russia broke out, and it was put aside. The same preoccupation was pleaded against taking up the Land question in the House of Commons. But in the Lords two or three peers introduced separate Land bills, and along with their schemes the Government measures of the preceding year were submitted to a select committee. In the Commons a committee had proved a convenient instrument for cutting down the original proposals, and in the Lords it was still more effective for the same purpose. The Tenants' Compensation Bill became the paltriest and meanest scheme for which any Cabinet had yet become responsible. The law of distress was maintained in full vigour, but scarcely a remnant of the principle of compensation was preserved, and the Ulster Tenant-

---

[1] It is proper to note that Lucas's position at the moment was damaged by the fact that he had advised a witness before the Corruption Committee to produce a note addressed to him by one of the Brigadiers which was marked "private." He vindicated his action under the circumstances of the case with great power and subtlety, but the current of opinion ran against him.

right was ignored, if it was not (as some contended) confiscated. When the bills reached the Commons, towards the close of the session, Sergeant Shee, on his own responsibility, proposed to defer all legislation till next year, as it was impossible at that late period to deal with the subject adequately. The Government cheerfully acquiesced, and the measures were withdrawn. Mr. Napier complained that the Whigs had taken possession of his bills, first defaced them, and then unduly delayed them; and Mr. Disraeli reminded the House that they had been doing nothing particular for some months, and might have been employed on this question. Lord John Russell, in the slow and discontented drawl which was his ordinary method, accounted for the delay by announcing that nothing had been done because it was not desirable to do anything. The Lord-Lieutenant and other persons in Ireland, with the best information, assured him that there was no longer need for legislation, there was a good harvest, a friendly feeling existed between landlord and tenant, and the question was settling itself.

On the face of God's earth there was not a country so miserable and hopeless as Ireland at that time. The population were flowing out of it like water from a vessel which is staved. The workhouses were crammed with inmates stricken with the diseases that spring from want and neglect, the landlords were still levelling homesteads and rooting out the native race, and nothing was to be done for remedy or alleviation. Nothing was to be done, and three-fourths of the representatives elected by the stricken people assented in silence, and three-fourths of the bishops, born and bred among them, sanctioned the perfidy. No ecclesiastic of any rank who had supported the Government abandoned them because they relinquished the Land question, any more than they had done when the fall of Sadleir and the disclosures before the Corruption Committee laid bare the character of Mr. Keogh's associates. It was no better in the North. The *Banner of Ulster* admitted that nothing was now to be hoped from the Government, but it continued its complaisance to the sordid traitors who had brought about this result.

The *Times*, which played the part of chorus in the tragedy, notified the point which the drama had now reached with commendable plainness—

At length the bubble has burst, and after trifling a year and a half with this particular form of Socialism, from the very touch of which they ought to have recoiled, Ministers have declared that they will countenance it no longer, and will not even support two cognate bills, admitted to be good in themselves, for fear that they should be made the vehicle of Tenant-right abominations."

The strongest nature is made stronger by the mesmeric sense of sympathy and support. But sympathy and support were gradually ebbing away from us. We were tasting what the poet calls "man's predestined lot—being beaten and baffled." The stay which upheld the Leaguers against all difficulties was conviction. They entirely believed that they were right. Some of them were endowed with great force of character, some were more liable to excitement and depression, but all were certain they were labouring for a great public end. An assembly like the House of Commons is rarely slow to recognise sincerity. It may hate it, and call it odious names, but it knows it for what it is. Genuine conviction and unfaltering will can no more conceal themselves than a man's stature or colour. There never was in Ireland before or since a political party more able, honest, or devoted, than the League of 1850. But the Land question was still in the pioneer stage—a stage through which all public questions fought by operating on opinion must inevitably pass.

Happily villainy is not an agreeable pursuit. I saw Mr. Sadleir at this time when he came to the House to vote on a party division, and his face was appalling. He had always been a dark mysterious person, but now he looked wild, haggard, and repulsive. None of us had any suspicion that he was an undetected forger and a swindler, but it seemed that thwarted ambition had turned his blood into liquid mud.

I have confined this narrative to the Tenant-right

contest, but the Irish members naturally applied themselves to other tasks. They endeavoured to obtain chaplains for Catholics serving in the army and navy, to secure religious equality in the Colonies, and they defended Maynooth College from an organised attempt to misrepresent and destroy it. It is enough to say that Lucas took the lead and Moore a notable part in these controversies. One instance in the Maynooth debate is worth recording as an illustration of the sort of evidence on which English opinion respecting Ireland is sometimes founded. Sir Francis Head, a retired Governor of Upper Canada, published a book entitled *A Fortnight in Ireland*, for which the Irish Constabulary furnished materials in the shape of violent speeches delivered at Tenant Right meetings, and reported by them to headquarters. Most of these speeches were made by the Reverend This or That; and they were naturally cited as illustrations of Maynooth discipline. Was a system to be tolerated which produced firebrands like these reverend orators? The Irish member who followed took up the reprehended speeches, and read three or four of the strongest of them amid ironical cheers. The sentiments, he said, seemed to him just and reasonable under the circumstances which existed in Ireland, but if the House differed with him in this opinion, he submitted at any rate that it was rash to hold Maynooth responsible (Oh !

oh! and more ironical cheers). He would only trouble them with a single fact in support of this conclusion; every speaker, without exception, whom he had quoted was a Presbyterian minister! There was an anonymous speech indeed in the collection particularly objectionable to Irish landlords, and it might seem impossible to relieve Maynooth from the imputation of having trained this unnamed speaker at any rate. But he undertook to prove a negative even in that case; for he recognised the passage in question as one from a speech which he had himself delivered in the Tholsel of New Ross!

NOTES ON CHAPTER VIII.

THE NORTHERNS AND THE LEAGUE FUNDS.

This letter will explain itself—

"PECULATION OF PUBLIC MONEY.

"It so happens that Tenant-right is the only question likely to bring in supplies of money from the rural districts, and the Dublin system of financial management is the excellent old plan which has already destroyed so many previous agitations, namely, that of having a small metropolitan clique who 'receive' all cash sent in—who 'vote' its appropriation, 'expend' it in accordance with their own votes, and then account for their disbursements, calling themselves all the while by different names according to the official characters temporarily assumed. At the very outset of the Tenant League the Northern members set themselves against this barefaced system of finance, and for a time they succeeded.

"At length, however, certain parties contrived to oust every respectable treasurer who could be appointed, and to re-establish the ancient *régime*. The incessant remonstrances of the North at length compelled the selection of three trustees, resident in Dublin, and chosen from among the friends of Messrs. Lucas and Duffy. The trustees had not been long in office until they peremptorily refused to sanction the money appropriations habitually voted, and they were consequently removed by a summary process, the nominal Council retaining in its own hands all funds transmitted to the League, without putting the trustees to any trouble in the matter."—*Banner of Ulster.*

"TO JAMES M'KNIGHT, ESQ., LL.D.

"SIR,—I find the above passage in your newspaper, and, as it implies charges of a kind which I will permit no man to connect, in any manner, with my name, I come straight to you for a prompt substantiation of them ; or such an apology as an offence so serious requires. I make full allowance for the exaggeration of party warfare. I am by no means sensitive to the ordinary assaults of the Press, of which I have had my full share without feeling a jot the worse for them. But on the subject of public funds I have spoken and written opinions which forbid me to endure the smallest imputation in silence. You will comprehend, therefore, that this is not a subject—as far as I am concerned—which can be despatched in generalities. My personal honour demands that it be fully retracted or scrupulously sifted to the bottom.

"I confidently believe your imputations on the Tenant League are totally unfounded. If you can establish any one of them I promise to separate myself from the League for ever. But I feel no necessity to undertake the defence of a public body which has many members better qualified and entitled to become its champion—I content myself with defending my own honour. As far, therefore, as you have presumed to connect my name with your allegations I pronounce them wicked and gratuitous inventions, false as a whole, and false in every particular.

"The gravamen of your very serious charge is this—That certain parties in Dublin (afterwards described as 'friends of Lucas and Duffy),' (1) contrary to the remonstrances of the Northern members, who were the watchful guardians of the funds, (2) contrived to oust every respectable treasurer who could be appointed, (3) till, at length, trustees were named ; but these officers peremptorily refused to sanction the money appropriations habitually voted, and (4) were consequently removed by a summary process.

"As far as I know or believe there is not one solitary item of truth in this very circumstantial statement. But to prevent mistakes I will take it in detail.

"1. The resolution of the League ordering the annual audit and publication of its accounts was not adopted at the instance of any of those whom you call Northern members. It was *my* proposal at the Preparatory Committee. They have accordingly been habitually audited, and laid before the public in the newspapers.

Almost the only concern I have ever had with the pecuniary affairs of the League was to vote year after year for this publication. Nobody resisted it; and I never heard, as far as I can recollect, any member resident in Ulster utter a word in remonstrance on the manner in which the funds were kept or accounted for.

"2. If any treasurer was ever 'ousted,' I pray you name him. The charge is that 'every respectable treasurer who could be appointed was ousted.' As far as my knowledge of the affairs of the League goes, there is not the colour of fact for this imputation in a single instance. Certain I am that I never deposed any person; or proposed, or suggested any person whatever for the office, or ever witnessed or was a party to any attempt of the kind imputed.

"3. 'The three trustees at length appointed (friends of Messrs. Lucas and Duffy) peremptorily refused to sanction the money appropriations habitually voted.' This is a tangible fact, and a clinching one. If this happened, then indeed we have a case to deal with, and I pray you specify it. In my entire connection with the League such a circumstance never came under my notice. No trustees ever made any such objection, or had the slightest ground for making it. The story is as purely imaginary as the last romance in the circulating libraries.

"4. 'The trustees were consequently removed by a summary process.' No trustees were ever removed by a summary process, or by any process whatever, as far as I know. If they were, who are they, and what was the process?

"But we must come to closer quarters. These charges mean nothing if they do not mean that the money of the League has been voted for some purposes in which Messrs. Lucas and Duffy had a personal interest. I challenge you to name one sum, however small, voted for any purpose in which I had the slightest personal interest. It is the usage of political bodies to buy and circulate newspapers containing reports of their proceedings. The League never circulated one copy of the *Nation*. It is the usage, I believe, to sustain friendly newspapers by high-priced advertisements. The high-priced advertisements of the League, such as its requisitions and audits, which cost much in unfriendly papers, were published *gratis* in the *Nation*. The few shillings a quarter paid for its ordinary advertisements, the secretary tells me, have been less to the *Nation* than to the *Telegraph*, and would amount to about as much since the formation of the League as I paid in one week for sending to Tyrone and Clare to report its meetings—rather less than it got in subscriptions out of the office of the *Nation*. This is true in every respect of the *Tablet* as well as the *Nation*—that is to say, of Messrs. Lucas and Duffy.

"But I am not content to stop here. I ask you to specify any money vote of the League which concerned me personally one straw whether it passed or not—any one vote which I had the smallest interest in more than a member residing in Belfast or Londonderry. I challenge you to show that I aim, or that I aimed to be, richer by the value of a postage-stamp from the funds of the League; that I had any interest to serve in it, that any of its treasurers were made or unmade by me, or, in short, that I had more to do with the management or expenditure of its funds than Dr. M'Knight.

"The actual fact is that for the three years the League has been in existence I have not taken part in a dozen of its votes on disbursements of money. I had something else to do than muddle over petty finances, and my duty to the public was, I conceived, fully discharged by taking care that competent auditors were appointed from time to time and the accounts published.

"I shall not condescend to retaliate charges, but assuredly my impression on the subject of the funds was this—that they had been almost exclusively furnished by the South and almost exclusively squandered by the North, as far as there were disbursements which were not indispensable. Of the very few votes which I originated (not, I believe, beyond a dozen) three were for advances to Northern gentlemen for the purpose of organising their respective counties; one of them did his duty very efficiently, and the other two spent the money and never made the smallest return for it. This is my experience.

"And now, sir, I demand your direct answer. Are you

prepared to substantiate charges with which you have connected my name? If you have any case whatever, speak out and let the public judge of it. If not, it can scarcely be necessary to suggest the course you should pursue.

"May I at the same time inquire how it has happened, if these suspicions were in your mind since the formation of the League, that you have maintained with me personally a frank and intimate correspondence on its proceedings, without ever having hinted a complaint? That, on the contrary, you were pleased, publicly and privately, to except me from the complaints you did make (which were never in relation to the funds).

"I separated from you; I did so with pain and hesitation, but peremptorily and publicly, when you became the advocate of men who had broken their solemn specific engagements for Treasury pay. This would account for angry feelings on your part, undoubtedly; but how it will account consistently with your honour for imputations never breathed before, and directed against a man whom you were accustomed to call your friend, it remains for you to show.—I am, sir, your obedient servant,

"C. GAVAN DUFFY.

"BLACKROCK, DUBLIN.
    October 13."

Dr. M'Knight did not attempt to sustain any one of the imputations, but withdrew the charge, grudgingly indeed, but unequivocally.

CHAPTER IX.

DR. CULLEN AND THE WHIG BISHOPS.

THE war still engrossed public attention, and in the ensuing session Irish business might be represented by a cipher. Outside of Parliament the League journals and a few League priests laboured to keep alive opinion, but the people seconded them feebly. That stage of depression was nearly reached when only the unconquerable do not despair. The leaders found themselves charged with all the costs as well as all the labour of the agitation. From lack of funds deputations defrayed their own expenses, and the subscription list showed large contributions from a few persons, instead of moderate contributions from all, as of old.[1] The harvest was a bountiful one; but the farmers in general regarded

[1] In 1852 the League received only £600, of which £170 were personal subscriptions of the Council and its most active members. This was the expenditure—Salaries, £220; the monthly periodical, £70; postage, £38; printing and stationery, £70; rent, £30; expense of deputations, £38.

this temporary gleam of prosperity less as an opportunity for renewing the struggle than as a lucky holiday, when they need take no thought for to-morrow. Our troubles were increased by a mesmeric feeling that Sergeant Shee was growing cold in the cause. His latest bill was only a shadow of his original proposal; and when a Leaguer refused to put his name upon such a pitiful scheme, the Sergeant crossed the house and substituted the name of one of the deserters. He was anxious, doubtless, to perform the task assigned to him like a gentleman, if it did not prove too inconvenient, but he had no deep feelings at stake, and the temptations to attorn were cogent. Another trouble to be noted at this time was the death of Maurice Leyne. He had gone to Tipperary to establish a local journal, which it might be hoped would make the continued ascendency of Sadleirism there impossible, was seized with typhoid fever and suddenly carried away in the maturity of his powers. Leyne had a gift of eloquence almost as electric as Meagher's, and a gift of humour to which Meagher made no approach.[1] He died in the arms of a man whom I had induced him to take with him in this enterprise — a young artist, from Bantry, who

---

[1] His squibs, signed "Zozimus," in the revived *Nation* were unfortunately on temporary topics chiefly, otherwise they would have proved of enduring interest. A specimen or two will be found in a note at the end of the chapter.

became known to me through some graphic contributions to the *Nation,* and who in the end made himself known to Ireland and Irishmen throughout the world as an orator of singularly persuasive power, a writer of rare *verve* and skill, and a patriot of unwavering devotion.[1]

In the progress of public business we now found the influence of Dr. Cullen at work against us at every step. In London, the Whig members boasted that they, not we, had the sympathy and confidence of the bishops. When Lucas contended for a more just and liberal arrangement with respect to Catholic chaplains in the army and navy, he was assured by members of the Government that the heads of his Church were content with what they had done. In effect the Apostolic Delegate was the leader of the Irish Whigs. When he came to Ireland the mission with which he was charged was understood to be to bring the Church into stricter harmony with the discipline of Rome. But to this legitimate and salutary purpose he very plainly added a design for which it was contended that he had, and could have, no authority, the design of regulating the politics of the country at his discretion. If such a task were admissible, it is difficult to conceive any one less qualified to undertake it. He was unacquainted with Ireland, unskilled in the principles of Parliamentary government, and slow to comprehend or accept new

[1] A. M. Sullivan.

ideas. He came from Rome enraged against the secret societies as the disturbers of Christendom, and confounded Parliamentary opposition with Continental Liberalism, which, from the necessity of its position, was driven to conspire. His idea of a social and political organisation for Ireland was understood to be one modelled on the Government of Rome, where the supreme authority resided in a few great ecclesiastics, and laymen counted for nothing. But Ireland was Democratic and Catholic to the core. Though the people were profoundly devoted to the Catholic faith, wrong and resistance of it had trained them into hatred of arbitrary power, and it would have been as difficult to induce them to accept the political rule of Rome as of London.[1] He was no doubt alarmed with absurd rumours and exaggerations by the Catholic gentry and officials who surrounded him; but he started with a profound confidence in his own judgment as a sure guide in all difficulties. When he changed his political action he offered no explanation, and would have been affronted if any one had expected him to justify himself. He was taking his course after the best consideration of the circumstances, and the business

---

[1] The young men of the day were described by an eminent contemporary poet as—

"Kindly Irish of the Irish,
Neither Saxon nor Italian."

of laymen was to follow, in admiring silence if possible, but, at any rate, without dissent or criticism. When he had to choose between the leaders of the Tenant League and the deserters from it, it ought not to have been a difficult task. On one side were men who renounced all the personal advantages which ambition seeks in a political career, that they might help a people in sore extremity; on the other, men who confessedly sought their own interest in the first place, if not exclusively. But it was with the latter he took his place. One of the tasks he undertook at this time was to establish a Catholic University. It was a wise and necessary work which carried with it the sympathy of every generous heart. But from the beginning the Archbishop aimed to control it by his individual will without the aid or concurrence of others who had as clear a duty, or as clear an interest in its success. Liberal contributions were given by the Irish all over the world—given indeed again and again—but funds are only one of the conditions of success. Dr. MacHale separated from him first, then the eminent man who had undertaken to control the institution as its Rector, the present Cardinal Newman; the best of the middle-class were driven to despair of the project by the method of government adopted at the outset. In the education of their children they were to have no part except to subscribe the necessary funds. The committee which he selected to revive Collegiate learning, which had once its virtual seat in this island, did not contain one layman of adequate intellect or culture. There were twenty-four members, of whom eight were bishops and eight priests; and eight were laymen—mere wooden figures, set up for show. The most notable were Thomas Meagher, M.P., a respectable citizen in his proper place; and Charles Bianconi, who, as some one suggested, was a man of large reading—but it lay among way-bills chiefly.

When the session closed, some of Lucas's friends in England, stung by the unfair treatment to which he had been subjected, determined to present him with a testimonial for his Parliamentary services to the cause of religion. The measure of Dr. Cullen's enmity is furnished by the fact that he wrote to an English bishop recommending him to discourage the tribute. Though he was gifted with an exceptionally vigorous physique, constant labour and responsibility began to tell upon Lucas by this time. Mr. Potter, one of our colleagues, was reported to be dying at Limerick, killed, like William Cobbett, by the total change of habits which the late hours in Parliament imposed, and I found myself in a scarcely more hopeful condition. A brain constantly overworked and a body stinted of fresh air and exercise brought on an intense dyspepsia which our public troubles were not calculated to allay. I was advised to travel for a time, and at the end of the session I went to make some personal acquaintance with the peasant proprietors of France and Belgium. The news which followed me from Ireland from time to time did not tend to make the excursion balsamic. A quarrel sprang up between Lucas and Shee, which found its way into the newspapers. A Conference was summoned as usual in the autumn; but the Parliamentary leader, instead of giving his assistance, wrote a letter to the Castle organ,[1] justifying himself for his refusal to attend. To carry his difficulties to such a confidant was a symptom which could scarcely be mistaken. "A Conference," he affirmed, "would be of no use till a union with the North was renewed," a union which he knew the North had broken by abandoning the principles of Crawford's bill and of Independent Opposition. But he was prepared to abandon these principles himself. His main reliance was on the Government, who had declared that legislation was no longer necessary—

"It is our duty, (he said,) as sensible and honest men, not to allow a most difficult question to be made an engine of internecine strife or party vexation, but to give to the Government under which we live our best assistance in a fair endeavour to effect its settlement."

Only two members of Parliament attended the Conference, and no Northern delegate, but there was a

[1] *Dublin Evening Post.*

considerable number of priests and farmers present. The original principles and policy of the League were re-affirmed, and it was resolved to appeal to the country through a series of county meetings.

A friend, who was a vehement Nationalist, but also a Catholic, as obedient to authority in its legitimate sphere as Lucas, wrote me at this time of a danger becoming more and more menacing—

"The Roman policy towards this country has undergone a complete change, and one hostile to its nationality. Until O'Connell's death Rome, or at least an influential party there, believed in the possibility of an independent Catholic State here, capable, with France, of strong action on England. Since O'Connell's death they see only the chance of a Red Republic. But England has shown extraordinary symptoms of conversion. These were recognised in the new Hierarchy and the Papal Aggression. Then they were again forced into an attitude of hostility. This all changes again, however, when Lord Aberdeen (who, to an extraordinary degree, enjoys the confidence of Roman statesmen) attains office, and offers it to the Catholics who defended 'Papal aggression.' Then Rome returns to her design of treating Ireland as an intrenched camp of Catholicity in the heart of the British Empire, capable of leavening the whole empire—nay, the whole Anglo-Saxon race—and devotes every nerve to that end. But the first postulate of it is the pacification of Ireland. Ireland must be thoroughly imperialised, loyalised, welded into England. Paul Cullen succeeds Castlereagh. You may well believe that it is slowly my mind has come to this conviction, but believe me it is the key that reads everything that has been meeting us, we knew not how, for the last two years. I will write upon it the minute you assent, and I think in a way well weighed and orthodox. The truth is it has so beset my mind for months that I can think of nothing else. And you meet whiffs of it everywhere in the air so that it seems to be like some huge atmosphere of choke damp, only needing a spark to kindle it. We [Nationalists] must give up Ireland unless we face it. And for a variety of reasons this is the very day, the very hour, and the very minute."

The theory described was undoubtedly the policy of the Apostolic Delegate; how far he acted under authority and instructions from the Holy See was still doubtful. It was a subject of complaint among ecclesiastics that he never exhibited the instrument which specified the nature and extent of his powers; and in the end it was discovered that the policy was entirely his own.

The first of the county meetings was fixed to be held at Callan early in November. It was preceded by a correspondence between Father Keeffe, secretary of the preliminary committee, and Sergeant Shee, in which it became too plain that the learned member for the county had gone quite over to the Government and was in training for the seat on the English bench which he finally obtained. When the correspondence seemed likely to endanger the Sergeant's re-election the Bishop of Ossory interposed with a mandate ordering Father Keeffe to pursue the controversy no further. As the day of meeting approached he followed up this measure by a more arbitrary stroke of authority. Father Keeffe was forbidden to attend the meeting in his own parish or to take any further part in the public affairs of Ireland. The *locus in quo* was a marvellous place for the experiment of excluding priests, to begin. Half the population had been already lost by cruel evictions, the churches were more than half empty, there were two thousand paupers in the workhouse, and two priests had already died of fever caught in attendance on them.

As one of the founders of the first Tenant Protection Society, Father Keeffe was a man who could not be spared; but the principle was of still more importance than the man. If a Whig bishop was at liberty to exclude a priest of unblemished character from public life, the example was sure to be imitated by other Whig bishops; and the public cause in which we were engaged must necessarily fail. The experiment was crucial. Already such of the clergy as thought it their duty to accept implicitly the direction of bishops in politics or who loved peace better than the public interest, and a few who had private ends to secure, were at the beck of the Castle; if the courageous and high-principled could be silenced by authority, what hope remained? It had been proved by repeated experiments that without the aid of the local clergy elections could not be won. There was no ballot to shelter the voter from the vengeance of his landlord; there was no Land law fencing him from eviction. For the chance of obtaining rights common to his class in all other civilised countries the Irish peasant had to stake his existence at the hustings almost as nakedly as a soldier does going into battle, and it is small wonder if men of simple minds saw the near and certain danger more clearly than the distant advantage. The League priests taught them where their true interest and safety lay, and this was their offence. After the lapse of a generation, when the facts can be judged dispassionately, I affirm that the class against whom this policy was directed were among the best ecclesiastics in the Irish Church and were drawn into politics by a generous sympathy with wrongs and sufferings of which they were the daily witnesses. If men who trafficked in Government places were to be supported by episcopal authority, and independent priests repressed, the contest was at an end. What must ensue we knew full well. In 1832 O'Connell obtained a body of forty Repeal members. A couple of years later he came to an agreement with the Whigs, and thirty of the forty procured offices or honours for themselves, and were heard of no more in National politics. In 1846 O'Connell's sons obtained a much smaller party, but it had gone in the same way. And once again were the representatives of Ireland to be set up for sale? It is insensate to speak of any corporation of men as if they were of strictly identical principles and feelings; and some priests were, no doubt, convinced Whigs from sympathy with the Catholic gentry, and a few, who had once wielded immense influence for public ends, had latterly set up political hucksters' shops, in which they bartered their influence for favours bestowed on their relatives and friends. But the bulk of them were by nature, experience, and sympathy, the truest friends and the safest guides the people could hope to find. Without their aid O'Connell could have no more united the Irish people than Charles Edward could have raised the Highlanders without the aid of their chiefs. But it was not on the platform or the hustings their service was most indispensable. No one could know Ireland without being familiar with cases in which a priest, unknown till the occasion called him forth, planted himself in the path of some local oppressor, like a *deus ex machina*. If these strong and skilful counsellors could be corrupted or cowed, the hope of saving the people vanished away.[1]

[1] An occasional contributor to the *Nation* described with rare insight and knowledge the conditions which go to make Irish priests controversialists of unusual power. " Birth, early associations, the course of studies at Maynooth, and the nature of the clerical life in country districts, all combine to give the Irish priest his most striking mental characteristic—*strength*. Sprung for the most part from the farmer class—a class who think directly if coarsely ; growing up among the fields, in vigour of body and mind ; fed at college on the old classics, on the masculine logic of the schools, on the subtle but accurate distinctions of moral theology, and the mighty eloquence of the Fathers ; coming forth into a position of labour, power, and responsibility ; open

When this transaction happened I was slowly returning from the Continent, still somewhat invalided. But a letter from Lucas communicating the facts drew me into the arena on the instant.[1] At Callan we had a hasty

to all the invigorating influences of nature, as many a stormy ride by night through the mountains might testify; and neither weakened by indolence nor by the emasculating influence of desultory and hasty reading, the Irish priest for the most part retains a hardiness of thought and language rare in this age. Coarse it may often be and unrefined, but still the stuff is in it— and we have never seen a sophism so completely strangled or a fallacy dashed so heartily to pieces as in occasional writings of the Irish clergy. When the New Reformation crusade was preached through Ireland some twenty years ago its orators were met almost in every parish by some obscure priest, who with vehement energy, with theology at his fingers' ends, with ridicule, anger, and indomitable logic, encountered and defeated them. When with this rude force and learning is combined the cultivation and mastery over language which familiarity with the *English* classic writers alone can give, the result is such writing as we occasionally see coming from some unknown country priest, and which it would be hard to parallel elsewhere—terse, eloquent, idiomatic— with a grip like a vice, and a broad vein of humour. But such a combination is rare. For the most part the talents and acquirements of the country clergy either lie torpid or else are unskilfully handled—the force occasionally running riot for want of this cultivation."

[1] "I hope you are quite strong again. We need you and all your strength. You may have seen that a meeting is to be held at Callan on Sunday next. This morning news came that in consequence of his letter to Sergeant Shee, in last week's *Nation*, the Bishop has *commanded* Father Mat. Keeffe to abstain in future from politics. This new order of things will require very careful and very resolute handling; and if there were no other reason, your presence at Callan will be absolutely necessary.

conference, and agreed upon a line of action, which was carried into immediate operation. To endure a stroke so fatal to the national interest in silence at any bidding would have been base, and we resolved to combat it with all our strength.

The meeting was remarkable for numbers and enthusiasm, but still more for the unequivocal manner in which it separated from the policy of the bishop and the county member. It was estimated that ten thousand farmers of Kilkenny and Tipperary attended. The chair was occupied by the archdeacon of the diocese who bore emphatic testimony against the party with whom Sergeant Shee was now associated. Another archdeacon, the able and venerable Fitzgerald, of Rathkeale, made it plain that the Ossory discipline was not likely to be tamely accepted by the second order of the clergy—

"I read in some old-world history (he wrote) of Lestock and Mathews, two captains, who, from mutinous or cowardly impulses, fled from the battle, leaving their rough old admiral, Benbow, to defeat and death. When they returned to England they were turned out of the service with ignominy, and their swords broken over their heads. Pity they had not to deal with the tenderhearted folks of Athlone, or Sligo, or Carlow. Bonfires and illuminations and triumphal arches would have awaited Lestock and Mathews. I can imagine the

Do, therefore, come, for God's sake, unless the field is to be abandoned at once."—Lucas to Duffy, Oct. 25, 1854.

Very Rev. Father ——, or the patriotic and eloquent Father ——, returning the swords and expressing a hope (a hope not likely to be disappointed) that they would use these weapons as nobly and honourably as before. (But irony, after a little, proved an inadequate vehicle of his feeling, which broke into naked indignation.) The representation of a borough or a county is the mightiest weapon for good or evil to the Celtic race and the Celtic Church that an Irishman can wield in our times; and is it not evil of the worst kind to commit that all-powerful weapon to the dishonest, traitorous hands—to the felon hands of those who falsely and perfidiously violate their solemn pledges? To me it would appear that the parties who select such as these to sit on that awful tribunal where the doom of the Irish race is in the balance is to share in the guilt of him who opened the gates of Rome to Alaric, or of the fisherman who piloted the Algerine Corsair into the haven of Baltimore to visit midnight slaughter on the sleeping and unsuspecting town."

Father Aylward, a leading priest of the diocese, moved a resolution, calling on Sergeant Shee to attend the next Conference, and accept its instructions respecting the bill with which he had been intrusted, on pain of forfeiting the confidence of his constituents. And Father Tom O'Shea, who lay as completely at the mercy of the Bishop as his colleague who had been silenced, spoke with his usual distinctness and vigour. Patrick Lalor, of Tinakill, called attention to the fact that Sergeant Shee, who was pledged to accept nothing less than the principles of Crawford's bill, had introduced a measure, as his latest proposal, which would leave the tenant in a worse condition than it found him.

Father Cahill declared that the most melancholy result of political desertion was that it led the people to distrust even those who were faithful. "For the future," he said, "when a Whig and a Tory contest a constituency in which I have an interest I will say to the people—Take your choice; one is as bad as the other. If a pledge-breaker stands I will support an open bigot, like Spooner or Chambers, in preference. But when a man makes his appearance professing the principles of Lucas, Duffy, and Moore, if I am satisfied from his antecedents that he is of sterling stuff, I will teach the people that he is of the creed outside of which there is no political salvation for Ireland."

Lucas addressed himself to the question which was uppermost in all minds. He announced that the well-beloved priest of Callan was forbidden by ecclesiastical authority to take any part whatever in public affairs. Father Keeffe was determined to practise the most exemplary obedience to his bishop. But the ultimate authority of the Church was the Supreme Pontiff who sits at Rome, the successor of St. Peter, whose Church is the mother and mistress of all Churches, who rules over all local ecclesiastical authority, and who has the right to decide in all causes in the last resort. As a loyal and obedient son of the Church, he and other members of Parliament were resolved to bring before the Holy See, for its official decision, the question, whether the honest clergy of Ireland were to be silenced by authority and their mouths closed for ever? What the clergy of Ossory, what the clergy of other dioceses in Ireland, might consider it their duty to do he was not in a condition to say; but as regards laymen and politicians, before a month was over some of them would cross the Channel and find themselves, with the blessing of God, beneath the shadow of the Vatican. "Let no man say," he added, "that in doing this—in making an appeal from the decision of Ossory to the decision of Rome—they are guilty of disrespect to the bishop of this diocese. The ablest and most pious bishop, with the best intentions, is, after all, but a fallible man. There is no infallibility under Heaven but in the Chair of St. Peter. If the final decision of the Church closed the mouths of honest priests, and upheld pledge-breakers, place-beggars, and all those who made politics a dishonest game, he, speaking in the name of some there present, but speaking, above all, his own conviction, would declare that he saw no other course for honest and sane men to take but to wash their hands of public affairs altogether, and to abandon all hope of protecting the rights and interests of Ireland in the Parliament of Great Britain."

At the public dinner which followed the meeting I

reiterated the declaration which Lucas had made on our behalf. I had come there, I said, almost without visiting my own home, because the stroke aimed at Father Keeffe, which was the first open exercise of a policy long pursued in secret, was one fatal to the people's interest. Whether the Bishop of Ossory had exceeded his legitimate authority I would not undertake to say, but of one thing I was certain, honourable men would decline to maintain a contest with bigots and oppressors in the House of Commons if they were to be betrayed at home by bishops of their own Church. No one was ignorant of the case of Father Doyle, of Ross, or of the withdrawal of Father O'Shea from the Louth election.[1] English bigots demanded an act to exclude priests from politics, and the Whig Bishops accommodated them with a discipline which was equivalent

[1] The result of this banishment of Father Doyle furnishes a curious illustration of the force of individual character. The parish was Ramsgrange, where he set to work at once with characteristic vigour to perform his new duties. He settled down for life, and has been for twenty years parish priest in his place of banishment, and has made it notable as the centre of fruitful and edifying work. It contains one of the largest churches in the diocese, efficient Catholic schools, a glebe house on the same scale as the church; out of proportion it seemed to the simple life of the pastor, till its real purpose was disclosed by its transformation into a convent for middle class education. The banished curate has become a Canon and one of the Council of the Diocese, and is still a tribune of the people, whose advice guides the county in any public emergency.

to an act. It was fortunate for religion that there was a tribunal to which a bishop must be as submissive as a layman, and to this tribunal the case would be carried—

"I will not anticipate the decision, but if there is not protection for the second order of the clergy—for that order whose zeal and devotion, whose sacrifices and whose courage won and maintained the liberties of the Irish Church—I, for one, will feel it a duty to throw up my seat in Parliament and not keep up the show of a battle in London which is betrayed and defeated at home."

The patronage of the Bishop did not protect Sergeant Shee from stern rebuke. Speaking to the toast of the Independent party in Parliament, Father O'Shea expressed a hope that the member whom they had elected with so much pains and with so much enthusiasm would not disgrace an honourable name; would not become a by-word, like Scully, Keogh, and Sadleir. He trusted he would not disgrace his constituents, and if he did he would be the first renegade of the party returned by the influence of the Irish Tenant League. He fancied he knew the whole soul and mind of Duffy and of Lucas—he thought he knew and understood the spirit and chivalry of Moore, the honesty of the member for Louth, and the integrity and highmindedness of M'Mahon; and he believed he himself would become a traitor when these men would sully their glorious cause.

The immense population of Tipperary was summoned to the second county meeting at Thurles. Five-and-twenty thousand persons were said to be present, and as many as sixty-two priests had signed the requisition. The principles of the League Bill and of Independent Opposition were reaffirmed as the creed of the party. On the Ossory discipline Moore confirmed what had been said by his colleagues at Callan—

"I solemnly declare, before God and man, that in what I say at this moment I am not guilty of the slightest exaggeration. I believe that to place an interdict upon the clergy—in their efforts to vindicate the social and religious rights of their people—to be the most wicked, because the most subtle and the most dangerous, of all the penal laws by which it has been sought to damn and degrade us."

It was vain to seek Tenant-right, it was vain to seek any honest end in Parliament, or to attempt the redress of any wrong till this question was decided. And he reiterated the pledge to retire and leave the responsibilities of public affairs on the bishops, if the appeal to Rome proved unsuccessful—

"If Father Tom O'Shea, whose name is a household word under every poor man's roof in Ireland—if Father Keeffe, whom every honest friend of the poor man's cause has learned to regard as one of its staunchest defenders, are no longer to have the right, in this free country, to exercise their own free will, to confront backsliding and rebuke bad faith, I for one will be but too well content to retire from a conflict in which success will be no longer possible, and perseverance scarcely honourable—until in the hour of peril and disaster, which inevitably follows upon perfidy and corruption, these shallow plotters shall seek to defend themselves against the results of their own miserable intrigues in the adoption of an honest policy."

It has been questioned by precipitate critics if the leaders were justified in retiring even in the worst contingency. This is hard, and somewhat unequal, justice. In recent times the defection of a single constituency, the opposition of a majority of his colleagues on one point of policy, if persisted in, has been held to justify the leader in threatening to resign his functions. But here there was not a single constituency since the general election which had *not* been guilty of defection; the majority of the party had openly deserted, and the districts in the island reputed to be most national—Tipperary, Cork, Limerick, Clare, and Galway —permitted their representatives to vote habitually against the policy and the leaders of the party.

Priests learned in canon law declared that the Church did not require blind obedience to exceptional rules, still less to arbitrary caprice. What she exacted was submission to well-understood and specific law, which she did not permit bishops any more than priests to violate. An appeal to Rome was therefore determined on. Father Keeffe resolved to carry his own case to Propaganda, and it was proposed to commission two deputations—one lay, the other clerical—to represent the public question to the Holy See.

When we took stock of our affairs at the opening of the new year, they might well seem desperate if this new stroke could not be averted. We had opposed to us the Government, the aristocracy, and the Established Church, and a decided majority of the Catholic bishops; the middle class, if not hostile, were indifferent, and the peasantry were weary of a contest which had yielded such trifling results. The party pledged to aid us in Parliament had gradually dwindled away, and not a single recruit was sent from Ireland to replace the deserters. A return of our losses in a three years' contest was published at the time, and, as it was strictly accurate, may be reproduced here as historical—

Deserters in 1852.

1. Castleross, Lord.
2. Fitzgerald, J. D. (now Lord Fitzgerald).
3. Higgins, Ouseley.
4. Keating, Robert.
5. Keogh, William.
6. Russell, J. W.
7. Sadleir, John.
8. Sadleir, James.
9. Scully, Francis.
10. Scully, Vincent.

Deserters in 1853.

1. Ball, John.
2. Burke, Sir Thomas.
3. Cogan, W. H. F.
4. Esmonde, John.
5. Fitzgerald, Sir John.
6. Grace, Oliver.
7. Kirk, William.
8. O'Brien, Cornelius.
9. O'Flaherty, Anthony.

DESERTERS IN 1854.

1. Bellew, Captain.
2. Bland, Loftus.

3. Shee, Sergeant.
4. Urquhart, Pollard.

DESERTERS IN 1855.

1. Greville, Colonel.[1]
2. Greene, John.
3. M'Cann, James.

4. O'Brien, Patrick (the present Sir Patrick O'Brien).

Not one Presbyterian minister remained in the Council of the League,[2] not one Catholic bishop was still an active member. In every election lost for two years quondam-members of the League co-operated with its opponents, and if a deserter had behaved with signal faithlessness he might count on presenting himself to the people, leaning, like Richard III., on two bishops. It was plain that if episcopal despotism could silence

[1] Colonel Greville was among the last to desert of those who did not remain faithful to the end. He became a Whig in 1855, and was created a peer in 1869.

[2] In the end Mr. Wm. Girdwood declared strongly for Independent Opposition, but the claims of his profession withdrew him from active politics; and he died very young. Mr. Underwood lingered on in the League, and when it ceased to exist was one of the founders of the Brotherhood of St. Patrick, a semi-revolutionary organisation. Mr. Bell, several years after the transaction described in this volume, withdrew from his office of Presbyterian minister, and associated himself in London and in New York with the Fenian Societies which had then come into existence.

the boldest priests who remained, no contest worth maintaining could be continued.

While the Roman mission was being organised Edmund Burke Roche, who from being a fiery Repealer in '44, and a Brigadier in '51, had become a steady Whig, was rewarded with a peerage. Cork, which he had represented for more than twenty years, became vacant, and the largest constituency in Ireland was called upon to pronounce upon the most urgent Irish interests. The Liberal electors were brought together in conference, and their proceedings illustrate the fatal make-believe which had succeeded to definite principles in so many minds. It was declared with much unction that they wanted a man who would promote not his own interest but the public interest, and who would represent not himself but his constituency. And it was solemnly resolved that the candidate accepted by them must act in opposition to all Governments not prepared to abolish the Church Establishment in Ireland, and pass Sharman Crawford's Land Bill. Several candidates presented themselves, among whom was Mr. Rickard Deasy, a successful barrister and a native of the county. He desired to enter Parliament as the directest road to promotion; but he is distinguishable from the Brigadiers by the signal fact that he made no mystery of his purpose. He declared that he would not join the party of Independent Opposition, and that if he were offered the office of Solicitor-General he would accept it.[1] After this declaration Mr. M'Carthy Downing, a member of the Council of the League,[2] inquired whether his acceptance of the office would not depend on the Government proffering it, making Sharman Crawford's bill a Cabinet question. Mr. Deasy was understood to reply in the affirmative. Some one else asked if he would act with Sadleir and Keogh, but he evaded giving an answer. Mr. Roche was a peer, and Dr. Power Governor of a Crown Colony, because they had followed these leaders; but Mr. Downing expressed himself perfectly satisfied. Three candidates went to the poll, but Mr. Deasy was elected. He became in succession Solicitor-General, Attorney-General, and a Baron of the Exchequer; and the Government, from whom he accepted these favours, no more proposed Sharman Crawford's Land Bill than Fergus O'Connor's Charter.

At the same time as the Cork election Cavan became vacant, and was addressed by a Tory and a Whig. The

[1] "He would never (he declared) sign the sentence of political ostracism which would be inflicted by the refusal to enter into the service of the Crown. The doctrine was unjust and unconstitutional, for it was the spirit of the Constitution that the servants of the Crown should be the representatives of the people. He would tell them that that was his ambition, provided he would not be compelled to sacrifice his principles for its attainment."—Speech of Mr. Deasy.

[2] Afterwards Home Rule member for the county Cork.

latter was a Catholic barrister, who had held office under Lord John Russell while he was passing his penal law against bishops. To support this candidate the Bishop of Kilmore took the field in person. With a cruel indifference to consequences he assured the people from the pulpit that they ran no risk in supporting Mr. Hughes, because even his opponents respected him. But the Whig bishop pleaded in vain; though the Catholic electors were in a great majority, the Tory was chosen.

With the mission to the Holy See the story of the League of North and South properly comes to an end. The appeal was necessarily a purely Catholic one, and Lucas's strong personal convictions and feelings intensified its character in this respect. But as some brief account of it is essential to complete the narrative of the marvellous rise and fall of the League. I furnish it in a concluding chapter.

NOTE ON CHAPTER IX.

MAURICE LEYNE'S SQUIBS.

Here are a couple of specimens—the first is a parody on a song of Maurice O'Connell's in the *Spirit of the Nation*; the second a parody on a well-known ballad by Thomas Davis—

RECRUITING SONG FOR THE "IRISH BRIGADE."

Air—"The White Cockade."

I.

Is there an idle patriot here
Whose pocket feels uncommon queer,
Who thinks "a seat," if not too dear,
Would bring him through another year?
    Come, let him wear the *white* cockade,
    And learn the spouter's blustering trade;
    'Tis for sich stuff a mimber's made;
    Oh, let him join the Brass Brigade!

II.

Who feared to speak in Forty-eight,
But slunk within the Castle gate,
And bowed and begged among the great,
A hungry spy, with outstretched plate?
    Come, let him wear, &c.

III.

Who's skilled to act as pamphleteer
To Clarendon or grim Napier,
And wheel about the coming year
If Aberdeen be new Premier?
    Oh, let him wear, &c.

IV.

Who fumed about the "Foreign Sec,"
Yet brings fat Saxons here on "spec"?
Who for the Tenants' rights can shout
Yet turn defaulting farmers out?
    Come, let him wear, &c.

V.

Who cants and roars about "the Church,"
Yet leaves his country in the lurch?
Who for a place when on the search,
Would shirk the case of Castle Birch?
    Come, let him wear, &c.

VI.

Who's weight to ride the recreant's race,
And take and hold the winning place?
Who to the Bishops can grimace,
But sell Kildare to Orange Naas?
    Come, let him wear, &c.

VII.

The people are our lawful prey;
Their suffrage keeps the dun at bay,
And Ultramontane pledges, they
Are "O'er the hills and far away."
    Then come and wear, &c.

VIII.

So, would you be our brave compeer,
Just drop a line to John Sadleir;
He'll do the job (and not too dear),
And straight you'll strut a Brigadier.
    Come then, and wear the *white* cockade,
    And learn the spouter's blustering trade;
    'Tis for sich stuff a mimber's made;
    Oh, come and join the Brass Brigade!

A BRIGADE BALLAD.

I.

Lord Derby is out, and the Brass Band is met,
And the member for Carlow is President yet;
With his glass in his hand, and the fox in his mien,
Cries he, "Comrades, a welcome to Lord Aberdeen!"
With bumpers and cheers they have done as he bade,
For Lord Aberdeen's 'listed the Irish Brigade!

II.

"Here's a health to the Pope!"—and they winked as they quaffed;
"Here's to old Sharman Crawford!"—and loudly they laughed;
"Good-bye to the pledges we took while ago,
Where Shannon and Barrow and Lough Corrib flow;
May we soon be in place!"—such a rumpus they made,
You'd have thought that mad drunk was the Irish Brigade!

III.

"Here's the list of appointments:" All silent they grow—
"For the Treasury, Sadleir; Solicitor, Keogh;
O'Flaherty's booked for a berth on Cork-hill;
All the rest will be paid from the Government till!"
So they rushed from their dinner, their claims to parade,
For tin is the want of the Irish Brigade!

IV.

They voted and speeched with this object in view,
Themselves to advance and the country to do,
But those who returned them as members of yore
Now angrily swear that they'll have them no more!
For a curse and disgrace to the cause they've betrayed,
Are the Traitors and Scamps of the Irish Brigade!

ZOZIMUS.

CHAPTER X.

THE MISSION TO ROME AND ITS RESULTS.

To Englishmen, so many of whom are persuaded that episcopal influence is supreme among Irish Catholics, these transactions will teach a lesson as new and significant as the union of North and South. Here was an archbishop who professed to be the confidential agent of the Pope, yet his policy was vehemently resisted by the mass of Irish Catholics. They appealed to the Pope to control him, because he was his agent, and in that character was using the powers conferred upon him at Rome to thwart and injure the interests of their country. Lucas, a Catholic Englishman warmly sympathizing with Ireland, and a trained polemic to whom ecclesiastical interests were the first consideration, naturally took up a position which corresponded with his individual convictions and duties—but the bulk of the Tenant Leaguers would have echoed the language in which O'Connell

THE MISSION TO ROME AND ITS RESULTS. 331

roughly embodied popular opinion in his day—"As much theology as you please from Rome, but no politics."

When it was determined to carry to the Holy See a complaint that the Apostolic Delegate was misusing his authority, it was a rare and exceptional circumstance that a layman was forthcoming, endowed with the knowledge, courage, and position necessary to prosecute such a complaint.

After consultation, it was agreed that a memorial, to be drawn up and signed by priests exclusively, should be put into immediate circulation, and when extensively signed be carried to Rome by a deputation of priests. That the Catholic members of Parliament should state the dangers which the Catholic interests intrusted to them suffered by the new policy in a memorial to be presented to the Propaganda by Lucas and one of our colleagues. The case of the two Callan curates— for Father O'Shea was ordered to refrain from politics immediately after the county meetings—was to be taken in charge by the clerical deputation, or by the appellants in person, as might be advised by competent counsellors in Rome. As far as opinion at home was concerned, Moore and I proposed to elicit a full expression of it on the subject of the appeal.

Lucas undertook his mission in no rash temper. At the outset he consulted theologians skilled in canon law and representative men among his constituents.

Dr. O'Hanlon, the Senior Professor of Theology in Maynooth College, advised that the appeal against the Ossory discipline was sound in principle and ought to be successful—

"I think (he said) the Holy See will never ratify the doctrine involved in the prohibition of the Bishop. To say that a priest should not interfere in politics is in other words to maintain that a priest, as such, in a vast variety of cases, should not employ either his influence or authority to deter or restrain men from the commission of sin. . . . . There is no use in concealing from ourselves the fact that the author of all this mischief is the Archbishop of Dublin. He has become far more willing and ready than poor Dr. Murray ever was to carry into effect the views of our Saxon Government in regard to this unfortunate country. In truth, he has been up to the present time regarded in Rome as the organ and mouthpiece of the Irish Church, and he has employed the influence thus acquired in endeavouring to subjugate prelates, priests and people, to the British Government. It is with this view that he has, in utter contempt of the recommendation of both priests and bishops, caused the rejection by the Holy See of several most worthy priests, and substituted in their places as prelates of our Church men who have little other merit than that of subserviency to his views and wishes."

Lucas reached Rome in the middle of December, and immediately waited upon several Irish prelates then in that city. In his first private report to his colleagues at home he said—

"I have seen and had conversations with Dr. MacHale, Dr. Derry, and Cardinal Wiseman. Dr. MacHale did not—nor did any one else—understand the whole scope of the business at first. On giving him a further explanation, and showing him the extent of the move we were making, he completely came round to our view, and expressed great satisfaction at the deputation, and spoke repeatedly with the greatest confidence as to the result. . . . The Archbishop had not read the memorial, but had heard of it, and thought some of the clauses about appointments to benefices, &c., might do harm. I made his Grace understand that the memorial was not drawn by me, but by the clergy, and expressed the genuine sentiments of those who drew it." [1]

The new Cardinal Archbishop of Westminster also took a favourable view of the mission. He was very gracious and friendly, and spoke with "a serious and composed earnestness which gave the impression of a fixed opinion and a settled purpose; and I may add (says Lucas) that both Dr. MacHale and Dr. Derry have been very favourably impressed with him."

Monsignore Talbot, brother of Lord Talbot de Malahide, was one of the Pope's chamberlains, and, from his constant access to his Holiness, a man of large influence. Lucas saw him a little later, and found him friendly, but not very sanguine.

Lucas's colleagues and clerical friends, who had undertaken to elicit and enlighten opinion in Ireland while he was at Rome, set to work vigorously. The priests' memorial was taken in hand by a clerical committee. Father Dwyer, of Doon, a prudent and gifted young curate of the archdiocese of Cashel, was secretary, and he had the aid of experienced friends, several of whom have since attained ecclesiastical rank

[1] Rome, 15th December, 1854.

or distinction, and two of whom are now bishops. The Callan priests prepared their own case, transmitted it to Lucas, and awaited further instructions. On behalf of the Parliamentary party, Moore and I threw ourselves on the country for sympathy and co-operation. Criticism on a bishop in Ireland, whenever a bishop had been subject to any criticism, had hitherto been uniformly meek and forbearing. But when the lives of the people and the essential liberties of the Church were at stake, forbearance was considered criminal, and long-repressed feeling burst out in a flood. The *Nation* took the lead: but several ecclesiastics wrote in the provincial Press, and others, at public meetings, exposed the fatal character of the new policy. Lucas had left no one behind to whom he would intrust this delicate task, and the *Tablet* restricted itself to copying articles from the *Nation* and reporting the provincial meetings—a circumstance which greatly increased my responsibility in dealing openly with questions which the community were accustomed to see passed over in silence. As the bishops aimed to control the politics of Ireland at their discretion, it was plainly declared that bishops had hitherto been the least intrepid or reliable class among the Irish people. At the Invasion a Synod of Bishops in Munster welcomed Henry II., and confirmed his claim to possess the island, an Ulster Synod, however, having taken a more patriotic course.

In the Middle Ages, bishops of English birth or selection were the bitterest enemies of Irish rights, and the worst defamers of the Irish name. At the Reformation a shameful proportion of the Episcopacy accepted the new doctrines to save their revenues. In the Confederation of Kilkenny, Charles I. had more partisans among the bishops than the Pope and the people together. In 1800 half the Episcopacy were Castle bishops, and supported the Union, and applauded Castlereagh and Cooke in language which would have been unbecomingly obsequious if addressed to Cardinal Fransoni or Cardinal Antonelli. If the second order of the clergy had accepted the advice of certain bishops a few years later no good Irishman would ever after have been permitted to attain a mitre. O'Connell declared that they favoured the project of giving the English Crown "an indirect but efficient power of nominating the Catholic bishops of Ireland, and vehemently discountenanced the opposition of the laity to that measure." The same spirit was still at work; every defeat of the League at the hustings was directly attributable to the influence of some Whig bishop. The Irish Church in its most disastrous days was saved from ruin by missionary priests and barefooted friars. There had always been patriot bishops who laboured and suffered and died for the people, but they were in a perpetual minority. If the doctrine of "No more priests in politics" was to prevail, it became necessary to inquire to whom was the political influence which priests now exercised to be transferred? Was it for their own benefit the Whig prelates meditated this portentous change? An article in the *Nation*, raising this grave question, concluded in these words—

"If they persist in enforcing the doctrine of 'No more priests in politics' it will become a clear duty in those who are not prepared to see the rights of this country jobbed away by English factions to push the principle to its natural limits, and insist upon 'No more bishops in politics.' . . . We believe it [the Episcopacy] will be disciplined and reduced to order by the authority of the Holy See. It is there the eyes of the country are turned. But if it be not, we foresee its political influence will not long survive its influence over the body of the priesthood. If it robs the priest of political power the people will strip it naked of the same, and the retribution will be just. If there are to be no more working priests in politics, why should there be any more mitred priests? If the priests who alone won Catholic Emancipation by strengthening the strong hands of O'Connell are to be silenced, let the episcopal priests, who (with some illustrious exceptions, past and present) were in courtly correspondence with the enemies of the people, be silenced also. If bishops insist upon no more priests in politics, let the people insist upon no more bishops."

It need scarcely be said that the proposal was to have "no more bishops" in politics, but the Whig Press declared that here was a project to abolish the Episcopacy; and a portion of the article, translated into Italian, was duly laid before the Propaganda by Dr. Cullen, to illustrate the evil designs and uncatholic opinions of the League party and Lucas's confederates at home.[1]

The Whig Press denied that any good Christian could desire to see priests engaged in politics. Had not St. Paul said, "*Nemo militans Deo implicat se in negotiis sæcularibus*"? The Leaguers naturally demanded, if this counsel of the Apostle meant that priests should refrain from public affairs, were all the cardinals and bishops who have been Ministers of State for the last fourteen centuries—were all the Nuncios and Legates who arbitrated peace and war and the disputed inheritance of realms—were all the priests and bishops who took sword in hand to fight for the liberty of their native soil or the secular rights of their people—were the Jesuits in Paraguay and in Europe—were the Irish priests, struggling for Catholic Emancipation, or the Belgian priests, fighting for national independence—living in rebellion to the law of God? Or was the instruction of St. Paul meant only for Ireland, and only in the latter half of the nineteenth century, and especially during the administration of Lord Aberdeen? Had it no force in the days of the Defence Association, when the Tories were to be ousted from power? And would it lose its authority the moment they resumed office? And was it intended for priests only, and not for bishops?

[1] Lucas's Correspondence.

Priests were very dangerously "entangled in secular affairs" when they were bartering their public support for some personal advantage—when they were scandalising the people by begging places for their own kith and kin—when they accepted free farms, or farms at a nominal rent, from oppressive landlords whom they sustained at elections—or when they discounted their ecclesiastical influence in any shape for personal advantage. But who would venture to say that the priest who was labouring to save the lives of his people in the land where their fathers died for the faith, to prevent their homesteads being rooted up, to check the exterminator and the Souper, and the lascivious bashaw of the parish—who would presume to contend that such a priest was not engaged in work of Christian charity? Who would say that he was entangled in secular affairs? In the history of Europe kings made scarcely a more prominent figure than ecclesiastical personages; they made laws and unmade them, founded States and plucked them down; framed treaties, and broke up alliances. The doctrine came from England; yet the early history of England was a history of priests. In the Saxon era it was open to debate whether the good St. Dunstan took the devil by the nose, according to the popular legend; but there was no doubt that he took a licentious king and a tyrannical nobility by the nose. In the Norman era St. Thomas a'Becket was a figure of as huge proportions as Henry II., and an ecclesiastic guided the barons who wrung the Magna Charta from the pusillanimous John. In our own day was not the sovereign of Rome a priest, and his Secretary of State and entire Executive ecclesiastics ?—

"Exclude priests from politics! It was for this object that English intrigue laboured for the last half century,"—*teste* Castlereagh's private correspondence with the Catholic bishops in '98 and '99; Quarantotti's controversy in 1814; Lord Clarendon's letter to the Archbishop of Corfu in '48. What brought Lord Minto to Rome? What brought Bulwer? What was Petre doing there at present? Whispering, lying, intriguing, with sleepless activity, for one end—to exclude Irish priests from Irish politics."[1]

If the policy succeeded, the people, hopeless of agitation, would fly to secret societies and violence. "No priests in politics" would set up the Ribbon Lodges again. It would fill to suffocation the stifling emigrant ship. The bigots predicted that the Catholic people would soon dwindle down to a minority in Ireland, and this policy gave the malign prediction a chance of being fulfilled.[2]

At the beginning of January the serious business of the mission commenced. Lucas had an official interview with Monsignore Barnabo, the Secretary of Propaganda. He was favourably known to this great official as Editor of the *Tablet*. But so far as he was a representative of

[1] *Nation.*   [2] *Ibid.*

the party of Independent Opposition he stood at a great disadvantage. Since Dr. Cullen had become a Whig his retainers in Dublin and at Rome vied with our natural enemies in misrepresenting us. It was reported to the Holy See that certain ungovernable priests who aimed to throw off the authority of their superiors, associated with laymen of a base ambition when they were not men of evil conduct and designs, were introducing disorder into the Church in Ireland. They thwarted the labours of the Apostolic Delegate to restrict the clergy to their natural duty—the cure of souls—mixed them up in worldly cabals, and even in violent and revolutionary designs. On one side, it seemed, were all the good ecclesiastics, who served God and performed their functions in silence; on the other, turbulent, reckless men, forgetful of their duty. The Apostolic Delegate was gradually restoring order, but it was necessary to strengthen his hand by new and more stringent rules of discipline by which evil-doers could be restrained, and, if necessary, punished; and the Secretary assured Lucas that new rules in the shape of Diocesan Statutes framed for Leinster were before Propaganda at that moment for their consideration.[1]

Lucas took the only course which promised the smallest success under the circumstances. He turned the tables on his opponents. He undertook to show that

Rome, December 23.

the Apostolic Delegate was not carrying out the policy of the Holy See, but a policy of his own, ill-conditioned in its nature and injurious to the interests of religion. That he had completely changed the tenor of his conduct in public affairs within two or three years, and was now repressing what he had before aided, and helping what he had hindered. That the priests whom he was discouraging were among the most pious and zealous in the Church, and that those whom he favoured were of a widely different character. That the laymen whom he was assailing had sacrificed every object of personal advantage and ambition to save a Catholic nation from extinction, while the laymen whom he favoured had habitually and notoriously sacrificed the interests of the poor and of religion to their personal advancement. That the prelates and other ecclesiastics whom he represented as the salt of the Church, living apart from political objects for the honour and glory of God, were, in truth, violent and often-selfish politicians, and had employed the tremendous spiritual powers conferred upon them for the service of God to promote the objects of the political party with which they were associated. It would be a calamity to create in Ireland a popular party opposed to the Church, and to set people loose in all public affairs from the influence of the Church and clergy; but if Dr. Cullen's views prevailed such would be the inevitable result, and they would mourn at Rome for many long years the troubles which bad advisers had brought upon them.

And he proceeded to contend, and demonstrate, that the proposed statutes, which were represented as necessary to restrain public scandals, would not at all restrain the only public scandals which had occurred in later times, but on the contrary were designed to repress those men who were zealous for the lives of the poor, and encourage those who bartered their influence for personal objects. He insisted that the Holy See was studiously misinformed on Irish affairs, and that it was invited, on the basis of this false information, to pursue a policy disastrous to the interests of the Catholic people and the Catholic Church; that O'Connell, after a long life of opposition to the English Government, had brought the greatest calamity on his country, and intensified the horrors of the famine, by an unhappy alliance with the Whig Government in 1846. The recent policy and proposed statutes of the Archbishop of Dublin were the embodiment and revival of these dangerous errors.

An indictment so clear and specific, raising such serious issues, and sustained by a man of the capacity and services of Lucas, seems to have alarmed the Secretary. He urged that a conference between Dr. Cullen, Dr. MacHale, and Lucas should be held at Propaganda, at which he would assist, and at which some middle course might be agreed upon.

THE MISSION TO ROME AND ITS RESULTS. 343

The conference with Dr. Cullen was finally brought about, it was believed, by the personal interposition of the Pope. The design was that an understanding might be arrived at which, if it proved acceptable to his Holiness, might be made a rule of action for the future—

"The conference (Lucas wrote to his friends) lasted two hours and a half, and of course I cannot give a shorthand report of it. A great deal turned on my speech at Callan, and on recent speeches and writings of others, also on Father O'Shea's conduct. On these things I said what may easily be imagined. Still speaking about the League, he took credit to himself for allowing perfect freedom of opinion, and alleged that he had recently promoted a clergyman whose connection with the League he regretted, and whom he had advised not to have anything to do with it; but still, though he continued a member of it, so unwilling was he to interfere with free opinion that he had actually made him a canon—Canon Redmond. Upon my honour he said that!

"I interrupted him by saying that his Grace forgot that before he made Redmond a canon, Redmond had done his best to damage the League, to serve the Government, and to damage those who had opposed the Government—namely, us. He said he did not see that there was any harm in supporting the Government; that if opposing the Government was a virtue, we ought in Italy to co-operate with Mazzini, and in Hungary with Kossuth; that the first duty of every Catholic was to support the Government, unless they attacked the Church. He then broke into a violent tirade against Duffy, whom he described as a wicked man, to act with whom after his conduct in 1848 was impossible until he had fasted fifty years on bread and water. I defended Duffy, as you may imagine, and referred to the evidence of Dr. Blake and Dr. Moriarty on his trial. At this time he became more violent. He said Duffy had been a party to getting the people massacred; ridiculed the notion of his being a pious man, declared he did not care what anybody had sworn; and turning upon me, said it was a shame, or discreditable, for me to say a word in behalf of such a man, or to act with him.[1]

"With regard to the services of any particular men in Parliament or elsewhere (which I did not press upon him, but somehow it got mentioned), he said Ireland would always produce plenty of excellent laymen; that if one set of men passed away, another would be there to supply their places. The meaning of this of course was that we might go to the devil if we liked. . . .

"I can't, of course, tell half that was said, but I have told enough to show the animus of the dialogue.

"On Dr. Cullen's part the conversation was carried on in a tone of shabby equivocation, ill-concealing, and not intended to conceal, a resolute purpose of defiance; and it rose into passion when he spoke of Duffy, whose recent articles seem not to have pleased him. But let all who read this understand that this passion and vehemence were the passion and vehemence of a man who is on the defensive, who has his back to the wall, who feels that his all is at stake, who, being

---

[1] A Castle bishop seems to be as inevitably an enemy and assailant of an Irish Nationalist as a Crown Prosecutor. More than a generation later Dr. Cullen's successor in the See of Dublin fell foul of my successor in the *Nation* at that time, with a condemnation as decisive. In the *Nation* of April 25, 1885, one may read this significant statement—"Talking to a distinguished foreign ecclesiastic on the day of the burial of the late A. M. Sullivan, he [Cardinal MacCabe] said—'The man they are burying to-day was a bad man; he was one of the wickedest men this country ever produced.'"—Letter of an Irish Catholic.

personally compromised with the Government, *cannot* do what the Pope wishes, and who is therefore determined to fight it out aginst the Pope and people, with every appearance of submission to the Holy See and compliance with its spirit."

The articles which had inflamed Dr. Cullen's temper to such a pitch were never rude or disrespectful, but they were painfully plain and direct. A specimen or two of the language most objected to are necessary to the veracity of the narrative—

"If some of the best priests in Ireland are sent to rot in bogs and morasses, if, among three thousand, no three have been found to undertake a mission to Rome in defence of their common right—if a bishop of the Church of God has mounted the platform with a man of the character and reputation of Mr. William Keogh—if the hopes of the country are low when they ought to be high and confident—if political profligacy has lost much of its horror in the eyes of people—we declare, in presence of God and man, that the chief cause of these perilous phenomena is the alliance between the Archbishop of Dublin and the Catholic agents of Dublin Castle. We see no reason for concealing it; on the contrary, the first step towards terminating the reign of terror is to proclaim it aloud—that fear of the Apostolic Delegate weighs like lead on the Irish priesthood, and renders all public action driftless and impotent. There is the fatal truth."[1]

And again—

"The *Times* accepts and adopts Dr. Cullen as a person 'who has merited the approbation and confidence of the English Government and Irish Executive;' 'who has

[1] *Nation.*

exercised his legatine powers with much discretion and in a manner to give satisfaction to the English Government;' and 'whose fall would be a loss to English interests and views.' There was a time, and Irish readers remember it well, when 'the Italian Monk,' with his 'pastorals against the polka,' and his 'astronomical craze,' was the favourite butt of the *Times*, and *Globe*, and *Advertiser*." [1]

Lucas was naturally of a different opinion from the archbishop about the necessity of plain speaking. Shortly after the conference he wrote to his wife—

"Tell Duffy I have read the *Nation* with real pleasure. I think he has done great service. When I wrote—if I wrote—querulously, it was because I was in exterior darkness, knowing nothing, and feeling shut out from the world. Let him know this. If Moore has not made up his mind to come before this reaches, let him not come at all. I am now in hopes that before he has started the affair may possibly be adjusted. Perhaps the Callan cases may make it linger; but it now looks nearer a settlement than it has yet done."

The most painful impression which this interview conveys is the disrespect with which Dr. Cullen treated Lucas throughout. From other sources I learned that he was imperious and contemptuous, and that Lucas was deeply wounded.[2] The space which separates an

---

[1] *Nation.*

[2] Ten years later I made the acquaintance at Rome of Father Mulhooly, then prior of San Clemente, who saw Lucas constantly during his mission, and sympathised warmly with him. He told me that in his judgment Lucas had no success, and could not, except in moments of temporary enthusiasm, have con-

archbishop, who was also an Apostolic Delegate, from a Catholic publicist, is naturally wide enough, but to Dr. Cullen it seemed immeasurable. Now that death has reduced both the interlocutors to their natural dimensions, his estimate will scarcely be confirmed by posterity. The publicist was a man endowed with rare and splendid gifts, with judgment, penetration, the patience that removes mountains, and the moral indignation which burns up false pretences like bramble; a man who, for the sake of God, devoted endowments which might have raised him to a first place in his own prosperous country, to the service of the poorest people and the most unprosperous nation in Christendom. When we are no longer dazzled by the cope and the mitre, which of us can fail to discern between Paul Cullen and Frederick Lucas that the layman was the better Christian and the born master?

Lucas had two interviews with the Pope, who treated him with special consideration, and applauded his

sidered that he had any. That in the interview with Dr. Cullen he was wounded and humiliated, and that his bitter disappointment was no doubt partly the cause of his illness, but he lived in Rome during an unhealthy season, and worked too closely at his Statement. In Father Mulhooly's opinion he had no chance of a victory at any time. In addition to Dr. Cullen's great position as Apostolic Delegate he had won the complete confidence of Monsignore Barnabo in '48, when he remained in Rome in charge of the Irish College while the other was in charge of the Propaganda.

defence of Catholic interests in the House of Commons, but signified mildly that he was less well content with his career as a journalist, as "the editor of the *Tablet* sometimes escaped from the kingdom of moderation into that of impatience." His Holiness at the close of the last interview intimated that if Lucas laid his views on Irish affairs before him in writing, he would give them his best attention. On this hint he determined to prepare an exhaustive Statement for the personal information of the Holy See, and began to work on it immediately.

While the business was proceeding in this fashion at Rome, the Castle Press in Dublin contained confident reports from week to week that Lucas had altogether failed. Cardinal Barnabo had received him coldly, it was alleged; and as he was not supported by any deputation from Ireland, and had produced no Memorial, he was regarded as merely fighting a personal quarrel of his own. His friends began to feel uneasy at the delay of the Priests' Memorial and Deputation. At public meetings in Tipperary, Wexford, and Mayo, which Moore and I attended in turn, the local clergy gave a warm sanction to the movement, agreed to emphatic resolutions, and applauded the strongest expressions of opinion. Sixty priests signed the requisition for the Wexford meeting, and the majority of them, with all their representatives in Parliament, assisted at the meeting and dinner; in Mayo the High Sheriffs for the past and present year sanctioned the movement; Moore spoke in the presence of a large body of priests, and the archdeacon of the diocese censured some of the Whig bishops by name. A number of signatures were gradually obtained for the Memorial, but they were not very numerous, and they were delayed or refused in places from which we were entitled to count on them most confidently. At the beginning of February Father Dwyer wrote to me in some dismay. He had received encouragement from every part of Ireland; but many priests who disapproved of Dr. Cullen's policy and desired to see it reversed, and were willing to express this opinion in their localities, made difficulties in signing a memorial attacking him so directly; and as respects the deputation, priests selected had pleaded ill-health, urgent local duties, and other excuses, which separately might be admitted, but, taken together, he thought, looked ominous. For want of willing seniors the committee had urged upon Father Dwyer to carry the Memorial and the correspondence to Propaganda himself, and he was disposed to do so if this were considered the best course—

"It is cruel (he said) to leave Lucas as he is; but is it worth while to send or go with our memorial at all? Letters which I have just received make me seriously ask this question. I find that only a few signatures of curates can be expected from Ferns. In Tuam it is an utter failure. We have forty-six signatures from Meath, the same number from Cashel, and not more than twenty-five from all the rest of Ireland. Father Doyle tells us to use the Wexford requisition and the clerical names attached to it and the resolutions at the meeting, instead of the memorial. That may be done; and the very numerous letters I have received from persons declining for special reasons to sign the memorial of which they approve, might also be used to show why the memorial is not more generally signed, whilst multitudes of priests are in their hearts in favour of it. . . . . Some dozen of the priests of Achonry, with the Vicar-General in the chair, passed strong resolutions in favour of the movement; their names were sent attached to the resolutions, but they have not yet signed the memorial. What do you think ought to be done?"

The difficulty which the Secretary encountered was increased by the personal entrance of the bishops into the controversy. Dr. Walsh wrote a letter to the Whig newspapers complaining that he was misrepresented in a document called a Memorial circulated for signature among priests in neighbouring dioceses. If he had exceeded the limits of his authority there was a right of appeal, and he courted an appeal to the proper tribunal. But the proper tribunal was not the public Press, or the people, or even the priests, but the Pope. After this publication many priests considered they were justified in refusing to sign a memorial arising out of a complaint where "inquiry was courted." To confine the remonstrance to the Callan case was the course they approved of. A little later the Archbishop of Dublin wrote a letter from Rome treating the appeal and the memorial as newspaper fictions. No memorial from Ossory or any other diocese complaining of any bishop or archbishop had been presented at the Propaganda; and no deputation lay or clerical was heard of at Rome, save one gentleman, who exhibited no credentials from any party.

These specific and authoritative statements had a decided success for a time, but there was a serious and damaging reaction when it became known that the Bishop of Ossory, who courted inquiry, refused Father Keefe permission to go to Rome to support his case—

"His lordship (a local priest wrote to me) peremptorily refused, and said he will not give him leave of absence unless he receives an official summons. Father Keefe assured him that he had received directions from his advocate, through Mr. Lucas, to go over at once to Rome, and he produced the letter. The Bishop replied that that was not a summons, and that he would not allow him to go. What law he acts under I don't know; certainly 'tis not canon law."

By this stroke the Callan complaint was indefinitely postponed. The secret influence of the Apostolic Delegate stopped the Memorial as effectually. It was at first believed that the Archbishop of Cashel, in whose diocese it had a multitude of supporters, was, at bottom, friendly to it. But when Father Dwyer requested his permission to carry the document to Rome, he positively refused. Some of his clergy urged him to reconsider this decision, but he replied that he would not interfere with Father Dwyer's liberty of action; he was free to go to Rome if he chose, but if he went he must sever his connection with the province of Cashel. Other bishops were sounded without success. "Our friends in the Episcopacy (one of the committee wrote) are fainthearted, vacillating, and afraid of their shadows. They shrink from being mixed up in any way with what might bring trouble on them at home or abroad." Those who were most disposed to assume that bishops must necessarily be right could least understand their prohibiting an appeal to the supreme authority.[1]

When Lucas learned that the hope of a deputation was at an end he was greatly moved. But his anger did not make him unjust. He made all the allowance that could reasonably be expected, and lamented the failure of the cause rather than his personal discomfiture. He felt relieved, he declared, from a necessity of consulting any one's wishes but his own in his further action, and intimated that the moral torpor in Ireland might necessitate his reconsidering his relations with that country.

[1] As Louis Napoleon figured as "Celui-ci" in the correspondence of the Opposition, Dr. Cullen was commonly spoken of as "Paul." His authority and influence as Apostolic Delegate seemed destined to last for a lifetime, and one of the two or three bishops who held by the League answered a request to aid the appeal to Rome by replying with a smile that such affairs could only be regulated satisfactorily in a *Paulo-post* future.

"ROME, *March 5th.*

". . . . I had written a much longer letter, but the receipt of your letter, and that of Fr. Dwyer's, of Doon, filled me with such indignation that I tore the letter up, intending at that moment to write nothing. Indeed, what is the use of writing at all, or of what value is Irish public opinion? In a matter which primarily concerns the priests, out of twenty-seven dioceses and 3,000 priests, not one can be found to give me an effective lift after I have spent three months in Rome upon an affair in which it is my personal interest to be defeated, and in which I am making every conceivable sacrifice of interest and convenience on public grounds alone. Fr. Dwyer, of Doon, has done his best, and I am heartily thankful; nor do I blame any individual, because I don't know who personally is to blame: but I feel that it is simply impossible to save or serve a people, 3,000 of whose picked men are capable of such inconceivable cowardice. Think of the Wexford priests! God help us! I am, it seems, to make their meeting and resolutions to stand in place of signatures to a memorial. I neither can nor will do anything of the sort. Simply in conversation I make it serve for proof of the reign of terror which prevails in Ireland, and which bows every head down to the dust in hopeless servility. My first impression was to send in no representation of my own, but to content myself with a formal presentation of the two memorials, and to return home content with having accomplished nothing. But calmer reflection has made me more inclined to the belief that, being here, it is a sort of duty to do what more I can do with little additional inconvenience—that is, to send in to the Pope statements of my own on points about which I know that information is needed. Perhaps ultimately this may be my decision; but after what has happened I have a right to say that I feel myself completely absolved from any obligation towards anybody else in this business; free to remain in Parliament, if elected, or to quit Parliament whatever turn the affair takes, and at liberty to break off from my labours here whenever I please."

I read this letter with something like consternation. The desertion of which he complained moved my anger as deeply as his own. But I differed from him as to the line of duty which this disaster prescribed. I could not admit that he was "completely absolved from any obligation to anybody else in the business." Some of us had not deserted him, or failed to do anything which we undertook. Some of us had staked the peace and happiness of life on the issue as unequivocally as he had. I wrote immediately to say that I held fast by the policy we had jointly announced at Callan, and which he had repeated at Propaganda and in his interview with the Pope—that if the new discipline could not be restrained by authority, we would retire from Parliament and leave the Whig bishops nakedly responsible for the failure of the people's cause. We could not succeed without the patriot priests, and I was not disposed to occupy a position where we would be merely a convenient screen for the Castle bishops. If he continued in Parliament to promote certain Catholic interests, as I surmised was his purpose, that was a design in which I, at any rate, would not engage. I entered the League and the House of Commons to preserve the Irish people from extermination, in the hope that they might afterwards be able to regain their national rights, and no other purpose, however good in itself, would be a substitute for this one. I was still of opinion that, if his mission had failed, we ought immediately to resign our seats.

In his reply Lucas contended that the time had not come for a decision; but though I continued of opinion that the time had come, and that the postponement would rob the transaction of character and significance, I postponed further controversy till his return from Rome.[1] It is probable that he did not determine his course at the moment, but he pondered more and more on the duty of concentrating himself on Catholic affairs. Constant labour and anxiety, and the climate of Rome since the southern heat had set in, tried his health seriously. He was suffering from asthma, bronchitis, and the sleeplessness which a brain disturbed with overwork or care rarely escapes. His personal interests and duties were postponed to the task he had undertaken,

[1] Lucas's reply on the cardinal point was, in these terms— "I hope to be home in time to consult with you and others about the course to be taken. My inclination is to make it a matter of common deliberation, and to act with you at all events, and with those friends out of Parliament whose opinion we jointly value. I take it that *in* Parliament nobody thinks of retiring but ourselves. . . . Put my name to your Smith O'Brien memorial. I think Alexander II. will disturb your programme of 'Gladstone or Bright at last.'"

but their ghosts could not always be laid; and though he was careful to assure his wife that his health was reasonably good, he sometimes forgot, I fear, in the absorbing interests of his mission, precautions without which no one is long well. His complete neglect of the *Tablet* would have been fatal to any journal less rooted in the confidence of its readers.[1]

His letters home were very touching; they vibrate with the passion of a strong, tender man, uttering the inmost feelings of his heart.

"I am ever thinking (he wrote to his wife) of my poor dear little Angy (his son Angelo, now Rev. Angelo Lucas) and it adds to my troubles and anxieties that I fear some day when he grows older he may look back to this very time when I am hazarding everything for what I believe to be my duty, and may reproach me in his own mind for having, in pursuit of a vain endeavour, thrown away his interests and neglected my duty to him. The fear that this may happen, and the thought that it may be in some degree true, are often very bitter to me. Poor, dear boy! I love him as my own soul. I sit and think of him and you almost for hours together sometimes;

---

[1] The *Tablet* was managed during his absence by Dr. Tormey, a young priest, who had won distinction in Maynooth as a Dunboyne student, and since he had been on the mission was known for discourses of striking vigour and freshness. In his correspondence home Lucas expressed his gratitude over and over again to Father Tormey, and Mr. Michael Dwyer, the assistant editor, for maintaining the spirit of the paper so effectually; and to Mr. O'Byrne, who had entire control of the business department. But the individuality of a great writer is the soul of his journal, and no zeal or ability can compensate for its absence.

and I pray God, if it be His will, to remove this burden from me and to take me out of public life. I hope you won't think from this that I am very downhearted. On the contrary, I am, on the whole, very cheerful and very ready to do the work in hand; but these thoughts come over me sometimes, and then I yearn with an inexpressible desire to get back to my wife and child."

Of personal discomfort he rarely uttered a complaint. In March he wrote to his friend Rev. Dr. Whitty, Provost of Westminster:—

"I am now for the first day in my more comfortable and expensive lodgings. They look out very pleasantly over chimney-pots and tiles, from the 3tio piano of 124 Via di Due Macelli on to the upper part of the palace and gardens of the Quirinal; and up to this hour, half-past two o'clock, the sun is on the bedroom, and it is very warm. . . . I am very well, and the weather heavenly."

The slow process of collecting facts and carefully authenticating them, so that nothing might be presented to the Pope which was not ascertained to be true, was a trying labour. His correspondence for this purpose was immense; and the slow, irregular post between Dublin and Rome doubled the toil. The memorial was gradually extending to a volume. In April he had written "as much as four or five long articles in the *Dublin Review*," and his work was far from being finished. There were still three or four chapters to write, but he expected to have them out of hand early in May.

"Suppose them done (he wrote towards the end of April), the Vice-Rector of the English College, Father Morris (a very warm friend, and very capable), will then revise them. We shall then take them to my avocat to revise and advise about. When my avocat shall have revised it, and the text is settled, the translation has then to be finished, but the translator works more slowly than I have done. Then it has to be presented, and then I have to wait to see if explanations are required."[1]

By the middle of May the work was completed, except a summing up to point the moral. The state of his health, which had become more and more troublesome, the desire to take part in a debate on Maynooth, fixed for the close of the month, and, above all, doubtless, an

[1] Not only Dr. Morris, but the professors generally of the English College, were friendly to his mission, while those of the Irish College were hostile. It may be noted here that Lucas was charged by certain priests of the diocese of Elphin with a complaint to Propaganda against their bishop. Lucas told them in reply—

"Dr. Brown is fully understood in Rome to be, from age and infirmity, incapable of managing his diocese; his acts are not approved, and he has received from the Holy See, '*a hundred times*,' hints and suggestions to resign his bishopric, upon which he has not thought proper to act. Great difficulty is felt about proceeding to extremities with him; but I venture to say that to be relieved from your present intolerable condition, your best course is great patience, and care to send to Rome well-authenticated statements of every misuse of power that takes place in your diocese."

This was the bishop who patronised Mr. Keogh in 1853, and who had gone to Conciliation Hall in 1846, to denounce the Young Irelanders as bad Catholics.

anxiety to join his wife and child, determined him to return home, leaving the bulk of the Statement in course of translation, and carrying a few chapters with him for further review. He was content with it as an array of facts. "Clearness and intelligibility," he said, "are the only merits I aspire to." But he promised that it would be at any rate "an Easy Lesson in Irish politics; the first Hornbook for Beginners." To my thinking it would be difficult to extract from the arcana of States a document written under a profounder determination to be just and veracious, and not for any motive to hide away essential truths, than that great State paper. Much of it is written with a merciless plainness of statement which can only be justified by the integrity of his motives and the importance of the end in view. While it was written his life was ebbing away, and before it was completed he was called on to prepare for death. On his death-bed he saw nothing to retract or mitigate: and this circumstance contributes to give the document its over-mastering force.

Towards the close of May, Lucas arrived in London, and came immediately to the House of Commons. A glance was enough to read the history of his mission. Baffled hopes and bitter disaster were written on his face. His countenance was cadaverous, his eye feverish, his cheeks hollow, and his flesh had so fallen away that he seemed to be wearing the clothes of a bigger man.

He told us with a painful smile that the door-keeper had stopped him as a stranger, and, in fact, he was barely recognisable by his intimate friends. The news which he had to hear was as discouraging as the news which he had to tell. The Independent party had dwindled to half a dozen, and the Land question in Parliament had fallen back to the condition in which the League had found it. There was a bill of Sergeant Shee's before the House, but the Government had struck out drainage, planting, and the redemption of bog from the improvements to be compensated; and, in a country where inordinate rents had made arrears universal, it was provided that no tenant in arrear should be entitled to make improvements or to claim compensation for improvements already made. In short, all our labours had been wasted by the policy of the Whig bishops and the success of the deserters.[1]

[1] But even this was not enough. The landlords mustered their friends in force, and struck out the principle of compensation for past improvements altogether, by a majority of thirty-six. When one came to inquire in what manner a majority was constituted for so iniquitous a project, it was generally found to consist of a score of Irish landlords defending their own fraud, with a dozen or so of their nominees and hangers-on, a batch of English squires, some of them having Irish property, and a string of the relatives and nominees of absentee proprietors and the usual chorus of Dundrearies and Dunderheads caught in the smoking-room or lobby and brought in to pronounce the solemn verdict of Parliament by an invitation to "Come along, like a brick, and vote against a d—d Irish craze."

The melancholy muddle of the Crimean war, Lord John Russell's intrigues and perfidy, the fall of Lord Aberdeen and the rise of Lord Palmerston, occupied Parliament during the mission to Rome; but they lie outside the purpose of this narrative. No change brought better prospects to Ireland, for the bulk of her representatives were voting servilely with the Minister in possession. Mr. Keogh, who remained in both Governments, and even got promotion, kept them in order by crumbs of patronage supplemented by liberal drafts on the Bank of Hope, which no one knew better than he how to draw.

Lucas became the guest of our colleague, Richard Swift, at Wandsworth, and there, after half a year's separation, we had an opportunity for a confidential *tête-à-tête*. So far as Propaganda was concerned, he admitted that his mission had failed, but he still hoped that when his Memorial was presented to the Pope it might bring about the change of policy we desired. He had reflected on the project of retiring from Parliament; it had been much pressed upon him by friendly ecclesiastics that he had duties to Catholic interests, not only in Ireland but throughout the Empire, from which the failure of his mission did not relieve him, and that he ought to remain in the House of Commons to perform them. He said, with a melancholy smile, that he could still be member for the Pope. I contended that our pledges were not conditional, but positive, and that they were too specific to be disregarded by men who had denounced pledge-breaking so mercilessly; and I insisted that the authors of the calamity which had befallen the Irish cause would not be recognised by the people on any other condition than our retirement. We debated the question late into the night without coming to an agreement. With or without his co-operation, I declared I would fulfil my undertaking; but I felt injured because a measure which was the policy of a party might, when adopted only by one man, have the appearance of personal caprice; and we parted for the first time in mutual displeasure.

I informed my private and political friends of my intention without delay. Some of them urged pleas in abatement; some frankly recognised that the time had come for telling the people that we could accomplish nothing for them under existing conditions. Out of a sheaf of letters I pick two, representing these different currents of opinion. The Bishop of Kerry, the most generous and considerate of private friends, urged delay:

"MY DEAR FRIEND (he wrote),—I commenced several times to write you a long letter, but I could never get time to give you all my mind. So I tore up what I had written; and now I ask one favour, that you come and spend a week with me in the mountains before you declare publicly your intention. Let me have the satisfaction of having done my best to keep you. We want honest and able men, and we cannot spare even one.

"The time is not far off when some who now disapprove will admit the rectitude of your views and motives, and regret that your policy had not been better supported. You were not able to do the best thing; then try the next best. You were always hopeful; you did not despond in darker days; why despair now? I feel anxiously on this matter.—Yours sincerely,

"✠ D. MORIARTY."

A man of stronger will, and destined in the end to occupy a higher position in the Church, came to a wiser conclusion. Dr. Croke wrote :—

"This much, however, I must say, that our party has been long since destroyed, and that there is no room in Ireland for an honest politician. For myself, I have determined never to join any Irish agitation, never to sign any petition to Government, and never to trust to any one man, or body of men living in my time, for the recovery of Ireland's independence. All hope with me in Irish affairs is dead and buried. I have ever esteemed you at once the honestest and most gifted of my countrymen, and your departure from Ireland leaves me no hope."

After a little, I told my constituents in a public address that it was no longer possible to accomplish the task for which I had solicited their votes, and that I would therefore resign my seat. To avoid the pain and humiliation of a controversy with Lucas in the face of rejoicing enemies, I allowed the fact that I was retiring in fulfilment of a pledge which we had made in common to fall into the background in my farewell address. And I have since paid the penalty in having the circumstance constantly misunderstood. I retired because I was pledged to retire if we failed to establish the independence of the second order of the clergy in politics; and we had failed. But I spoke of my own intentions solely, and made no allusion to the purpose or duty of any one else.[1] Some journals naturally assumed that

[1] I invite the reader's attention to the terms of the announcement:—"I have determined to retire from the office to which your favour raised me, and, *till better times arrive*, from all share and responsibility in the public affairs of Ireland. The Irish party is reduced to a handful, the popular organisation is deserted by those who created it, prelates of the Irish Church throng the ranks of our opponents, priest is arrayed against priest, and parish against parish, a shameless political profligacy is openly defended and applauded, the special opportunity sent by Heaven for our deliverance is bartered away to an English faction, and the ultimate aim for which alone I laboured—to give back to Ireland her national existence—is forgotten or disdained. *Till all this be changed*, there seems to be no more hope for the Irish Cause than for the corpse on the dissecting-table. I have done my best to change it. For the last twelve months I have spared no pains in public or private to rally the National party—but in vain. A preternatural apathy broods over the country, disheartened by corruption and pampered by a false and temporary prosperity. When all external circumstances favour a National movement, it is repudiated at home. God knows I have done my best. One step alone remains. I promised, in such a fatal contingency, to throw up my seat in Parliament, in order that the truth might not be screened from the people, nor the crisis pass without some emphatic warning and protest. The time for this duty has come."
[I should, perhaps, note that this catalogue of crimes proper to be denounced and errors proper to be amended has been described

Lucas was about to take the same course, and he wrote a note to the *Times* denying that he had any such intention. He still spoke in private of returning to Rome to present his Memorial, and insisted that his health was considerably better since his arrival in England.

The failure of the mission had coerced me to quit Parliament; the paralysis of national feeling induced me to quit Ireland also. A country where Mr. Keogh was the popular patriot, surrounded by huzzaing partisans, and Dr. Cullen the dominant ecclesiastic, was one where life would be a long torture. I was then and always a Catholic of the school of Newman and Montalembert, not at all of the school of Dr. Cullen or M. Veuillot: and I knew William Keogh at that moment as well as all Ireland knows him now. I told my constituents that the motive which induced me to take up the Land question was the belief that it was not a substitute for, but a step towards, national self-government, and an essential preliminary without which nothing could be accomplished in the larger enterprise. Some might believe that the national cause could be asserted by a people who had not secured the means of living like men, but I did not believe it.

in later times as a statement by me that " Ireland was as dead as a corpse on a dissecting-table "—a manifest and disingenuous misrepresentation.]

"If there be any who honestly think so (I said), let them try, and may God prosper them. For me, I have tried. For seven years I have kept the green flag flying alone, or with but a handful of friends; for twice seven years I have thought, written, and acted to one sole end. In these years I have been five times prosecuted by the English Government—in '42, in '44, in '46, in '48, and '49,—and wasted thirteen months of my life in English prisons. I have 'spent and been spent' cheerfully in fortune, health, peace, the duties of home and the rights of my children; often with less aid than opposition from those who professed the same opinions, always in exhausting personal conflict with a hired Press, and all who lived, or hoped to live, by corruption."

Meantime some of the friends nearest to Lucas assured me that he was in a much more dangerous condition than he supposed, and that he would be for a long time, perhaps for ever, unfit for serious labour. I was deeply touched by a calamity brought on by the constancy and courage with which he had performed his task at Rome, and I wrote to him to put our recent controversy out of his mind, as I went into exile remembering only the good battle we had fought together for a good cause. The last letter which I got from him came in reply:—

"I was delighted, my dear Duffy, to receive your very kind note on my return to Brighton from London on a visit to the doctor. The little scene to which you refer was most painful to me, and I am, above all things, delighted that we may now consider the affair at an end. There may be a difference of opinion, but I am sure you acquit me of entertaining towards you anything but kind and affectionate feelings, such as I have no doubt whatever you entertain towards me. . . . It is to me a subject of the deepest regret that you are going from Ireland—not only on public grounds, with regard to which I consider it a calamity—but on private grounds, and because the absence of such a friend as I have always felt you to be makes our wretched politics very much more distasteful than they have hitherto been."

Before quitting Parliament there was some work which it was my peculiar duty to do. After the escape of Meagher and Mitchel the Government allowed Smith O'Brien and his remaining associates to return to Europe with the sole condition that they must not revisit the United Kingdom. It is a significant tribute to the character of O'Brien among men who knew him well that I had little difficulty in obtaining the signatures of a hundred and fifty members of Parliament to a memorial requesting that this restriction might be withdrawn. Sir Fitzroy Kelly and Henry Baillie, Spooner and Alexander Hamilton, Whiteside and Napier signed as willingly as Cobden, Bright, Lord Godrich,[1] or Milner Gibson. The Secretary of the Admiralty and the Secretary of the Board of Control[2] felt free to urge this measure on the Cabinet of the Administration to which they belonged; and Mr. Disraeli, then leader of the Opposition, authorised me

[1] The present Marquis of Ripon.
[2] Mr. Phinn and Mr. Danby Seymour.

to tell Lord Palmerston that he approved of the proposal. But all I could accomplish at the moment was to get the question considered; their unconditional return to Ireland was long delayed by official timidity.

The tragic story of Lucas's sudden relapse and premature death need not be detailed here. He died on Monday, 20th October, in his forty-fourth year, and was buried at Brompton Cemetery. His last thoughts were given to the public cause. The Rev. Dr. Whitty, his closest friend in life, and the confessor who prepared him for death, immediately after that event wrote these touching words to Monsignore Morris, to whom the Memorial was intrusted for presentation to the Pope :—

"From the most complete and intimate knowledge of his sentiments, I may add that, as in life, so at the near approach of death, his one desire and prayer was that the Holy See should be made acquainted with the whole truth, and determine on all these questions what would be for the welfare of the Church in these kingdoms."

Touching testimonies of public confidence and affection followed him to the grave. For my part, I did what I could to honour the memory of my lost colleague. When his approaching death was announced I declined on the instant a farewell banquet prepared by political friends in Ireland, and a second by literary friends in London, of which it is pleasant to remember that John Stuart Mill was chairman, and James

Hannay, author of *Singleton Fontenoy*, and Edward Whitty, author of the *Friends of Bohemia*, the Secretaries. At the same time, but on other grounds, I refused a pecuniary testimonial. After fourteen years spent in public labours, during which I possessed the chief property in a popular journal, I did not carry away a hundred pounds from its profits to begin life anew. I sold my interest in the *Nation*, indeed, at a fair price, to A. M. Sullivan and one of his friends; but the purchase-money was spent in wiping out the responsibilities of a public and Parliamentary career in which, after the treason of Sadleir and Keogh, the leaders paid the expenditure for the most part out of their private resources. I was resolute, however, not to mix up the necessary public action of laying down my office with any private interest or convenience whatever.[1]

But I accepted aid which I might hope to repay if

[1] I may quote a few lines from a letter of the period to explain the animus of my refusal:—"I declined a public tribute in '44 when a State prisoner in Richmond; in '46, when amerced by a Government prosecution; and in '49 (tendered by Father Mathew), when a State prisoner in Newgate. Not because I was insensible of the generous kindness that prompted it, nor because I denied that it may sometimes be wisely and properly tendered by the people to those who suffer in their cause; but from personal feeling alone. To maintain an impregnable Nationality in Ireland against scepticism and corruption, I fear it is necessary to keep it clear not only of the bribes of the Castle but even of the largesse of the people."

I did not utterly fail in the new country. The friend whom I loved best in life, after Thomas Davis, came to me with his hands full of bank-notes, which he insisted I should borrow till better times came; an Irishman in the public service of England, whom I had never seen, and knew at that time only as a Protestant Nationalist of remarkable literary gifts (which, happily, he still employs in the same cause), offered me the savings of his lifetime, to be repaid at discretion; and an Irish lady, married to a staff officer in the English army, proffered me the law library of her uncle, an English judge, as I meditated practising as a barrister in Australia. It is good to know that any man who has served the Irish cause honestly has never failed to win gratitude and confidence from the Irish race.

One question to be determined before I left Ireland was the future of the Tenant League. I urged on the Council the policy of dissolving it forthwith, in order that the fact might stand out in naked significance that the cause had been destroyed by Whig bishops. Another rally might be made later, and would be more successfully made, I contended, if in the interval there was no pretence of agitation to create false hopes. But some adventurous persons who had become members of the Council in later times, of whom the most notable was Mr. MacNamara Cantwell, insisted that they could use the organisation for good results, and it was resolved to keep the League alive. The new leaders began their labours by summoning a selected number of the Irish party to take counsel at Dublin; but they did not understand the men they proposed to deal with. Mr. Tristram Kennedy, Mr. J. F. Maguire, Mr. Swift, and others answered their invitation by informing them that some of the members they were invited to meet had habitually and ostentatiously betrayed the popular cause, and that it was an insult and a blunder to ask honest men to confer with them. This rebuff was fatal. Moore, Maguire, Archdeacon Fitzgerald, Father Tom O'Shea, Father Dowling, and others still made generous efforts to keep public feeling alive, but it gradually ebbed away. In Parliament there remained four or five men true to their principles; but Moore, the only one fit to lead, lost his seat at the first general election, and those who remained, and one or two others sent to support them, did not choose a leader and submit themselves to his control, rarely consulted together, and had no common centre of authority. They naturally accomplished nothing—

"All fighting without lead and without method,
  A dreary, hopeless, desultory war."

Such is the history of the League; a brilliant and marvellous beginning, a singularly successful Parliamentary career for a time, and then—treachery, desertion, and defeat. We failed at that time and place, because we were betrayed by prelates in whom the people had a blind confidence. It is a popular tradition that after the battle of the Boyne Sarsfield declared that if the two armies could change kings he would fight it over again and win; and if we could have changed the bishops of 1855 for the bishops of 1885 the Land question would have been settled triumphantly thirty years earlier. At any rate, the founders of the League awakened and formulated for the first time the opinions destined to prevail in the end, as surely as Wilberforce and Clarkson awakened opinion in favour of the slave, or John Keogh and Wolfe Tone in favour of the trampled Catholic: and they taught the principle of Independent Opposition, which alone could insure success. The League inherited that weapon from the Young Irelanders of 1848, and bequeathed it to the Irish party of 1886.

In a narrative which turns so essentially on the personal character of a few men, readers unacquainted with the local circumstances will probably desire to learn the fate of the *dramatis personæ*. Time is a sharp test of character; and character, tried by life and death, throws a searching retrospective light on events. The young priests who fell under the disfavour of the Apostolic Delegate are still living. Nearly twenty years after the transactions which I have recorded the

See of Ossory became vacant by the death of Dr. Walsh, and the parish priests of the diocese expressed their verdict on the character and career of Father Matthew Keeffe by electing him at the head (*dignissimus*) of the list of three priests submitted to the Holy See from which to select the new bishop. But Dr. Cullen was still the chief counsellor on Irish affairs, and Dr. Moran, his nephew, was the choice of the Propaganda. The new bishop—acting solely in the interest of religion, no doubt, but who certainly started with no prejudice in favour of the " Callan Curates "—found in them his most efficient colleagues. The official theologian of his diocese was the Very Rev. Canon O'Shea, P.P., once Curate of Callan; his brother was Archdeacon; and the Very Rev. Canon Keeffe, P.P., was a Prebendary of Ossory—one of the bishop's consultative Council of Four, and Precentor of the Diocesan Chapter.

Of the young priest banished from New Ross, whom friends were fond of naming the "Iron Curate" after another man of steadfast will, the "Iron Duke," I have already spoken. His colleagues, the "Carbonari Curates," either died at their posts or entered religious orders that they might perform the duties of the priesthood under severer discipline and in harder labour than the life of a secular priest exacts.

Archdeacon Fitzgerald and all the parish priests who took a leading part in the League are dead. Of the younger men, the curates who aided it, many are also dead. Father Dwyer, who managed the Memorial movement, and Father Cahill, who expounded and justified it with distinguished ability, are dead; but Father Dwyer's closest associate and counsellor is now Bishop of Limerick; the young curate who induced many priests of Down and Connor to sign the Priests' Memorial, and set them the example, is now Bishop of these united dioceses.[1] The parish priest, who came most promptly from the far West to the consultations of the Council, is now Bishop of Clonfert; the young professor who welcomed the leader of the League to the ecclesiastical capital of Connaught with the most vigorous oratory, is now Archbishop of Tuam; and the other young professor, who sketched an effectual organisation for encountering the serried power of the exterminators, is now Archbishop of Cashel.

Dr. M'Knight is also dead, having struggled to the end for the interests of the tenant-farmers on the new and perplexing theory of duty which he adopted after the establishment of the Aberdeen Administration. Rev. John Rogers is a Professor in the Queen's College, Belfast, and has not, I think, abandoned any of the opinions which he taught with such persuasive power thirty years ago. Rev. David Bell, when the League fell, despaired of constitutional agitation, and allied

[1] Both have died while this narrative is passing through the press.

himself with the Fenian movement. He now resides in the United States, and holds a secular office under the Republic. Several others of the Presbyterian ministers are living, and cannot, I am persuaded, regret the work of Christian charity in which they were engaged when the League banner of orange, green, and blue, was lifted to the sky.

Sergeant Shee was made a judge by Lord Palmerston, being the first Catholic who had reached that office in England since the flight of James II. On circuit he considered it his duty, as one of the Queen's judges, to go in state to the Protestant cathedral in the circuit town, as his colleague, a Protestant, naturally and properly did. This humiliating ceremonial will enable all men of honour of whatever creed to estimate Mr. Justice Shee's consistency and courage.

I may assume that the fate of John Sadleir and William Keogh is known to all my readers. Detected in swindling on a gigantic scale, Sadleir either committed suicide by the strange device of going to Hampstead on a winter evening and swallowing a dose of poison on the open heath, or, as many persons are persuaded, got a body conveyed to that place, which the coroner's jury were induced to accept as his, and made his escape to new regions to enjoy his plunder at leisure. A gifted woman, who announced the news to me at the Antipodes, remarked that she was "shocked but not surprised, as he always looked like a man who had sold himself to the devil." His brother and accomplice was expelled from Parliament, fled from justice, and has been heard of no more. After these exposures, Mr. Keogh, like Jeffries, whom he resembled in vigour of intellect, laxity of principle, and disregard of truth, clambered at an early age to the Bench. In that position he bid for English sympathy by assailing the bishops on whose shoulders he had risen to office, was held in respect neither by those whom he joined nor those whom he deserted, and ended a tempestuous life by a miserably tragic death.

Dr. Cullen, the chief factor in these transactions, maintained his influence at Rome unimpaired up to his death. He was created a Cardinal, being the first Irishman ever invested with the purple. Of his episcopal career I am no competent judge, but I can confidently affirm that his political action was deeply disastrous to Ireland. After the lapse of a generation we can estimate it by its results. He separated the priests from the people in his archdiocese, and Dublin has been the seat of a murderous conspiracy, conducted by humble and illiterate, but, as the judge who tried them affirmed, "not naturally evil-disposed men," whom he had deprived of the counsel and guidance in public affairs which might have retained them in the path of morality. He raised the episcopal authority in politics to a new and unprecedented standard, and more and more aimed to accumulate all power in his own hands. A National journalist formulated his constantly contracting system in language of equal wit and truth:—"No priests in politics—except bishops." "No bishops in politics—except archbishops." "No archbishops in politics—except the Apostolic Delegate." The result was that the influence of the episcopal office fell lower than it had ever done since the coming of St. Patrick, till wiser counsels re-established it. His immediate successor, who followed in his footsteps, not only lost all authority in public affairs over the mass of the people, but was subjected to disedifying personal rebuffs unprecedented in Irish history. And the eminent ecclesiastic who fills his office at present has formally reversed his policy by restoring the freedom of the clergy in public affairs. There is now scarcely one bishop who sympathises with the theory of Cardinal Cullen, and not one who acts upon it. It is needless to further debate a system on which his own Order have pronounced so significant a verdict.

Of myself I may venture to say a word in the last book I shall write on the history of my own times. Dr. Cullen's successful resistance of the appeal to Rome induced me to quit my native land; but I served the Irish race more effectually elsewhere than I could have done in Ireland at that time. Neither here nor anywhere else on the face of the earth have Irishmen attained so open and successful a career as in the land where I laboured twenty years for that result. Irishmen proved, what it was very essential in the interest of Irish nationality to demonstrate, that Irish Celts were fit to govern, and would exercise with honourable and scrupulous fidelity the trusts which they accepted. Many difficulties disappeared before that demonstration; even the intractable prejudices of the Cardinal at length gave way. When I returned to Ireland, after ten years' absence, the Catholic University was largely officered by my political associates in Young Ireland, and a National Association was at work of which my life-long friend, John Dillon, was the leader. When the authorities of the University invited me to an entertainment, and John Dillon urged me to enter the Association and share with him the responsibility of its management, I was entitled to infer that the patron of the University and of the Association had been consulted on these measures. But I considered the political system, though somewhat amended, still incurably bad, and declined to re-enter Irish politics by that door. Ten years later still, when I again visited Dublin at the era of the O'Connell Centenary, the Lord Mayor, Alderman M'Swiney, who was for the moment a personage of unusual importance, invited me to a conference of three persons at the Mansion House, the purpose of which was to found a new Repeal Association on the old lines of 1843, and a National journal to sustain its policy. I inquired who was to furnish funds for so costly an undertaking as a daily paper, and he told me, after some hesitation, that in addition to his own large contribution the Cardinal promised a substantial share of the capital. I demanded if the Lord Mayor knew that his Eminence regarded me, who was invited to direct these operations, as a man who ought to endure a long penance on bread and water before being permitted to serve the country again. He rejoined that the Cardinal had quite altered his opinion upon this point. I replied that I had not altered mine. I still thought that the policy of excluding priests from politics to make way for bishops, and excluding bishops to make way for archbishops, was execrable; that I had always striven to rear a people able to judge and act for themselves; to rear men and citizens, not grown children or obedient mutes; and that I would be mad to undertake the task he designed for me, where there existed difference of principle so fundamental and unchangeable.

Immediately afterwards my old friends, the veterans of the Tenant League, made a proposal which was much more seductive. Father Peter O'Reilly, P.P. of Kingscourt, invited as many of them as he could muster, including the Callan curates (now become ecclesiastical rulers where they had been confessors and martyrs), to meet me under his hospitable roof, and with them a county member, Mr. Ennis, of Meath, who was prepared to resign his seat to make a vacancy for me. But I discovered that Mr. Ennis expected me to adopt the policy of Mr. Butt, which formally excluded Independent Opposition, and included a scheme of making the Irish members a legislature for Ireland in the intervals of their attendance on the Imperial Parliament. The project had never been scrutinised by men familiar with national constitutions, and in truth it was hopelessly and incurably defective. It was a melancholy spectacle to me to see Irish members pledged to a scheme which would never be accepted either by England or Ireland when they came to understand it; and as it would have contradicted the practice of my life to profess and defend opinions which I did not hold, I declined this test. The scheme is now not only abandoned, but is as obsolete as the Penal Laws. I would not re-enter Parliament; but to the measure of my powers and opportunity I served my race in whatever position I found myself, and vindicated to unfriendly audiences the principles which I had contributed to plant in Irish minds.

This narrative is now completed, and it contains much which I deem it important that Irishmen should know. It is our reproach that we are *incuriosi suorum*. How few of us are familiar with the marvellous story of John

Keogh's struggle for Catholic Emancipation, which he almost won while O'Connell was still a lad at college! How many of the young men of to-day know that in 1833, when the Established Church in Ireland was docked of bishops and revenues by Parliament, its complete disendowment might perhaps have been accomplished, and was rendered only a question of time? And if in 1856 all the labours of the Tenant League seemed wasted, it was not so. Truths had been uttered which, once heard, are never forgotten, and the principles embodied in recent land legislation were first formulated by the League of 1850. The revived contest for them was conducted under the immense advantages of the ballot and an extended franchise, and with the aid of prelates who shared the sentiments and labours of the Tenant League. There is scarcely a notable ecclesiastic in Ireland past sixty, a Land Leaguer, at present, who was not openly or confidentially allied with the Tenant Leaguers thirty years ago. If we were defeated in 1854, they also were defeated. If they are successful now, a liberal share of the merit belongs to those who toiled for the truth in evil days.

APPENDICES.

APPENDICES.

I.

TOUR THROUGH IRELAND IN 1849.

PART of this tour was made in company with Thomas Carlyle. In notes of that visit to Ireland, published since his death (a publication to be greatly deplored, I think), he mentions my meeting and conferring with several of the public men who afterwards became founders of the League. But he scarcely does justice to his personal feelings at certain spectacles which we encountered. I borrow a page from my own diary of the same period—

"We travelled slowly from Limerick to Sligo, and we found everywhere the features of a recently conquered country. Clare was almost a wilderness from Kilrush to Corofin. The desolate shores of Lough Corrib would have resembled a desert but that the stumps of ruined houses showed that not Nature, but Man, had been the desolator. Between Killala Bay and Sligo, during an entire day's travel, we estimated that every second dwelling was pulled down; and not cabins alone, but stone houses fit for the residence of a substantial yeomanry.

"The degradation which had fallen on the generous and spirited Celtic race was a sight such as I had nowhere seen or read of. The famine and the landlords have actually created a *new race* in Ireland. We saw on the streets of Galway crowds of creatures more debased than the Yahoos of Swift—creatures having only a distant and hideous resemblance to human beings. Grey-headed old men, whose idiotic faces had hardened into a settled leer of mendicancy, and women filthier and more frightful than the harpies, who at the jingle of a coin on the pavement swarmed in myriads from unseen places; struggling, screaming, *shrieking* for their prey, like some monstrous and unclean animals. In Westport the sight of the priest on the street gathered an entire pauper population, thick as a village market, swarming round him for relief. Beggar children, beggar adults, beggars in white hairs, girls with faces grey and shrivelled; women with the more touching and tragic aspect of lingering shame and self-respect not yet effaced; and among these terrible realities, imposture shaking in pretended fits to add the last touch of horrible grotesqueness to the picture! I saw these accursed sights, and they are burned into my memory for ever. Poor, mutilated, and debased scions of a tender, brave, and pious stock, they were martyrs in the battle of centuries for the right to live in their own land, and no Herculaneum or Pompeii covers ruins so memorable to me as those which lie buried under the fallen roof-trees of an 'Irish extermination.'"

In the West we were shown the residence of a baronet who spent in London a rental of £30,000 a year drawn from his Irish tenantry. He had ejected 320 persons within a few months, and was in arrears with his poor-rate. In a workhouse in the county of Kilkenny, described as one of the best-conducted in Ireland, and managed by a paid vice-guardian, we found a crowd of infant children as visibly fading away as if they had been sentenced to death. They were crowded into a single small room, the mephitic atmosphere of which would poison a grown man

II.

JOHN MITCHEL, THE LEAGUE, AND GAVAN DUFFY.

WHEN the League was fighting the battle of the Irish tenant-farmers against the landlords, the British Government, Sadleir, Keogh, and the Parliamentary deserters who had betrayed the people for office or patronage, and the Whig bishops who lent them a fatal support, Mr. Mitchel escaped from Tasmania and resumed the office of journalist at New York. The first work he took in hand was, not to aid the organisation which had so many enemies, but to denounce it as entirely worthless. Nothing, he affirmed, would ever be obtained for the tenant-farmers from the British Parliament; their best hope was an Irish expedition from the United States, with arms in their hands, which might be expected perhaps before another year had elapsed. What patriotic Irishmen ought to do with the League was to renounce and repudiate it. It is no longer necessary to invite the judgment of posterity on that policy; a generation has since lived and died; all the League demanded has been won from Parliament, and the expedition which Mr. Mitchel was expected to lead never set out: neither the Crimean War, the Indian Mutiny, nor the heat between England and France, which at one time threatened an explosion, having furnished the opening for which he was waiting. Towards the close of his life he visited Ireland to preach the kindred doctrine of refusing to seek Home Rule in Parliament (where it could never be obtained), and of electing only such members as were resolved *not* to sit in the House of Commons, and whose seats would necessarily be given by that body (as his own seat was given) to the enemies of the people. That policy, also, has been effectually tested by time, and need not be debated.

It was a curious aggravation of Mr. Mitchel's attacks on the League that while he was issuing them from his bureau in New York, Dr. M'Knight, at Belfast, was holding some of us responsible for having been the friends and confederates of a man who denied that it "is a crime, or a wrong, or even a peccadillo, to hold slaves, to buy slaves, to sell slaves, or to keep slaves to their work by flogging or other needful coercion." This theory of human rights has also been removed from the region of controversy, having received final judgment at Richmond before the sword of General Grant.

The ground upon which the Nationalists who supported the League justified themselves was very simple—It is easy (they said) for you to be heroic and transcendental at New York; but we who stand face to face with the enemy know that it is impossible to accomplish anything except by the tedious and exhausting process of Parliamentary action; without it our people will be altogether defenceless, and our manifest duty is to recognise the institutions which exist, and employ them for their benefit. The most conclusive verdict on this controversy is that a dozen years later, when the Southern States of America had the same problem to solve, Mr. Mitchel adopted the identical policy there which he insisted on the League rejecting in Ireland. "There was no longer a Confederate Government (he wrote)—it had disappeared from human eyes; and inasmuch as a country cannot be without a Government, and the only Government then in fact subsisting being the Federal Government of the United States, I owed to it, from that instant, full obedience, which obedience I at once yielded in good faith, as I think my fellow-citizens at the South very generally did at the same time ; and for the same reason I am therefore no longer a Secessionist nor a rebel ; but a Unionist and a lawful citizen." Mr. Mitchel's attacks on the League were supplemented by attacks upon me. He found it embarrassing, when challenged by common friends, to justify that procedure. When he was an attorney in a northern village I offered him a position and an income as a contributor to the *Nation*, which enabled him to change that obscure stage for the one on which his reputation was won ; and after three years' intimate daily connection I can ask no better testimony than his own how my relations with him were conducted. When we separated in January, 1848, he wrote to me—

"I do not blame you, (he said in the note announcing his retirement from the *Nation*) I do not blame you in the *slightest particular ;* and, moreover, I am quite certain I could not have worked in subordination to *any other man alive* near so long as I have done with you. And lastly, that I give you credit in all that is past for acting on good and disinterested motives, with the utmost sincerity, and also with uniform kindness to me personally."

After his attacks had continued for nearly three months, during which I copied them weekly into the *Nation*, I replied, in a "Letter to John Mitchel from Charles Gavan

Duffy," which excited wide attention in Ireland and in America. Its most significant result was that Mr. Mitchel never attacked me any more, and several years later repudiated with great warmth a suggestion in the *Nation*, then edited by Mr. A. M. Sullivan, that he still assailed me whenever an opportunity offered. As far as I am concerned, here the matter might have ended for ever, but Mr. Mitchel had not the grace to blot out from his *Jail Journal* the imputations which I had shown to be untrue and impossible, and they are still read by thousands of our countrymen. I labour under the additional disadvantage that my "Letter to John Mitchel" appeared in pamphlet form, as a supplement to the *Nation*, and owing to its diminutive size, is rarely bound with the volume to which it belongs. In short, it has disappeared from publication, while the libels which it answers and rebuts remain in currency. Under these circumstances, while I was engaged in writing the history of the period, I resolved to republish a few paragraphs from it for readers who desire to know the truth. Mr. Mitchel answered it elaborately in his newspaper, the *Citizen*; but as he is now where he cannot defend himself, where I also must soon be, I shall not reprint any statement which he did not in express terms or by direct implication admit to be true. Allegations which he either denied or disputed I shall leave out of account. But I am entitled that the facts of a case, which his brilliant book will keep long in memory, should be accurately known.

Mr. Mitchel's gravest charge was that I lowered the National cause by producing Father Mathew, Dr. Blake, and other witnesses to speak of my past career, and by allowing Meagher to prove that a letter bearing his signature was inserted in the *Nation* during my absence. This was my reply—

"And now, sir, let us consider your charges on their merits.

"The first amounts to this: that I was guilty of crime and cowardice in producing witnesses to character on my trial, and permitting it to be proved that certain of the articles in the indictment were not written by me. Before defending that course, I wish to inquire how it comes you selected *me* for reprobation on this score? I was the *last* tried of the State prisoners: six months after Martin—five months after O'Brien and Meagher—four months after O'Doherty and Williams—and that which you charge as a crime upon me, every soul of them did months before me! Mark; there is not a single feature of my defence which was not anticipated by the prisoners you left behind you in Van Diemen's Land, or rejoined in America. And there is not one of them but was tried and convicted long before my first jury was sworn.

"The earliest tried was John Martin. In your *Jail Journal*, you described him as your main reliance for revolutionary vigour in Ireland; others you pronounced 'not sufficiently desperate; your chief trust was in Martin and Reilly.' . . . Martin was tried six months before me, and what was his defence?

"Did 'the unfortunate man, bowed and prostrate to the earth,' produce witnesses to prove 'his legal and constitutional character'?

"Did 'the poor man try to evade the responsibility of some of the prosecuted articles, by proving that they were not written by himself'?

"Mr. Martin did precisely what you are pleased to describe in these terms. His brother, James Martin, was produced to prove that so recently as the March of the same year, and a month after the French revolution, he had delivered a speech in Newry, in which he declared for the 'Constitution of '82'—advocated 'the authority of the Queen, Lords, and Commons' of Ireland—disavowed any intention to 'unsettle property'—disowned 'insurrection,' and said unequivocally, 'let it be understood, then, that for one Repealer I do *not advocate violence or war*, and I am just as peaceful in my views now as before the recent events which have created such a warlike spirit in some of my countrymen.'

"The most dangerous articles in the indictment against Martin were James Finton Lalor's. An order of Court was obtained to remove Lalor from Clonmel to Dublin, for the purpose of acknowledging his own writings; and he was not examined in the end, only because it was found his testimony, on the whole, would be dangerous to the prisoner [in fact it might have been elicited that Martin had read proofs in prison of the articles in question]. But in lieu of his personal evidence, a '*subpœna duces tecum*' was served on the Attorney-General to produce a letter which Lalor had addressed to him, claiming the responsibility of the articles; and a similar letter of Reilly's was read to the court and jury in the course of the defence. In the end, the charge of the judge turned chiefly on the question —whether Martin was cognisant of, and responsible for, these particular articles. And Mr. Butt requested permission to read two queries 'written by the prisoner himself,' to bring the mind of the jury to bear directly on the injustice and absurdity of convicting him for the work of others: First—Whether the jury believed that *John Martin* intended to depose the Queen, or make war against her? and (second), whether *John Martin* expressed both or either of these intentions?

"This was the first of the State trials. Mr. Martin adopted the practice universal in such circumstances—the practice of increasing, by every legitimate means, the difficulty an arbitrary Government found in convicting him. He employed the only defence admissible in an English court—he pleaded 'not guilty' by the evidence as well as by his answer to the arraignment. I do not blame him in the smallest degree—but for you, Mr. Mitchel (who knew these facts), I fear me your indignation is not heroic rage after all, but only the black bile of personal malevolence.

"The Clonmel trials followed next. O'Brien summoned his Parliamentary and private associates to say what he was and what were his opinions. Mr. Monsell, Sir Denham Norreys, Bolton Massey, Sir David Roche, and others were examined with this view. The cause of which he was the leader had been stained by brutalities of sentiment which revolted him, and he separated himself peremptorily from them by this evidence. I most confidently believe his anxiety at that momentous hour was less for his life than that his character might stand right with his people then and thereafter. But whatever were the specific motives, he did that in September which you assail me for doing in the April after.

"Terence M'Manus is not reputed to want courage. Well; Mr. M'Manus thought it not unbecoming to produce merchants of Cork, Waterford, and Kilkenny, literally 'to bear witness to his good character in private life,' as a commercial man. The Castle press had described him as an English Chartist, and that practical intellect which before and since had guided him out of the hands of his enemies suggested the natural answer—to confront them with the truth.

"But what did Thomas Meagher? He proved that he had separated himself peremptorily from Mr. John Mitchel, rejected his theories, and supported the resolutions which resulted in driving him from the Irish Confederation. In short, he put his true character before the jury and the country—for Thomas Meagher was a revolutionist of the sword, not of the shambles.

"All these men were tried before me—their trials were published as widely as mine—you have been living under the roof with one of them, and in familiar intercourse with the rest for the last three or four years, and know their story like the alphabet—yet you think it is quite fair to ignore their cases—to ignore your friend John Martin's case; to ignore Thomas Meagher's, and M'Manus's, who are at hand to answer for themselves; to ignore O'Brien's, the most conspicuous man among us, in order to fasten upon your accustomed quarry—myself. This is what you consider fair play and open dealing.

"I now come to my own defence. I scorn to rest it upon precedent; I took the course I did, not because all my comrades had set me the example, but because it was the wisest, best, and boldest open to me at that hour. But you were a prisoner in Van Diemen's Land, and I refrained from specifying one of the chief motives of my elaborate defence. You, Mr. Mitchel, furnished that motive. The clumsy libels of Balfe and Birch might precipitate my conviction by ruining me with the jury; your more subtle slanders, shaped to defame me with the people, weighed heavier on my mind. I had been silent under bitter provocation for the sake of the cause, but I was not poison-proof. You had not utterly failed; and when I read in my cell in Newgate that I was 'about to plead guilty on the eve of O'Brien's trial,' I felt to the marrow of my bones that, if any man believed the foul lie, I owed it to you. I reviewed in my mind the battle I had maintained through a stormy era with the most unscrupulous of adversaries, the Castle hack and the Jacobin, and then, and on that reflection, I determined to set my whole life before the jury and the country. I determined to snatch away the hobgoblin my enemies had laboured to create, and set an honest man in his place. So help me the good God that will judge me, I embarked in the movement of '48 believing that I had on one side the English gibbet, if we failed; and on the other, the hand of some fanatical assassin, whom your slanders would arm against me, if we succeeded. And in putting myself on my country by my defence, I was not alone answering Lord Clarendon—I was answering you. How did you misrepresent my character? I will specify two or three overt acts traceable to yourself, by which I apprehend you and I, Mr. Mitchel, will be better understood for the future.

"You were an habitual reader of the *Northern Star* in '48; every number of your paper contained extracts from it. You were in personal communication with the Irish Chartists, and spoke at two of the three meetings they held in Dublin that year. In the *Star*, Mr. Fergus O'Connor published a biography, describing how you sacrificed your noble professional income to be a mere writer in the *Nation*; and how you were compelled to break away from that unworthy journal, because the cowardly proprietor, Gavan Duffy, not only trammelled the free expression of your sympathy with the English Chartists, but himself wrote infamous reactionary articles about digging deeper the gulf between Ireland and them. Afterwards Mr. Dyott adorned his speech with this story at one of the Chartist meetings in Dublin, and improvised an effective comparison between Mr. Duffy of the *Nation* and Mr. Conway of the *Post*. His speech was, of course, transferred to the *United Irishman*, but this paragraph was adroitly omitted. You chuckled, I have no doubt, at the odium that was created against me among large masses of men in England and Ireland, and at your own growing Chartist popularity. Will you chuckle now, when I disclose the fact that, of these reactionary anti-Chartist articles I was not the writer, and—you, Mr. John Mitchel, were !

"In our relations at that moment a sensitive gentleman would have burned with impatience to assume the responsibility of his own work ; he would have walked into a furnace rather than shelter himself from reproach behind me. But you took the benefit of the fable ; and I, for my part, left you your miserable triumph, rather than distract the Confederation by an exposure.

"Rev. John Kenyon's second letter, assailing O'Connell while his body was still unburied, was refused insertion in the *Nation* till a more fitting occasion. ' Free opinion and free discussion,' said the *Nation*, 'are good in their time and place. But this kind of gladiatorial combat over a dead body has been disused since the Trojans and well-booted Greeks fought over the corpse of Menoeiades.' Father Kenyon nursed his wrath till the appearance of the *United Irishman*. In the first number he congratulated you that, unlike the *Nation*, *you* would not curtail dissent and extinguish thought by rejecting unpalatable communications. In the third number he sent you the identical rejected epistle, and you inserted it, observing it would be in the public memory that it was *suppressed* by the *Nation* in the previous June. It was beautiful to contemplate the contrast between your generous and gallant reception of 'free opinion' and my cowardly suppression of it. In that day, when men's minds were preternaturally suspicious, no reader could fail to carry away so patent a conclusion.

"Oh, soul of candour and chivalry! it was *you* who suppressed Kenyon's letter in the *Nation*; it was you who notified that this kind of gladiatorial combat over a dead body had ceased with the pagan times! And I, after that equivocation, once again held my peace, lest a new quarrel would deliver our divided ranks a prey to the enemy.

"It is not enough that I answer for my own acts, or acts done in my presence or with my authority. Your generous friendship credits me with the sins of others; and with sins that had no existence. This is your next charge, miraculously elicited from one number of a daily paper, the transactions running over weeks—

"'The doctor has sent into my cabin a *Daily News* which came by the mail on Sunday. Now, why could not Mr. Duffy have made ballads in some quiet place all his days? As if purposely to relieve the enemy from all embarrassment in the "vindication of the Law," he has allowed a petition to Government to be got up, very extensively signed, praying that as he is totally ruined—as he has already been long confined—as he is an admirable private character—as his health is delicate—as the violent and revolutionary articles in his newspaper appeared during a period of great excitement, and extended over but a few weeks—the enemy would, of their mercy, forbear to persecute him further—the very thing they wished to have any decent excuse for. I say he has allowed this petition, because no petitioners could make such *implied promises of amendment* without his sanction, and especially because he has not disowned the mean proceeding. It is quite in keeping with his miserable defence upon his last trial, his production of evidence to *character*, his attempt to evade the responsibility of articles published by himself. Sir Lucius O'Brien, too, who presents this memorial to Lord Clarendon, takes occasion to admit the "guilt" of the culprit. With what joy the enemy must gloat upon this transaction, and exult over us and our *abandoned cause!*'

"Unhappy man! Did you indeed people your solitude

with these hideous spectres of a diseased heart? I am fain to throw down my pen. That hell of envy and rancour carried in your bosom to the Antipodes and back again, making the daylight dark and truth falsehood to your eyes, is its own Nemesis.

"Of all the rash and ungenerous conclusions to which you rush, over the chance number of a paper, which yesterday's or to-morrow's might correct, so much as one is not true. Not one.

"Nobody made 'promises of amendment' on my behalf, 'implied' or expressed. On the contrary, the memorialists were met with a flat and insolent refusal on the ground (to cite the language of Lord Clarendon) that I had 'exhibited no signs of repentance, and had not expressed the smallest regret.' Our cause was trampled under the feet of soldiers and spies; the country was in a panic; the arm of the law was strong and merciless; the malice of my enemies desperate and vindictive, but I had 'not exhibited the least regret for my course.' I accept it as my epitaph.

"And let me tell you now, sir, what has never dropped from my pen before. On the eve of the fifth commission, when it had become a point of honour with the Government not to be defeated, and I had everything to fear from their vengeance, I was offered a release if I consented to enter a plea of 'Guilty.' It is not my habit, Mr. Mitchel, to clamour over my own achievements; and, except to Meagher and O'Brien, who read it at the time, my refusal was unknown beyond the circle of my own family, and has so remained to this day.

"The 'cause' was not 'abandoned'; on the contrary, it was regaining courage and confidence at that hour by the demonstration that English law might be resisted with success. You had made it ridiculous by threats unaccomplished; my forty days' combat, face to face with the law, was making the pulse of the people beat fast again. They felt that for one man to exhaust and defeat all the resources of a powerful State was a more unexampled victory (whatever its intrinsic value) than if Ballingarry had been made a Bannockburn.

"Sir Lucius O'Brien 'admitted the guilt' of the culprit! What then? The opinion of a man unknown to me—with whom I have never had the slightest communication then or since—an opinion contradicted by his companions as soon as it was uttered, the opinion of a man who repudiated his own brother, an opinion uttered behind my back, and over which I had no possible control—am I to be slandered on grounds like these? I cannot think that even in the Banbridge Petty Sessions this would have passed for evidence. It belongs to your later studies—the Jurisprudence of the Lamp-post.

"But I did not disown the memorial. No, indeed; I looked on with unmixed satisfaction while twenty thousand citizens of Dublin, including the foremost in every profession and pursuit, while some hundreds of the Irish priesthood—while men I had never heard of, and places I had never seen, proclaimed their sympathy with my life and character, and demanded my release. The reasons urged were their reasons, not mine. What I gloried in was the answer such a demonstration furnished to my slanderers—come what might, *they* had failed—*you* had failed, and the aim of my life would not be misunderstood.

"I did not forbid the movement; nor did Meagher and O'Brien forbid a similar memorial at the same moment against their sentence being carried out. They let it take its course. When will you spit your poisonous rheum upon them; or is it only in me it is a crime to have friends?

"Your last charge is that I sent O'Brien to Ballingarry and that the insurrection was (in consequence, no doubt) a contemptible failure. That I sent O'Brien to Ballingarry is utterly untrue; but I decline to debate a question of which you know nothing. The failure I am in no way bound to defend; I was not there; the time, place, or *modus operandi* were not of my choosing; but it passes human patience to hear *you* disparage it.

"'The Ballingarry failure (you say, and one might fancy it was Mr. Birch was sneering at O'Brien and his associates instead of Mr. Mitchel) is hardly, I suppose, to be treated as a criterion. A gentleman—a very estimable and worthy gentleman certainly—goes with three or four *attendants* (!)

(who are wholly unknown to the people they go amongst) into the counties of Kilkenny and Tipperary, and there tells several persons they are to rise in insurrection under his guidance, and free the country. He has no money, this gentleman, to pay troops, no clothing or arms to give them, no food to keep them alive. He just exhibits a pike, and bids them follow him and free the country!'

"Whatever was the value of that plan of campaign, there is one thing a man may safely aver—it was at least better than yours; an opinion which may be predicated of any plan since the Tooley Street plot. One looks back on the *United Irishman*—at its promises, its performances, its plan of operations, its adjustment of means to ends (that grand secret of all human success) with feelings which even the interests at stake cannot keep grave. One must smile or swear. Your theory of revolution was reducible to two maxims worthy of Bedlam—that whatever was meditated against the English Government should be proclaimed beforehand, and that officers or preparation were superfluous. You neglected every precaution; the greatest as well as the smallest. You had no agent in France, no agent in America, no agent in Canada, no agent among the discontented Chartists of England. When you were arrested you had not a barrel of gunpowder, or a case of muskets. You did not know where to lay your hand upon pickaxes or crowbars to make the first barricade. Your resources literally began and ended in an ink-bottle. Your system of tactics consisted in uttering threats which you were not able to fulfil; in denouncing the puerility and cowardice of being adequately prepared; and in disparaging, as Reactionaries, the men who took the precautions which you neglected. Your labours had indeed one computable result; you begot among the Confederates an angry and unscrupulous faction, who spent their nights and days in denouncing the best men in the movement. But of these 'Montaguards' not one took the field with O'Brien; on the contrary, some of them behaved with signal cowardice, one with disgusting treachery, and a third was unmasked as a Government spy. O'Brien's failure might have befallen any cause; it had befallen some of the noblest in the annals of mankind; destiny may repeat or may reverse it—but nothing can rob it of its intrinsic greatness. In the midst of a generation who did not believe in heroic sacrifice he offered up his life for the common weal. That is an event of the grandest interest even on the obscurest stage. No generous enemy would undervalue it; only the *un*generous enemy who masquerades in the disguise of a friend."

I desire to add to these extracts a single fact with which I think the reader ought to be acquainted. I published in the *Nation* every line Mr. Mitchel wrote against me; I published his answer to my letter. Of my vindication or retaliation he never allowed a line to appear in the *Citizen*. He crowded his paper week after week with letters from third parties sustaining him or assailing me, but my vindication he utterly excluded from readers before whom I had been systematically assailed. Every other Irish-American journal in New York, and, as far as I know, in the United States, copied it, and several purely American journals also, without curtailing it of a syllable; the *Citizen* alone, where its appearance was a manifest right, excluded it.

LONDON: RICHARD CLAY & SONS, PRINTERS.

www.ingramcontent.com/pod-product-compliance
Lightning Source LLC
Chambersburg PA
CBHW050847300426
44111CB00010B/1160